ACTION RESEARCH

A GUIDE FOR THE TEACHER RESEARCHER

THIRD EDITION

Geoffrey E. Mills
Southern Oregon University

PEARSON

Merrill
Prentice Hall

Upper Saddle River, New Jersey
Columbus, Ohio

Library of Congress Cataloging-in-Publication Data

Mills, Geoffrey E.
  Action research: a guide for the teacher researcher/Geoffrey E. Mills.—3rd ed.
    p. cm.
  Includes bibliographical references (p.   ) and index.
  ISBN 0-13-172276-X (paperback)
  1. Action research in education—United States—Handbooks, manuals, etc.
2. Teaching—United States—Handbooks, manuals, etc. I. Title.
LB1028.24.M55 2007
370.7'2—dc22   2005058673

Vice President and Executive Publisher: Jeffery W. Johnston
Publisher: Kevin M. Davis
Development Editor: Autumn Crisp Benson
Editorial Assistant: Sarah N. Kenoyer
Production Editor: Mary Harlan
Production Coordinator: Trish Finley
Design Coordinator: Diane C. Lorenzo
Text Design: GGS Book Services
Cover Design: Janna Thompson Chordas
Cover Image: Corbis
Production Manager: Laura Messerly
Director of Marketing: David Gesell
Marketing Manager: Autumn Purdy
Marketing Coordinator: Brian Mounts

This book was set in Garamond by GGS Book Services. It was printed and bound by
R.R. Donnelley & Sons Company. The cover was printed by R.R. Donnelley & Sons
Company.

Pearson Education Ltd.   Pearson Education Australia Pty. Limited
Pearson Education Singapore Pte. Ltd.   Pearson Education North Asia Ltd.
Pearson Education Canada, Ltd.   Pearson Educación de Mexico, S.A. de C.V.
Pearson Education–Japan   Pearson Education Malaysia Pte. Ltd.

10 9 8 7 6 5 4 3 2 1
ISBN 0-13-172276-X

For Ernie Mills, Audrey Mills, Dr. Milton H. Brown, and Catherine S. Brown—
Your love, support, and spirit live with me always.

MERRILL PRENTICE HALL

Teacher Preparation Classroom

Your Class. Their Careers. Our Future. Will Your Students Be Prepared?

We invite you to explore our new, innovative and engaging website and all that it has to offer you, your course, and tomorrow's educators! Organized around the major courses pre-service teachers take, the Teacher Preparation site provides media, student/teacher artifacts, strategies, research articles, and other resources to equip your students with the quality tools needed to excel in their courses and prepare them for their first classroom.

This ultimate on-line education resource is available at no cost, when packaged with a Merrill text, and will provide you and your students access to:

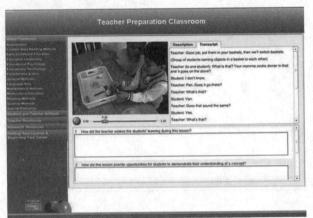

Online Video Library More than 150 video clips—each tied to a course topic and framed by learning goals and Praxis-type questions—capture real teachers and students working in real classrooms, as well as in-depth interviews with both students and educators.

Student and Teacher Artifacts More than 200 student and teacher classroom artifacts—each tied to a course topic and framed by learning goals and application questions—provide a wealth of materials and experiences to help make your study to become a professional teacher more concrete and hands-on.

Research Articles Over 500 articles from ASCD's renowned journal *Educational Leadership*. The site also includes *Research Navigator*, a searchable database of additional educational journals.

Teaching Strategies Over 500 strategies and lesson plans for you to use when you become a practicing professional.

Licensure and Career Tools Resources devoted to helping you pass your licensure exam; learn standards, law, and public policies; plan a teaching portfolio; and succeed in your first year of teaching.

How to ORDER *Teacher Prep* for you and your students:

For students to receive a *Teacher Prep* Access Code with this text, instructors **must** provide a special value pack ISBN number on their textbook order form. To receive this special ISBN, please email: Merrill.marketing@pearsoned.com and provide the following information:

- Name and Affiliation
- Author/Title/Edition of Merrill text

Upon ordering *Teacher Prep* for their students, instructors will be given a lifetime *Teacher Prep* Access Code.

Preface

The Role of Action Research in Effecting Educational Change

Action research has the potential to be a powerful agent of educational change. Action research helps to develop teachers and administrators with professional attitudes, who embrace action, progress, and reform rather than stability and mediocrity. In addition, the action research process fosters a democratic approach to decision making while, at the same time, empowering individual teachers through participation in a collaborative, socially responsive research activity.

Commitment to action research positions teachers and administrators as learners rather than experts. Those committed to action research will willingly undertake continued professional development because they believe that there is a gap between the real world of their daily teaching practices and their vision of an ideal one.

Incorporating action research into preservice teacher education programs and professional development programs for inservice teachers will help make action research an ongoing component of a professional teacher's practice. Such action will ultimately help teachers incorporate action research alongside other critical components of teaching, such as curriculum development, authentic assessment strategies, classroom management strategies, teaching strategies, and caring for children. Such actions will encourage teachers to embrace change.

It is my hope that this book will, in some small part, help us keep moving forward, even in difficult times. Action research is an invitation to learn, a means to tackle tough questions that face us individually and collectively as teachers, and a method for questioning our daily taken-for-granted assumptions as a way to find hope for the future.

Conceptual Framework and Organization of the Text

This book has emerged over a number of years based on my experience of doing and teaching action research. During this time I have had the opportunity to work with some outstanding teachers and principals who were committed to looking systematically at the effects of their programs on children's lives. This book's organization has grown out of these experiences and has been field tested by numerous students and colleagues.

Each chapter opens with an action research vignette that illustrates the content that will follow. These vignettes, most of which have been written by teachers and principals with whom I have worked, show readers what action research looks like in practice and who does it. The order of these chapters roughly matches the action research process, an approach that I have found successful when teaching action research.

Contents of This New Edition

Chapter 1 defines action research and provides historical and theoretical contexts for the rest of the book. The chapter also reviews various models of action research and concludes with the four-step process (identifying an area of focus, collecting data, analyzing and interpreting data, and developing an action plan) and the dialectic model on which this book is based. The remaining chapters mirror these steps.

Chapter 2 helps action researchers choose an "area of focus." Guidelines for selecting an area of focus are offered, along with step-by-step directions for how to do a literature review using many online resources as well as traditional university library resources. New for this edition is an expanded discussion of how to write a literature review. Readers will also find a new example of a completed review of literature on the Companion Website for the book. The chapter culminates with an action research plan that provides a practical guide for moving teacher researchers through the action research process.

Chapter 3 offers a comprehensive discussion on qualitative data collection that covers the "3 Es" of data collection: experiencing, enquiring, and examining. New for this edition is a comprehensive discussion of quantitative data collection techniques as a corollary to the qualitative data collection techniques discussion.

Chapter 4 addresses important data collection considerations such as validity, reliability, and generalizability to ensure that the data collected will be "trustworthy."

New to this edition, Chapter 5 provides an expanded discussion of ethical guidelines and poses an ethical dilemma vignette to spark teacher researchers' thinking about how best to resolve ethical dilemmas if and when they arise.

Chapter 6 describes selected techniques of data analysis and data interpretation and distinguishes between the goals of the two processes. New to this edition is an expanded discussion of data analysis and interpretation with examples of each. For example, a new annotated example of the analysis of a transcripted interview with themes and categories identified has been added.

Chapter 7 helps teacher researchers take action using a helpful Steps to Action Chart. The chapter also discusses potential obstacles to change and suggests strategies for overcoming these obstacles.

Chapter 8 provides practical guidelines for writing up action research and ways that teacher researchers can "get the word out." A reprinted action research article with marginal notations gives researchers an example of the general structure and components of written action research. A self-evaluation rubric helps teacher researchers make sure their write-up is ready for publication. New to this edition is a published action research article from an online action research journal, which is available on the Companion Website. There is also an expanded discussion of using the *Publication Manual of the American Psychological Association* (5th ed.) during the writing process.

Finally, Chapter 9 discusses the importance of bridging the gap between research and practice and following through with the complete action research cycle to ensure that the research findings have an impact on student learning. The importance of sharing, critiquing, and celebrating action research is also covered, along with valuable guidelines for using the action research resources offered on the Internet, including action research Web sites, listservs, and online journals.

Appendix A contains an extended example of action research through a case study of Curtis Elementary. This case study follows the process described throughout the book and includes an evaluation of the project on the basis of criteria for judging the quality of action research. Appendix B contains a brief discussion of descriptive statistics (mean, mode, median, and standard deviation) and how they can be applied to the analysis and interpretation of teacher research. New for this edition are examples showing how to use a calculator to derive these descriptive statistics. Appendix C, "Displaying Data Visually," presents a variety of examples of visual displays of data—bar graphs, tables, and a concept map—from action research projects. Using these display techniques helps teachers "see" data for better analysis and more effective communication of their findings.

Features of the Text

The text's user-friendly format includes chapter objectives, Key Concepts boxes, Research in Action checklists, chapter summaries, and questions for further thought. The text also includes many practical illustrations of the action research process that will help teacher researchers apply the process in their own school or classroom setting. The information in Chapter 9, which provides online action research resources, will be a welcome feature to those who wish to interact with other action researchers and access the multitude of action research resources available on the Internet.

Companion Website

You can find the Companion Website at **www.prenhall.com/mills**. This online learning site helps students master course content through chapter overviews, challenging application problems, interactive self-assessment quizzes and essay questions, Internet links to explore related action research Web sites, as well as an example of a review of literature and a link to an article published by an online journal.

Online PowerPoint® Slides

To enhance class lectures, Online PowerPoint® slides are available on the Instructor's Resource Center. To access the Online PowerPoint slides, go to **www.prenhall.com,** click on the Instructor Support button, and then go to the Download Supplements section. Here you will be able to log in or complete a one-time registration for a user name and password.

Acknowledgments

I would like to thank the reviewers, who invested a great deal of time and provided critical feedback during the development of this book. These reviewers include Jennifer Esposito, Georgia State University; Christine Fox, University of Toledo; Patricia McCollum, Piedmont College; and Amira Proweller, DePaul University.

I would also like to acknowledge the staff at Merrill/Prentice Hall without whose guidance (and patience!) this book would not have become a reality. In particular, I thank Kevin Davis, Publisher and Executive Editor, for working with me on a third edition of the book so as to build on what we achieved with the previous editions, and Autumn Benson, Development Editor, who worked diligently to ensure a quality, user-friendly text.

I would also like to extend my gratitude to the hundreds of students at Southern Oregon University who responded to various drafts of previous editions of this book and also endured my ramblings about the importance of being reflective practitioners and self-renewing professionals. Their insights into what makes a text user-friendly have been greatly appreciated and are reflected in the text. Similarly, I have had the pleasure of working with hundreds of teachers throughout Oregon who taught me what needed to be included in a "helpful" book.

Finally, I appreciate the support and encouragement of my wife, colleague, and best friend, Dr. Donna Mills (Southern Oregon University), who endured my mood swings and weekend writing commitments throughout this lengthy process. And I thank my son Jonathan, who gave up play time with his dad and continually reminded me of three important things: (1) what it means to be a teacher and a learner, (2) that I must exercise every day so that I keep up with his energy and enthusiasm for life, and (3) that it's always the computer's fault when things don't work the way they are meant to! The writing of this third edition was tackled immediately following another long writing project, the eighth edition of *Educational Research: Competencies for Analysis and Applications* (Gay, Mills, and Airasian, 2006). My sincere thanks to Donna and Jonathan for their patience and support during the past three years.

Geoff Mills

RESEARCH NAVIGATOR: RESEARCH MADE SIMPLE!

www.ResearchNavigator.com

Merrill Education is pleased to introduce Research Navigator—a one-stop research solution for students that simplifies and streamlines the entire research process. At www.researchnavigator.com, students will find extensive resources to enhance their understanding of the research process so they can effectively complete research assignments. In addition, Research Navigator has three exclusive databases of credible and reliable source content to help students focus their research efforts and begin the research process.

How Will Research Navigator Enhance Your Course?

- Extensive content helps students understand the research process, including writing, Internet research, and citing sources.
- Step-by-step tutorial guides students through the entire research process from selecting a topic to revising a rough draft.
- Research Writing in the Disciplines section details the differences in research across disciplines.
- Three exclusive databases—EBSCO's ContentSelect Academic Journal Database, *The New York Times* Search by Subject Archive, and "Best of the Web" Link Library—allow students to easily find journal articles and sources.

What's the Cost?

A subscription to Research Navigator is $7.50 but is available at no additional cost when ordered in conjunction with this textbook. To obtain free passcodes for your students, simply contact your local Merrill/Prentice Hall sales representative, and your representative will send you the Evaluating Online Resource Guide, which contains the code to access Research Navigator as well as tips on how to use Research Navigator and how to evaluate research. To preview the value of this website to your students, please go to www.educatorlearningcenter.com and use the Login Name "Research" and the password "Demo."

Brief Contents

CHAPTER 1: **Understanding Action Research**   1

CHAPTER 2: **Deciding on an Area of Focus**   22

CHAPTER 3: **Data Collection Techniques**   50

CHAPTER 4: **Data Collection Considerations: Validity, Reliability, and Generalizability**   80

CHAPTER 5: **Ethics**   100

CHAPTER 6: **Data Analysis and Interpretation**   116

CHAPTER 7: **Action Planning for Educational Change**   140

CHAPTER 8: **Writing Up Action Research**   162

CHAPTER 9: **Sharing, Critiquing, and Celebrating Action Research Online**   188

APPENDIX A: **Action Research in Action: A Case Study of Curtis Elementary and an Article Critique**   211

APPENDIX B: **Descriptive Statistics and Action Research**   223

APPENDIX C: **Displaying Data Visually**   231

Contents

CHAPTER 1: **Understanding Action Research**   1

What Motivates Unmotivated Students?   1

A Brief Overview of Educational Research   2

Defining Action Research   5

Origins of Action Research   5

Theoretical Foundations of Action Research   6
    Critical Action Research • Practical Action Research

Goals and Rationale for Action Research   8

*Justifying Action Research: The Impact of Action Research
on Practice*   10
    Action Research Is Persuasive and Authoritative • Action Research
    Is Relevant • Action Research Allows Teachers Access to Research
    Findings • Action Research Challenges the Intractability of
    Reform of the Educational System • Action Research
    Is Not a Fad

Making Action Research a Part of Daily Teaching Practices   14

The Process of Action Research   15

Summary   20

For Further Thought   20

CHAPTER 2: **Deciding on an Area of Focus** 22

Interactive Teen Theater 23

Clarifying a General Idea and an Area of Focus 25

Criteria for Selecting a General Idea/Area of Focus

Reconnaissance 26

Gaining Insight Into Your Area of Focus Through Self-Reflection • Gaining Insight Into Your Area of Focus Through Descriptive Activities • Gaining Insight Into Your Area of Focus Through Explanatory Activities

Review of Related Literature 29

Searching Online Resources • Searching the Internet and the World Wide Web • Becoming a Member of Professional Organizations • Visiting a University Library • Evaluating Your Sources • Abstracting • Analyzing, Organizing, and Reporting the Literature • Writing Tools and Suggestions

The Action Research Plan 44

Write an Area-of-Focus Statement • Define the Variables • Develop Research Questions • Describe the Intervention or Innovation • Describe the Membership of the Action Research Group • Describe Negotiations That Need to Be Undertaken • Develop a Timeline • Develop a Statement of Resources • Develop Data Collection Ideas • Put the Action Plan Into Action

Summary 48

For Further Thought 48

CHAPTER 3: **Data Collection Techniques** 50

Reflection on Action Research 51

Qualitative Data Collection Techniques 56

Triangulation

Experiencing Through Direct Observation 57

Participant Observation • Fieldnotes

Enquiring: When the Researcher Asks 61

Informal Ethnographic Interview • Structured Formal Interviews • Focus Groups • E-Mail Interviews • Questionnaires

Examining: Using and Making Records   68

    Archival Documents • Journals • Making Maps, Videotapes, Audiotapes, Photographs, Film, and Artifacts

Quantitative Data Collection Techniques   73

    Teacher-Made Tests • Standardized Tests • School-Generated Report Cards • Attitude Scales • Other Measurement Techniques

Realign Your Area of Focus and Action Research Plan When Necessary   76

Summary   77

For Further Thought   77

CHAPTER 4: **Data Collection Considerations: Validity, Reliability, and Generalizability**   **80**

Improving Student Understanding and Motivation of Multiplication Facts   81

Validity   84

    Guba's Criteria for Validity of Qualitative Research • Maxwell's Criteria for Validity of Qualitative Research • Anderson, Herr, and Nihlen's Criteria for Validity in Action Research • Wolcott's Strategies for Ensuring the Validity of Action Research

Reliability   94

    The Difference Between Reliability and Validity

Generalizability   96

Personal Bias in the Conduct of Action Research   97

    Propositions

Summary   98

For Further Thought   98

CHAPTER 5: **Ethics**   **100**

The Use of Technology to Enhance Mathematics Achievement   101

The Ethics of Research   103

    Informed Consent and Protection from Harm • Deception

Doing the Right Thing: The Role of Ethics in Action Research   *107*

Ethical Guidelines • Flinders's Conceptual Framework for Ethics in Qualitative Research

Summary   *114*

For Further Thought   *114*

CHAPTER 6:   **Data Analysis and Interpretation**   **116**

Emphasizing Learning by Deemphasizing Grades   *117*

Ongoing Analysis and Reflection   *121*

Avoid Premature Action

The Role of Analysis and Interpretation   *122*

Data Analysis Techniques   *123*

Identifying Themes • Coding Surveys, Interviews, and Questionnaires • Analyzing an Interview • Asking Key Questions • Doing an Organizational Review • Developing a Concept Map • Analyzing Antecedents and Consequences • Displaying Findings • Stating What's Missing • Using Computer Software to Assist with Data Analysis

Data Interpretation Techniques   *135*

Extend the Analysis • Connect Findings with Personal Experience • Seek the Advice of "Critical" Friends • Contextualize Findings in the Literature • Turn to Theory • Know When to Say "When"!

Sharing Your Interpretations Wisely   *137*

Summary   *138*

For Further Thought   *138*

CHAPTER 7:   **Action Planning for Educational Change**   **140**

Reflecting on Admission Criteria   *141*

Developing Action Plans   *143*

Levels of Action Planning • Action Should Be Ongoing • The Importance of Reflection

Some Challenges Facing Teacher Researchers   *151*

Lack of Resources • Resistance to Change • Reluctance to Interfere with Others' Professional Practices • Reluctance to Admit Difficult Truths • Finding a Forum to Share What You Have Learned • Making Time for Action Research Endeavors

Facilitating Educational Change   *155*

Teachers and Administrators Need to Restructure Power and Authority Relationships • Both Top-Down and Bottom-Up Strategies of Change Can Work • Teachers Must Be Provided with Support • Every Person Is a Change Agent • Change Tends Not to Be Neat, Linear, or Rational • Teacher Researchers Must Pay Attention to the Culture of the School • The Outcome of Any Change Effort Must Benefit Students • Being Hopeful Is a Critical Resource

What Do Teachers Gain Through All of This Work?   *159*

Summary   *160*

For Further Thought   *160*

CHAPTER 8: **Writing Up Action Research**   **162**

Why Should I Formally Write About My Action Research?   *164*

Format and Style   *165*

Sample Annotated Action Research Article   *166*

Rituals and Writing   *173*

Establishing a Writing Routine

An Outline for an Action Research Report   *175*

Other Structures in Action Research Reports   *176*

General Guidelines for Submissions to Journals   *178*

Choosing a "Journal" Style • APA *Publication Manual* Conventions • Self-Assessing Your Write-Up • Integrating Teaching, Research, and Writing • How Long Should the Write-Up Be? • Seeking Feedback • What's in a Title? • Polishing the Text

Summary   *186*

For Further Thought   *187*

CHAPTER 9: **Sharing, Critiquing, and Celebrating Action Research Online**   **188**

Reflecting on Reflective Teaching   *189*

Sharing Action Research   *191*

Electronic Means for Sharing Action Research   *192*
A Word on Quality Control on the Internet

Using the Internet to Get Connected   *193*

What Different Types of Online Resources Can I Use?   *194*
Action Research Web Sites • Listservs • Online Journals

Online Action Research: Challenges and Cautions   *202*
The Challenge of Technophobia • The Challenge of the Ever-Evolving Internet • Caution: Monitor Your Time Online

But Is It Really Research?—Criteria for Judging Action Research   *204*

Personal Reflection   *206*

Celebration—It's Time to Party!   *207*

This Is Just the Beginning!   *208*

Summary   *209*

For Further Thought   *209*

APPENDIX A: **Action Research in Action: A Case Study of Curtis Elementary School and an Article Critique**   **211**

The Setting: Curtis Elementary—A Professional Development School   *211*

The Area of Focus: Constructing Meaning in Reading   *213*

Reviewing the Literature   *215*

Creating an Action Plan   *215*

Creating Meaning in Reading   *215*

Sharing the Findings   *219*

Critiquing Action Research **220**

Audience • Format • Prejudices • Professional Disposition • Reflective Stance • Life Enhancing • Action • Action-Data Connection • Impact • Changes • Colleague Response

Celebrating Action Research **222**

Final Thoughts **222**

Summary **222**

For Further Thought **222**

APPENDIX B: **Descriptive Statistics and Action Research** **223**

Count What Counts! Using Descriptive Statistics **223**

Why Use Descriptive Statistics? • Measures of Central Tendency • Measure of Variability: Standard Deviation • An Illustration • Be Careful About Your Claims

APPENDIX C: **Displaying Data Visually** **231**

Example 1: Writers Workshop and ESL Students' Written Work and Attitudes **231**

Example 2: Teaching Mathematics Using Manipulatives **234**

Example 3: The Impact of Book Sharing on Student Motivation to Read **237**

Example 4: Mapping Teacher's "Locus of Control" and "Movement" **237**

Example 5: Concept Map **237**

Summary **239**

References **241**

Author Index **244**

Subject Index **246**

Note: Every effort has been made to provide accurate and current Internet information in this book. However, the Internet and information posted on it are constantly changing, so it is inevitable that some of the Internet addresses listed in this textbook will change.

Understanding Action Research

This chapter introduces action research by providing an example of an action research project from a real teacher researcher, an exploration of the historical and theoretical foundations of action research, a discussion of the goals and justification for action research, and an explanation of the action research process.

After reading this chapter you should be able to:
1. Define action research.
2. Describe the historical foundations of action research.
3. Identify the similarities and differences between critical/postmodern and practical theories of action research.
4. Describe the goals of and justification for action research.
5. List the four stages of the action research process.

What Motivates Unmotivated Students?
Deborah South

Deborah South, a teacher in a rural Oregon high school, was a participant in an action research class. She shares the challenges she faced when, owing to a last-minute teaching assignment, she found herself working with a group of "unmotivated" students. Deborah's story illustrates the wide variety of factors that can influence students' learning and a teacher's willingness to critically examine her teaching methods and how they affected the children in her classroom. Although Deborah's interpretation of the results of her study did not validate her practice, it did provide data that Deborah and the school's principal could use to make changes to the existing curriculum for unmotivated students.

Teaching students who are unmotivated and apathetic can be a difficult challenge for any teacher to overcome. These students typically can be disruptive and negative and often require an extraordinary amount of teacher time to manage their behavior. My concern with teaching unmotivated students has existed almost since I began teaching 5 years ago. As an educator, one tries all kinds of possible strategies to encourage students to be successful. However, these strategies do not work with unmotivated students who are apathetic and exhibit unacceptable behavior. Eventually the patience runs out and, as ashamed as I am to admit it, I stop trying to find ways to reach these particular students. It soon becomes enough that they stay in their seats, be quiet, and do not disturb anyone.

However, last term my attitude was forced to change. I was given a study skills group of 20 of the lowest achieving eighth graders in the school. This new class consisted of 16 boys and 4 girls. My task was to somehow take these students and miraculously make them motivated, achieving students. I was trained in a study skills program before the term started and I thought that I was prepared: I had the students, I had the curriculum, and I had the help of an outstanding aide.

Within a week, I sensed we were in trouble. My 20 students often showed up with no supplies. Their behavior was atrocious. They called each other names, threw various items around the room, and walked around the classroom when they felt like it. Their attitudes toward me were negative. I became concerned about teaching these students. In part, I felt bad that they were so disillusioned with school and their future; I also felt bad because the thought of teaching in this environment every day for another 14 weeks made me wish summer vacation were here.

Given this situation, I decided to do some reading about how other teachers motivate unmotivated students and to formulate some ideas about the variables that contribute to a student's success in school. Variables I investigated included adult approval, peer influence, and success in such subjects as math, science, language arts, and social studies, as well as self-esteem and students' views of their academic abilities.

I collected the majority of the data through surveys, interviews, and report card/attendance records in an effort to answer the following questions:

- How does attendance affect student performance?
- How are students influenced by their friends in completing schoolwork?
- How do adults (parents, teachers) affect the success of students?
- What levels of self-esteem do these students have?

As a result of this investigation, I learned many things. For example, for this group of students attendance does not appear to be a factor—with the exception of one student, their school attendance was regular. Not surprisingly, peer groups did affect student performance. Seventy-three percent of my students reported that their friends never encouraged doing homework or putting any effort into homework.

Another surprising result was the lack of impact of a teacher's approval on student achievement. Ninety-four percent of my students indicated that they never or seldom do their homework to receive teacher approval. Alternatively, 57 percent indicated that they often or always do their homework so that their families will be proud of them.

One of the most interesting findings of this study was the realization that most of my students misbehave out of frustration at their own lack of abilities. They are not being obnoxious to gain attention, but to divert attention from the fact that they do not know how to complete the assigned work.

When I looked at report cards and compared grades over three quarters, I noticed a trend. Between the first and second quarter, student performance had increased. That is, most students were doing better than they had during the first quarter. Between the second and third quarters, however, grades dropped dramatically. I tried to determine why that drop would occur, and the only common experience shared by these 20 students was the fact that they had been moved into my class at the beginning of the third quarter.

When I presented my project to the action research class during our end-of-term "celebration," I was convinced that the "cause" of the students' unmotivated behavior was my teaching. I had concluded through my data analysis and interpretation that the one experience these 20 children had in common was participation in my study skills class. This conclusion, however, was not readily accepted by my critical friends and colleagues in the action research class who urged me to consider other interpretations of the data. For example, perhaps the critical mass of negativity present in one classroom provided the children with a catalyst to act out against the teacher. After all, this was the only class shared exclusively by these 20 students. Afterward, I shared the findings of my study with my school principal. As a result, she decided not to group these students together homogeneously for a study skills class the following year.

A s you can see, action research is a "wonderfully uncomfortable" (Lytle, 1997) place to be—once we start our journey of investigation, we have no way of knowing in advance where we will end up. Action research, like any other problem-solving process, is an ongoing creative activity that exposes us to surprises along the way. What appeared to matter in the planning stages of an action research investigation may provide us with only a hint, a scratching of the surface, of what is really the focus for our investigations. How we deal with the uncertainty of the journey positions us as learners of our own craft, an attitude that is critical to our success. This book attempts to foster an openness in the spirit of inquiry guided by action research.

A Brief Overview of Educational Research

When you hear the words *scientific research*, you probably think of a scientist in a white lab coat (usually a balding, middle-aged man with a pocket full of pens!) mixing chemicals or doing experiments involving white mice. Traditional scientists, like the one pictured in this rather trite image, proceed with their research under the assumption that "all behaviors and events are orderly" and that all events "have discoverable causes" (Gay, Mills, & Airasian, 2006, pp. 5–6). This traditional belief that natural phenomena can be explained in an orderly way using empirical sciences is sometimes called **positivism**.

Human beings, however, are very complicated organisms, and compared with chemicals—and mice, for that matter—their behavior can be disorderly and fairly unpredictable. This presents a challenge to educational researchers, who are concerned with gaining insight into human behavior in educational environments such as schools and classrooms.

The goal of traditional educational research is "to explain, predict, and/or control educational phenomena" (Gay et al., 2006, p. 5). To do this, researchers try to manipulate and control certain **variables** (the factors that might affect the outcomes of a particular study) to test a **hypothesis** (a statement the researcher makes that predicts what will happen or explains what the outcome of the study will be).

For example, researchers might be interested in studying the effects of a certain phonics program (the independent variable) on the rate at which children learn to read (the dependent variable). The researchers may hypothesize that the use of this phonics program will shorten the time it takes for students to learn to read. To confirm or reject this hypothesis, they might study the reading progress of one group of children who were taught using the phonics program (the **experimental group**) and compare it with the reading progress of another group of children (called the **control group**) who were taught reading without the phonics program. Children would be **randomly** assigned to either the experimental or the control group as a way to reduce the differences that might exist in naturally occurring groups. At the end of the **experiment**, the researchers would compare the progress of each group and decide whether the hypothesis could be accepted or rejected with a predetermined level of **statistical significance** (for example, that the difference between the mean for the control group and the mean for the experimental group is large, compared with the standard error). Finally, the researchers would present the findings of the study at a conference and perhaps publish the results.

This process may sound very straightforward. In classroom and school settings, however, controlling all the factors that affect the outcomes of our teaching without disrupting the natural classroom environment can be difficult. For example, how do we know that the phonics program is the only variable affecting the rate at which students learn to read? Perhaps some students are being read to at home by their parents; perhaps one teacher is more effective than another; perhaps one group of students gets to read more exciting books than the other; perhaps one group of children has difficulty concentrating on their reading because they all skipped breakfast!

Action researchers acknowledge and embrace these complications rather than try to control them. In addition, action researchers differ from traditional researchers because they are committed to *taking action* and *effecting positive educational change* based on their findings, rather than being satisfied with reporting their conclusions to others. Another difference is that whereas educational research has historically been done by university professors, scholars, and graduate students on children, teachers, and principals, action researchers are often the schoolteachers and principals who were formerly the subjects of educational research. As such, they participate in their own inquiries, acting as both teacher and researcher at the same time. Teacher research is gaining a high priority in the United States as part of the George W. Bush education agenda No Child Left Behind. According to

Imig (2001), this legislation is "profound," "sweeping," "intrusive," "far reaching," and "unprecedented." As part of this legislation, states will be required to test students in reading and math every year in grades 3 through 8, with sanctions for schools that fail to make "adequate yearly progress" (Imig, 2001, p. 2). The link between this kind of legislation in America and action research is clear: How can teachers show that they are making a difference with their teaching for all students? Action research provides teachers with a philosophy and practice that allows them to systematically study the effects of their teaching on student learning.

Finally, research is also categorized by the methods the researchers use. Simply put, different research problems require different research approaches. These approaches to educational research are often classified as either quantitative or qualitative research. **Quantitative research** focuses on controlling a small number of variables to determine cause-effect relationships and/or the strength of those relationships. This type of research uses numbers to quantify the cause-effect relationship. Quantitative researchers generally have little personal interaction with the participants they study, since most data are gathered using paper-and-pencil, noninteractive instruments. **Qualitative research** uses narrative, descriptive approaches to data collection to understand the way things are and what it means from the perspectives of the research participants. Qualitative approaches might include, for example, conducting face-to-face interviews, making observations, and recording interactions on videotape. Key Concepts Box 1–1 compares traditional research and action research.

Although different, the two approaches need not be considered mutually exclusive; a study might incorporate both quantitative *and* qualitative techniques. Studies that combine the collection of quantitative and qualitative data in a single study are called **mixed-methods research designs**. For example, researchers interested in the relationship between student achievement and self-esteem might

KEY CONCEPTS BOX 1–1

A Comparison of Traditional Research and Action Research		
WHAT?	TRADITIONAL RESEARCH	ACTION RESEARCH
Who?	Conducted by university professors, scholars, and graduate students on experimental and control groups.	Conducted by teachers and principals on children in their care.
Where?	In environments where variables can be controlled.	In schools and classrooms.
How?	Using quantitative methods to show, to some predetermined degree of statistical significance, a cause-effect relationship between variables.	Using qualitative methods to describe what is happening and to understand the effects of some educational intervention.
Why?	To report and publish conclusions that can be generalized to larger populations.	To take action and effect positive educational change in the specific school environment that was studied.

begin their inquiry by comparing the grade point averages of high school students with the students' numerical scores on a multiple-choice questionnaire designed to measure their self-esteem. To gain a broader understanding of this complicated relationship, researchers might also interview and observe a number of students to gather additional data.

The area of focus or **research question** identified by the researcher will determine the most appropriate approach (quantitative and/or qualitative) to use. Because most action researchers use narrative, descriptive methods, the emphasis in this book will be on the use of qualitative research, although Chapter 3 includes a section on "Quantitative Data Collection Techniques."

Defining Action Research

Over the past decade, the typical "required" research course in many schools, colleges, and departments of teacher education has changed from a traditional survey class on research methods to a more practical research course that either focuses on or includes the topic of action research. But what is action research, and why is it capturing the attention of teachers, administrators, and policy makers?

Action research is any systematic inquiry conducted by teacher researchers, principals, school counselors, or other stakeholders in the teaching/learning environment to gather information about how their particular schools operate, how they teach, and how well their students learn. This information is gathered with the goals of gaining insight, developing reflective practice, effecting positive changes in the school environment (and on educational practices in general), and improving student outcomes and the lives of those involved.

Action research is research done *by* teachers *for* themselves; it is not imposed on them by someone else. Action research engages teachers in a four-step process:

1. Identify an area of focus.
2. Collect data.
3. Analyze and interpret data.
4. Develop an action plan.

Before we elaborate on these four steps, however, we will explore the historical antecedents of action research and the theoretical foundations of current action research practices. As you read these descriptions, consider which philosophy best fits your beliefs about action research, teaching, and learning. Then consider how you might incorporate action research into your professional life.

Origins of Action Research

The history of action research has been well-documented and debated (c.f. Adelman, 1993; Gunz, 1996; Kemmis, 1988; Noffke, 1994). Kurt Lewin (1890–1947) is often credited with coining the term *action research* around 1934. After a series of practical experiences in the early 1940s, he came to view action research as a process that "gives credence to the development of powers of reflective thought, discussion, decision and action by ordinary people participating in collective research on 'private troubles' that they have in common" (Adelman, 1993, p. 8).

The many "descendants" of early action researchers follow different schools of action research thought, including the American action research group, with its roots in the progressive education movement, particularly in the work of John Dewey (Noffke, 1994); the efforts in the United Kingdom toward curriculum reform and greater professionalism in teaching (Elliott, 1991); and Australian efforts located within a broad-ranging movement toward collaborative curriculum planning (Kemmis, 1988).

As is evident, the geographical locations and sociopolitical contexts in which action research efforts continue to evolve vary greatly. However, the primary focus of all these efforts, regardless of the context, is on enhancing the lives of students. As Noffke (1994) reminds us, reading the accounts of action research written by people housed in universities does little to illuminate the classroom experiences of teachers and what they hope to gain from participating in action research activities. Therefore, this book focuses on teachers examining issues related to the education of children and on partnering with teachers, administrators, counselors, and parents in the action research process.

Theoretical Foundations of Action Research

The theoretical perspectives and philosophies that inform the practices of today's teacher researchers are as varied as the historical roots for action research. The following sections briefly review the two main theories of action research: critical (or theory-based) and practical.

CRITICAL ACTION RESEARCH

Critical action research is also known as emancipatory action research because of its goal of liberation through knowledge gathering. The term *critical action research* derives its name from the body of critical theory on which it is based, not because this type of action research is critical, as in "faultfinding" or "important," although it may certainly be both! The rationale for critical action research is provided by critical theory in the social sciences and humanities and by theories of postmodernism.

Critical theory in action research and the social sciences and humanities shares several fundamental purposes (Kemmis, 1988). These similar interests or "commonalities of intent" include:

1. A shared interest in processes for enlightenment.
2. A shared interest in liberating individuals from the dictates of tradition, habit, and bureaucracy.
3. A commitment to participatory democratic processes for reform.

In addition to its roots in the critical theory of the social sciences and humanities, critical action research also draws heavily from a body of theory called **postmodernism**, which challenges the notions of truth and objectivity on which the traditional scientific method relies. Instead of claiming the incontrovertibility of fact, postmodernists argue that truth is relative, conditional, and situational, and that knowledge is always an outgrowth of previous experience. For example, historically there has been little or no connection between research and practice in education—an apparent failure of research to affect teaching. This is not news for teachers! Research has been viewed as something done *on* them, not *for* them.

According to Kennedy (1997), the lack of influence of research on practice has been attributed to the following qualities of educational research:

- It is not persuasive and has lacked the qualities of being compelling to teachers.
- It has not been relevant to teachers' daily practices—it has lacked practicality.
- It has not been expressed in ways that are accessible to teachers.

The postmodern perspective addresses many of these concerns by advocating for research that challenges the *taken-for-granted assumptions* of daily classroom life and presenting *truths* that are relative, conditional, situational, and based on previous experience. So although research may provide insights into promising practices (from research conducted in *other* teachers' classrooms and schools), action research conducted in one's *own* classroom/school is more likely to be persuasive and relevant and the findings expressed in ways that are meaningful for teachers themselves.

Postmodern theory dissects and examines the mechanisms of knowledge production and questions many of the basic assumptions on which modern life is based. Thus, it inspires us "to examine the ordinary, everyday, taken-for-granted ways in which we organize and carry out our private, social, and professional activities" (Stringer, 1996, p. 156). Action research gives us a means by which we can undertake this examination and represent the classroom teachers' experiences that are contextually and politically constructed.

The values of critical action research dictate that all educational research should be socially responsive as well as:

1. Democratic—Enabling participation of people.
2. Participatory—Building a community of learners.
3. Empowering—Providing freedom from oppressive, debilitating conditions.
4. Life-enhancing—Enabling the expression of people's full human potential. (Stringer, 2004, p. 31)

Although this critical theory-based approach has been criticized by some for lack of practical feasibility (Hammersley, 1993), it is nonetheless important to consider because it provides a helpful heuristic, or problem-solving, approach for teachers who are committed to investigate through action research the taken-for-granted relationships and practices in their professional lives. Key Concepts Box 1–2 summarizes the most important components of a critical perspective of action research.

PRACTICAL ACTION RESEARCH

Practical action research places more emphasis on the "how-to" approach to the processes of action research and has a less "philosophical" bent. It assumes, to some degree, that individual teachers or teams of teachers are autonomous and can determine the nature of the investigation to be undertaken. It also assumes that teacher researchers are committed to continued professional development and school improvement and that teacher researchers want to systematically reflect on their practices. Finally, the practical action research perspective assumes that as decision makers, teacher researchers will choose their own areas of focus, determine their data collection techniques, analyze and interpret their data, and develop action plans based on their findings. These beliefs are summarized in Key Concepts Box 1–3.

Components of a Critical Perspective of Action Research	
KEY CONCEPT	EXAMPLE
Action research is participatory and democratic.	You have identified an area in your teaching that you believe can be improved (based on data from your students). You decide to investigate the impact of your intervention and to monitor whether it makes a difference.
Action research is socially responsive and takes place in context.	You are concerned that minority children (for example ESL [English as a Second Language] students) in your classroom are not being presented with curriculum and teaching strategies that are culturally sensitive. You decide to learn more about how best to teach ESL children and to implement some of these strategies.
Action research helps teacher researchers examine the everyday, taken-for-granted ways in which they carry out professional practice.	You have adopted a new mathematics problem-solving curriculum and decide to monitor its impact on student performance on open-ended problem-solving questions and students' attitudes toward mathematics in general.
Knowledge gained through action research can liberate students, teachers, and administrators and enhance learning, teaching, and policy making.	Your school has a high incidence of student absenteeism in spite of a newly adopted district-wide policy on absenteeism. You investigate the perceptions of colleagues, children, and parents toward absenteeism to more fully understand why the existing policy is not having the desired outcome. Based on what you learn, you implement a new policy and systematically monitor its impact on absenteeism levels and students' attitudes toward school.

Goals and Rationale for Action Research

Although the critical/postmodern and practical theories of action research draw on vastly different worldviews, these two distinctly different philosophies are united by common goals that go a long way toward bridging whatever philosophical, histori-cal, social, and regional variations exist.

Action research carried out according to both philosophies creates opportuni-ties for all involved to improve the lives of children and to learn about the craft of teaching. All action researchers, regardless of their particular school of thought or theoretical position, are committed to a critical examination of classroom teaching principles and the effects teachers' actions have on the children in their care.

Components of a Practical Perspective of Action Research	
KEY CONCEPT	EXAMPLE
Teacher researchers have decision-making authority.	Your school has adopted a school-based decision-making approach that provides teachers with the authority to make decisions that most directly impact teaching and learning. Given this decision-making authority, you decide as part of your continued professional development to investigate the effectiveness of a newly adopted science curriculum on students' process skills and attitudes.
Teacher researchers are committed to continued professional development and school improvement.	Based on the results of statewide assessment tests and classroom observations, the teachers and principal at your school determine that reading comprehension skills are weak. Collaboratively, the staff determines the focus for a school improvement effort and identifies the necessary professional development that will be offered to change the ways teachers teach reading.
Teacher researchers want to reflect on their practices.	You are a successful classroom teacher who regularly reflects on your daily teaching and what areas could be improved. You believe that part of being a professional teacher is the willingness to continually examine your teaching effectiveness.
Teacher researchers will use a systematic approach for reflecting on their practice.	Given a schoolwide reading comprehension focus, you have decided to monitor the effectiveness of a new reading curriculum and teaching strategies by videotaping a reading lesson (once per month), administering reading comprehension "probes" (once per week), interviewing children in your classroom (once per term), and administering statewide assessment tests (at the end of the school year).
Teacher researchers will choose an area of focus, determine data collection techniques, analyze and interpret data, and develop action plans.	To continue the example above, you have focused on the effectiveness of a new reading curriculum and teaching strategies. You have decided to collect data using videotapes of lessons, regular "probes," interviews, and statewide assessment tests. During the year you try to interpret the data you are collecting and decide what these data suggest about the effectiveness of the new curriculum and teaching strategies. When all of the data have been collected and analyzed, you decide what action needs to be taken to refine, improve, or maintain the reading comprehension curriculum and teaching strategies.

By now it should be evident that educational change that *enhances the lives of children* is a main goal of action research. But action research can also *enhance the lives of professionals.*

Osterman and Kottkamp (1993) provide a wonderful rationale for action research as a professional growth opportunity in their "credo for reflective practice":

1. Everyone needs professional growth opportunities.
2. All professionals want to improve.
3. All professionals can learn.
4. All professionals are capable of assuming responsibility for their own professional growth and development.
5. People need and want information about their own performance.
6. Collaboration enriches professional development. (p. 46)

Action research is largely about developing the *professional disposition* of teachers, that is, encouraging teachers to be continuous learners—in their classrooms and in their practice. Although action research is not a universal panacea for the intractability of educational reform, it is an important component of the professional disposition of teachers because it provides teachers with the opportunity to model for their students how knowledge is created.

Action research is also about incorporating into the daily teaching routine a *reflective stance*—the willingness to critically examine one's teaching in order to improve or enhance it. It is about a commitment to the principle that as a teacher one is always distanced from the ideal but is striving toward it anyway—it's the very nature of education! Action research significantly contributes to the professional stance that teachers adopt because it encourages them to examine the dynamics of their classrooms, ponder the actions and interactions of students, validate and challenge existing practices, and take risks in the process. When teachers gain new understandings about both their own and their students' behaviors through action research, they are empowered to:

- Make informed decisions about what to change and what not to change.
- Link prior knowledge to new information.
- Learn from experience (even failures).
- Ask questions and systematically find answers. (Fueyo & Koorland, 1997)

This goal of teachers to be professional problem solvers who are committed to improving both their own practice and student outcomes provides a powerful reason to practice action research.

Justifying Action Research: The Impact of Action Research on Practice

At the beginning of a course on action research, I often ask teachers to reflect on what they do in their schools and classrooms; that is, what are the assumptions they take for granted in their schools and what are the origins of those practices? Often the responses include the following:

> In elementary grades, it is important to do the "skill" subjects in the morning and the "social" subjects in the afternoon because that is when young children can concentrate better and learn more.

The best way to do whole-group instruction with young children (grades K–3) is to have them sit on the "mat" in a circle. That way they are close to the teacher and pay more attention to what is being said.

In high schools the optimal time for a learning period is 43 minutes. Anything longer than that and the students get restless and lose concentration. Therefore, I think that the proposal for "block scheduling" is just an attempt to make us more like elementary school teachers.

If you simply share scoring guides with children, they will automatically do better on the test. There's no need to change instructional approaches.

In a science laboratory if children spend less time collecting data, they will develop a deeper understanding of the science concepts being taught.

Although these are real examples of just a few of the naïve theories about teaching and learning that I have heard, they also indicate the gap that has existed between research and practice in the field of education. To what extent has teaching practice been informed by research? Is teaching informed by folklore? Do teachers acquire the culture of teaching through years of participation and observation, first as students and then as neophyte teachers? How did teachers get to be the way they are? Are some of the derogatory Hollywood portrayals of teachers and teaching (for example, as characterized in *Ferris Bueller's Day Off, Mr. Holland's Opus*, etc.) really warranted? What is it about research that makes teachers, in general, snicker at the thought that it can in some way improve practice? What is the potential for this discussion to put action into action research efforts?

According to Kennedy (1997), studies of the connection between research and practice and the apparent failure of research to affect teaching has provided the following insights:

- Teachers do not find research persuasive or authoritative.
- Research has not been relevant to practice and has not addressed teachers' questions.
- Research findings have not been expressed in ways that are comprehensible to teachers.
- The education system itself is unable to change or, conversely, it is inherently unstable and susceptible to fads.

Many teacher researchers may consider Kennedy's hypotheses to be statements of the obvious; however, these statements provide yet another rationale for why many teachers have chosen to be reflective practitioners: to address the intractability of the educational system. These hypotheses also speak to the desire to put action into ongoing action research efforts.

ACTION RESEARCH IS PERSUASIVE AND AUTHORITATIVE

Research done by teachers for teachers involves collection of persuasive data. These data are persuasive because teachers are invested in the legitimacy of the data collection, that is, they have identified data sources that provide persuasive insights into the impact of an intervention on student outcomes. Similarly, the findings of action research and the actions recommended by these findings are authoritative for teacher researchers. In doing action research, teacher researchers have developed solutions to their own problems. Teachers—not outside "experts"—are the authorities on what works in their classrooms.

ACTION RESEARCH IS RELEVANT

The relevance of published research to the real world of teachers is perhaps the most common concern raised by teachers when asked about the practical applications of educational research—either the problems investigated by researchers are not the problems teachers really have or the schools or classrooms in which the research was conducted are vastly different from their own school environment. In reviewing the last two decades of research on schools and teaching, however, Kennedy (1997) cites the seminal works of Jackson's (1968) *Life in Classrooms* and Lortie's (1975) *Schoolteacher* as ways to illustrate the relevance of the findings of these studies. Kennedy's review (1997) found that classroom life was characterized by crowds, power, praise, and uncertainty:

- Crowds—Students are always grouped with 20 or 30 others, which means that they must wait in line, wait to be called on, and wait for help.
- Power—Teachers control most actions and events and decide what the group will do.
- Praise—Teachers give and withhold praise, so students know which of their classmates are favored by the teacher.
- Uncertainty—The presence of 20 to 30 children in a single classroom means there are many possibilities for an interruption in one's work.

Kennedy (1997) argues that one of the aims of research is to increase certainty by creating **predictability** within the classroom, because "Routines increase predictability and decrease anxiety for both teachers and students" (p. 6).

One of the outcomes of action research is that it satisfies the desire of all teachers to increase the predictability of what happens in their classrooms—in particular, to increase the likelihood that a given curriculum, instructional strategy, or use of technology will positively affect student outcomes. And although these desirable outcomes come at the initial expense of predictability—that is, they have emerged from the implementation of a *new* intervention or innovation—the findings of your action research inquiries will, over time, contribute to the predictability of your teaching environments.

ACTION RESEARCH ALLOWS TEACHERS ACCESS TO RESEARCH FINDINGS

Kennedy (1997) also hypothesizes that the apparent lack of connection between research and practice is due to teachers' poor access to research findings. This apparent lack of impact of research on teaching is, in part, credited to teachers' prior beliefs and values and the realization that teachers' practices cannot be changed simply by informing them of the results of a study. After all, if we reflect on how we currently teach and what we hold as sacred teaching practices, we are likely to find that our beliefs and values stem from how we were taught as children ("It worked for me and I'm successful. I'm a teacher.") and how we have had teaching modeled for us through our teaching apprenticeships (student teaching).

Simply informing teachers about research is unlikely to bring about change. Therein lies the beauty, power, and potential of action research to positively affect practice. As a teacher researcher, you challenge your taken-for-granted assumptions about teaching and learning. Your research findings are meaningful to you because *you* have identified the area of focus. *You* have been willing to challenge the conventional craft culture. In short, *your* willingness to reflect on and change your thinking about your teaching practices has led you to become a successful and productive member of the professional community.

ACTION RESEARCH CHALLENGES THE INTRACTABILITY OF REFORM OF THE EDUCATIONAL SYSTEM

Kennedy's (1997) final hypothesis is that the lack of connection between research and practice can be attributed to the educational system itself, not the research. Kennedy (1997) characterizes the American educational system as a system that:

- Has no consensus on goals and guiding principles.
- Has no central authority to settle disputes.
- Is continually bombarded with new fads and fancies.
- Provides limited evidence to support or refute any particular idea.
- Encourages reforms that run at cross-purposes to each other.
- Gives teachers less time than most other countries do to develop curricula and daily lessons.

Given this characterization, it is little wonder that the more things change, the more they stay the same! Again, action research gives teacher researchers the opportunity to embrace a problem-solving philosophy and practice as an integral part of the culture of their schools and their professional disposition, and to challenge the intractability of educational reform by making action research a part of the system, rather than just another fad.

ACTION RESEARCH IS NOT A FAD

One insight that Kennedy does not address when discussing the apparent failure of research to affect teachers' practices is the belief of many classroom teachers that researchers tend to investigate trendy fads and are interested only in the curricular approach or instructional method *du jour*. Therefore, it is not surprising to hear critics of action research say: "Why bother? This is just another fad that, like other fads in education, will eventually pass if I can wait it out!" But action research is decidedly not a fad for one simple reason: *Good teachers have always systematically looked at the effects of their teaching on student learning.* They may not have called this practice action research, and they may not have thought their reflection was formal enough to be labeled research, but action research it was!

Making Action Research a Part of Daily Teaching Practices

The first step in making action research a part of daily teaching practices is to become familiar with the process and recognize how much action research is already a part of daily life as a classroom teacher. Consider this analogy that reveals how similar the act of teaching is to the act of doing action research. In any individual lesson, you plan, implement, and evaluate your teaching, just as a teacher researcher does when undertaking action research. You develop a list of objectives (a focus area), implement the lesson, reflect on whether the children achieved the objectives through summative evaluation statements (data collection), spend time at the end of a lesson reflecting on what happened (data analysis and interpretation), and spend time at the end of the day considering how today's lesson will affect tomorrow's lesson (action planning). Like action research, the act of teaching is largely an intuitive process carried out idiosyncratically by both experienced and novice teachers.

I was recently reminded by a teacher enrolled in one of my action research classes that in my fervor and enthusiasm to illustrate data analysis and interpretation in practice (based on some of my own research), I had unwittingly made her feel that research was something that could realistically be done only by a full-time researcher who did not have a "real" job to contend with—namely, teaching 28 very lively first graders! The teacher felt that action research was so difficult and time consuming that it was unreasonable to expect a mere mortal to undertake the activity. She felt as if she needed "Super Teacher" to burst into the classroom and take over business! Not so. If the process of action research cannot be done without adversely affecting the fundamental work of teaching, then it ought not to be done at all.

Throughout this text, we will explore practical, realistic ways that action research can become a normative part of the teaching-learning process. There will be an initial commitment of time and energy as one learns the process but that time is an investment in enriching the education of students. If one is to realistically incorporate the process of action research into daily teaching practices, a few things need to happen:

- *Try the process and be convinced that the investment of time and energy is worth the outcomes.* First, undertake an action research project that is meaningful to you and addresses the needs of your students. Once the project is completed, you will see the contribution your new understanding of the subject will make to your teaching or your students' learning (or ideally, both!). Only then will you be fully confident that action research is a worthwhile investment of your time and energy. Your beliefs and attitudes about action research will be changed after you have tried it for yourself.
- *Know that action research is a process that can be undertaken without having a negative impact on your personal and professional life.* For example, action research, as it is described in this book, is not intended to be just "one more thing" for you to do. Teachers already have too much to do and not enough time in which to do it! The action research process advocated in this book is intended to provide you with a systematic framework that can be applied to

Making Action Research a Part of Your Daily Teaching Practice

_____ Actually *try* the process to convince yourself that the investments of time and energy are worth the outcomes.

_____ Recognize that action research is a process that can be undertaken without negatively affecting your personal and professional life.

_____ Seek support from your professional colleagues.

your daily teaching routines. The investment of time as you learn how to do action research will be worth the outcomes. The process may also produce unexpected positive outcomes by providing opportunities for collaborative efforts with colleagues who share a common area of focus. This book provides strategies you can use to develop your *reflective practice* utilizing many of the existing data sources in your classroom and school. It will provide you with a model that can be shared with like-minded colleagues who also are committed to improving the teaching-learning process in their classrooms.

- *Ask for support from your professional colleagues with implementation.* Although such strategies as studying theory, observing demonstrations, and practicing with feedback enable most teachers to develop their skills to the point that they can use a model fluidly, skills development by itself does not ensure skills transfer. Relatively few persons who learn new approaches to teaching will integrate their skills into regular practice unless they receive coaching (Joyce, Hersh, & McKibben, 1983). That is why seeking support and guidance from other teacher researchers is critical to your success as an action researcher. These suggestions are summarized in Research in Action Checklist 1–1.

The Process of Action Research

Now that we have defined action research, described its historical and theoretical foundations, and explained why teachers do it, let's explore the process of action research. Many guidelines and models have been provided over the years for teacher researchers to follow, for example:

- Kurt Lewin (1952) described a "spiraling" cyclical process that included planning, execution, and reconnaissance.
- Stephen Kemmis (1988) created a well-known representation of the action research "spiral" (see Figure 1–1) that includes the essential characteristics of Lewin's model. Kemmis's model includes reconnaissance, planning, first action step, monitoring, reflecting, rethinking, and evaluation.
- Emily Calhoun (1994) described an Action Research Cycle (see Figure 1–2) that includes selecting an area or problem of collective interest, collecting data, organizing data, analyzing and interpreting data, and taking action.

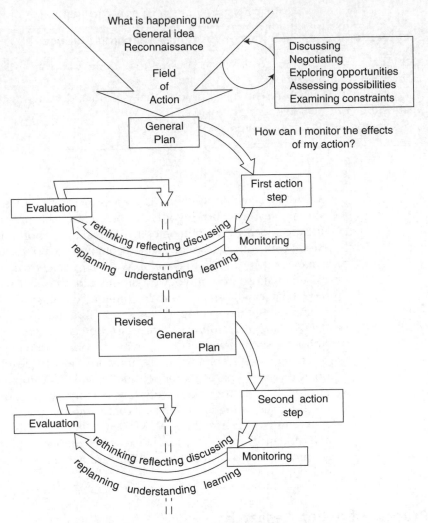

FIGURE 1–1   A Representation of Lewin's Action Research Cycle

Source: *Action Research in Retrospect and Prospect* (p. 29), by Stephen Kemmis, 1988. Victoria, Australia: Deakin University Press, distributor. Copyright 1988 Deakin University. Reprinted with permission. All rights reserved.

- Gordon Wells (1994) described what he calls an Idealized Model of the Action Research Cycle (see Figure 1–3) that includes observing, interpreting, planning change, acting, and "the practitioner's personal theory" (p. 27), which informs and is informed by the action research cycle.
- Richard Sagor (2000) described a seven-step process that includes selecting a focus, clarifying theories, identifying research questions, collecting data, analyzing data, reporting results, and taking informed action.
- Ernest Stringer (2004) described an Action Research Helix (see Figure 1–4) that includes looking, thinking, and acting as "phases of the research (are) repeated over time" (p. 10).

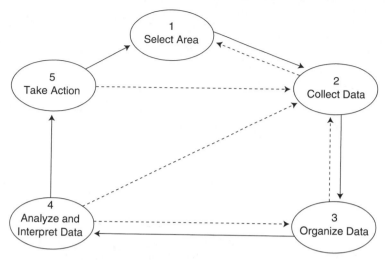

FIGURE 1–2   The Action Research Cycle

Source: *How to Use Action Research in the Self-Renewing School*, p. 2, by Emily Calhoun, 1994, Alexandria, VA: Association for Supervision and Curriculum Development. Copyright ©1994 ASCD. Reprinted by permission. All rights reserved. The Association for Supervision and Curriculum Development is a worldwide community of educators advocating sound policies and sharing best practices to achieve the success of each learner. To learn more, visit ASCD at www.ascd.org.

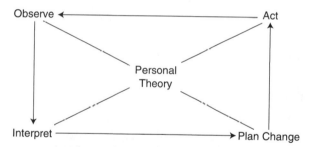

FIGURE 1–3   An Idealized Model of the Action Research Cycle

Source: *Changing Schools from Within: Creating Communities of Inquiry*, p. 27, by Gordon Wells, 1994, Toronto, Ontario: OISE Press. Copyright 1994 OISE Press. Reprinted by permission. All rights reserved. U.S. rights granted by permission of Gordon Wells: *Changing Schools from Within: Creating Communities of Inquiry* (Heinemann, A division of Read Elsevier, Inc., Portsmouth, NH, 1994).

- John Creswell (2005) described action research as a dynamic, flexible process that involves the following steps: determining if action research is the best design to use, identifying a problem to study, locating resources to help address the problem, identifying necessary information, implementing the data collection, analyzing the data, developing a plan for action, and implementing the plan and reflecting on whether or not it makes a difference.
- Cher Hendricks (2006) described an action research process that follows the principle of "systematic inquiry based on ongoing reflection" (p. 9) that is heavily influenced by the work of Lawrence Stenhouse (1981) from the Center for Applied Research in Education at the University of East Anglia in England (see Figure 1–5).

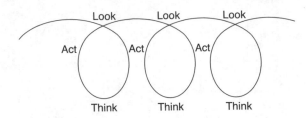

FIGURE 1–4 Action Research Helix

Source: *Action Research in Education* (p. 12), by Ernest Stringer, 2004, Upper Saddle River, NJ: Prentice Hall.

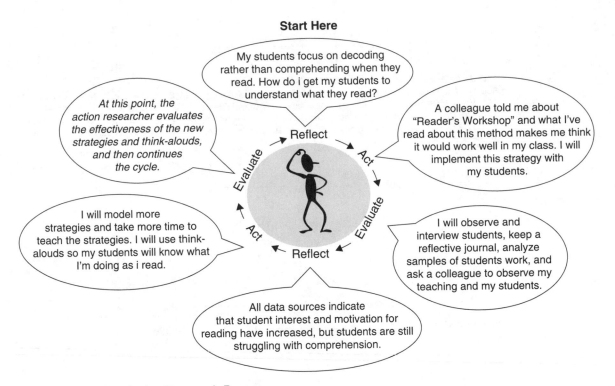

FIGURE 1–5 The Action Research Process

Source: *Improving Schools through Action Research: A Comprehensive Guide for Educators* (p. 9), by Cher Hendricks, 2006, Boston, MA: Allyn and Bacon.

All these models have enjoyed varying degrees of popularity, depending on the context in which they have been applied. For example, these action research models have been applied to agriculture, health care, social work, factory work, and community development in isolated areas.

Clearly, these action research models share some common elements: a sense of purpose based on a "problem" or "area of focus" (identification of an area of focus), observation or monitoring of practice (collection of data), synthesis of information gathered (analysis and interpretation of data), and some form of "action" that invariably "spirals" the researcher back into the process repeatedly (development of an action plan).

These shared elements are what we will focus on in this book. The following chapters will address in detail how to proceed with an action research process that includes the four elements mentioned above: **identifying an area of focus**, **collecting data**, **analyzing and interpreting data**, and **developing an action plan**. Key Concepts Box 1–4 illustrates the action research process used by Deborah South, described at the beginning of this chapter.

This four-step process, which I have termed the **Dialectic Action Research Spiral**, is illustrated in Figure 1–6. It provides teacher researchers with a practical guide and illustrates how to proceed with inquiries. It is a model for research done *by* teachers and *for* teachers and students, not research done *on* them, and as such

KEY CONCEPTS BOX 1–4

Steps in the Action Research Process Based on Deborah South's Example of "Unmotivated" Students	
KEY CONCEPT	EXAMPLE
Identifying an area of focus	The purpose of this study was to describe the effects of a "study skills" curriculum on student outcomes. In particular, the study focused on the variables of student attendance, peer influence, adult influence, and students' self-esteem.
Collecting data	Data was collected through surveys, interviews, and report card/attendance records.
Analyzing and Interpreting the data	Attendance did not appear to be an issue—children attended school regularly. Peer groups did affect performance. Students encouraged each other not be complete homework assignments. Teacher approval of student work appeared to have little effect on students' work habits, whereas about half of the children indicated that they were motivated to complete their homework to receive parental approval. On average, student grades had dropped dramatically during the term in which they were enrolled in the study skills class. Interpretation: The study skills class was having a negative impact on student outcomes, behavior, and attitudes.
Developing an action plan	It was determined that students would not be homogeneously grouped for a study skills class the following year because of a "critical mass of negativity" that appeared to emerge from the students as they fed off each other's lack of motivation. The study skills curriculum would continue to be used and monitored with a heterogeneous grouping of students.

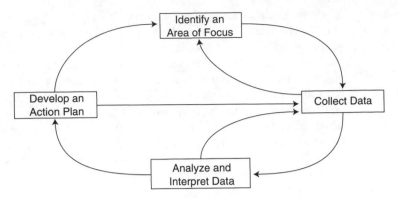

FIGURE 1–6 The Dialectic Action Research Spiral

is a dynamic and responsive model that can be adapted to different contexts and purposes. It was designed to provide teacher researchers with "provocative and constructive ways" of thinking about their work (Wolcott, 1989, p. 137).

Summary

Action research is systematic inquiry done by teachers (or other individuals in the teaching-learning environment) to gather information about—and subsequently improve—how their particular schools operate, how they teach, and how well their students learn.

The geographical settings and theoretical contexts in which action research efforts evolved are diverse. Two main philosophical perspectives inform current action research practice: **critical action research**, which has its roots in critical and postmodern theory and emphasizes democracy and liberation; and **practical action research**, which takes a more applied and contextualized approach to action research.

The shared goal for all types of action research is to improve the lives of students and teachers. Classroom teachers are often skeptical of research because of its historical failure to connect to classroom practice and the experiences of teachers and students. Action research is not a passing fad because good teachers have always critically reflected upon their practices. This text will provide realistic strategies and practical guidelines for incorporating action research into teachers' daily classroom practices.

Although there are a number of models for doing action research, the basic process consists of four steps: **identify an area of focus**, **collect data**, **analyze and interpret data**, and **develop an action plan**. The following chapters will explore these four steps in greater detail.

For Further Thought

1. How would you describe the purpose(s) of action research?
2. How do the tenets of the critical/postmodern perspective support the need for action research?

3. Suppose that the students in your class are not progressing in essay writing as you had hoped. Using the four steps in the action research process described in this chapter, sketch out briefly what you might do to systematically examine this issue.
4. Your school has received a large professional development grant focused on improving children's scores on a national reading test. You believe that your existing reading program is strong. What kind of action research study might you conduct to address the differences between your current reading program's outcomes and the concepts tested on the national test?

2 Deciding on an Area of Focus

This chapter provides guidelines for clarifying a general idea and an area of focus for action research efforts. Procedures are described for doing reconnaissance and reviewing related literature using online resources such as ERIC, the Internet, university library resources, or articles found in journals published by professional organizations for educators. Finally, this chapter tells how to create an action research plan.

After reading this chapter you should be able to:
1. Select an appropriate area of focus.
2. Do reconnaissance.
3. Review related literature using online resources.
4. Write an action plan to guide your work.

Interactive Teen Theater

Cathy Mitchell

Cathy Mitchell is a substitute teacher who also works with teen theater companies. Her story helps us to see how serendipity can play a role in developing an area of focus. In the beginning of the action research process, Cathy was unsure of her area of focus. However, as the result of an unexpected "intervention" to her teen theater production when an actor did not turn up for a performance, Cathy decided to systematically investigate the effects of improvisation on audience participation.

For the past 10 years I have directed peer education teen theaters. These companies create and perform original plays based on company members' experiences and ideas. The plays are collections of dramatic scenes, comic sketches, and songs; the topics are current issues of concern to young people, including self-esteem, substance abuse, teen pregnancy, love versus lust, violence, family relationships, and sexually transmitted diseases. We tour extensively, performing for high schools and middle schools as well as at juvenile detention facilities.

Although the company is generally very well received, I have felt that there is something stale in the actor/audience relationship. The audience sits attentively, laughs in recognition, and enjoys the variety in their class day, but remains essentially passive. Question sessions after the show, initially planned to generate discussion about important topics, frequently degenerated into boring adulation questions, such as "How long have you been rehearsing this?" or "Do you want to be an actor when you grow up?"

Two years ago, a few actors had to miss a performance. When we arrived at the high school we were scheduled to perform at, we realized the opening scene had two small roles that we could not eliminate but didn't have enough actors to fill. I asked two children from the audience to volunteer, taught them their lines backstage while the rest of the scene was going on, and they walked on stage and finished the scene. The audience was instantly galvanized. Even

with this very small change we had broken the division between actor and audience.

This began my experience into interactive theater. For me, this has meant bringing some of the improvisation techniques that we use to develop material during rehearsals onto the stage and inviting the audience to participate in limited ways. I found that involving the audience changed the dynamics from a passive spectator sport to a more participatory dialogue.

Through my research I have arrived at a working description for interactive theater: A short scene is played by workshop actors. The audience is asked to look for opportunities to improve the resolution. The scene is played again, and any time anyone wants to intervene and take any character's place to show a better way of handling the situation, they just shout "Stop!" and take over the role. One scene may be played many times. Often no closure is evident, and the scene ends in unresolved issues and heightened emotions. The actors and audience then discuss the issues generated by the scene.

The purpose of my study was to determine the effects of audience interaction with the actors in teen theater productions on their ability to identify issues and transfer learnings into similar problems in their lives. For example, in the current production of Duct Tape Theater, a company I direct, there is a well-written scene called "Sticks and Stones," which is a collage containing poetry, a song, short monologues, and scenes. It lasts about 20 minutes and confronts issues of prejudice, discrimination, and violence. I decided, as my intervention, to replace this scene with an interactive theater piece developed with the audience. For three performances we included "Sticks and Stones" (my control groups), and for three other performances we included what became known as the "Violence Improv" audience interaction scene. This gave us six audiences: three control groups and three interactive groups.

Some of my methods of data collection for this project—my personal journal and the actors' journals, which are required for actors receiving credit for the class—were already in place. I also asked each teacher to write me a letter commenting on what they observed during the performance. None of these gave me the data I really wanted but which was most difficult to collect—data from the audience. I decided to have my acting company develop this data collection source with me. The actors and I developed a questionnaire to be filled out directly after the performance and a group interview technique that involved three company members meeting with a small group of audience members for about 15 minutes. The goal was to generate as many responses as possible to the scenes about teen violence and harassment. One actor served as the interviewer, one as the scribe, and one kept a running tally of comments and responses.

The data showed four clear themes:

1. The audience clearly judged the performance containing the "Violence Improv" as more relevant to their lives than the control performance of "Sticks and Stones."

2. More individuals participated in discussing the issues of violence and harassment, with more overall comments and more comments that were considered "right on." This data showed that more audience members were able to both identify issues in the performance and relate these issues to their own lives.

3. The clearest negative response was that the interactive piece made the performance feel "rushed." These data told me that the interactive material threw off the timing of the show. I often wrote in my own journal that I feel exhausted at the end of performances, and teachers wrote to me that we were running into break time and past the end of the period "trying to squeeze everything in."

4. The biggest letdown to me was that there wasn't any significant increase in the number of different issues identified or solutions suggested between the two audiences. Even though the interactive improvisation generated more answers and much more participation, the issues and solutions were pretty much the same.

My action research project confirmed to me that my methods for making teen theater work more meaningful are on the right track. It also became clear, however, that the format I am using is not the best one. I plan to continue working with the teen theater groups, to modify the format I have used in the past, and to monitor the effects of the changes on participants' transfer of learning to their real lives. For me, this is critical work, and the most important result of this project is that I feel renewed energy for my work. Last year at this time I was busily seeking a replacement for myself and announcing to everyone that I wasn't going to direct teens anymore. I didn't even consider that I could examine the problem, address it, and remedy it. It feels really good to expect something to happen in my working life as a result of my own research and reflection.

NOT EVERYONE COMES TO AN ACTION RESEARCH SETTING with an area of focus in mind. In fact, many teachers initially resist participating in the process. It is not uncommon for teachers and administrators to skeptically claim, "I'm only here because I have to be. No action research—no teaching/administrator license!" In this teen theater example, the "intervention" and "area of focus" emerged quite unexpectedly and led to some important understandings about how to increase audience understanding and participation.

We'll assume, then, that you may not have identified an area of focus. However, you probably do have several interests and concerns: perhaps your content area, a self-contained special education classroom, an at-risk program, an alternative education program, a multi-graded classroom, a single fourth-grade classroom, a reading specialist program, a block-scheduled team teaching program, or even a one-room schoolhouse, to name a few!

Every teacher and administrator who undertakes an action research project starts at the same place: making explicit a question or problem to investigate, or defining an **area of focus**. Finding an area of focus can be hard work if your action research inquiry is going to be engaging and meaningful for you. Taking time in the beginning to ensure that your topic is important—for you—is a critical step in the action research process. No one should tell you what your area of focus is or ought to be. The following guidelines can help you focus your research question.

Clarifying a General Idea and an Area of Focus

In the beginning of the action research process, you need to clarify the general idea that will be the area of focus. The general idea is a statement that links an idea to an action and refers to a situation one wishes to change or improve on (Elliott, 1991). Here are some examples, phrased in the form of a statement based on an observation, and followed by a question about how the situation could be improved:

- *Statement/Observation*: Students do not seem to be engaged during teen theater productions.
  Question: How can I improve their engagement?
- *Statement/Observation*: Students take a lot of time to learn problem solving in mathematics, but this process doesn't appear to transfer to their acquisition of other mathematics skills and knowledge.
  Question: How can I improve the integration and transfer of problem-solving skills in mathematics?
- *Statement/Observation*: Parents are unhappy with regular parent-teacher conferences.
  Question: How can I improve the conferencing process using student-led conferences?

Taking time in the beginning of the action research process to identify what you feel passionate about is critical. For some, this will be a relatively short activity—you may have come to an action research setting with a clear sense of a student-centered, teacher-centered, or parent-driven area of focus. For others, gaining a sense of the general idea will be more problematic. Don't rush it. Take time to talk to colleagues, reflect on your daily classroom life, and carefully consider what nags at you when you prepare for work every day.

Identifying Your Area of Focus

Is your area of focus an issue that
____ Involves teaching and learning?
____ Is within your focus of control?
____ You feel passionate about?
____ You would like to change or improve?

CRITERIA FOR SELECTING A GENERAL IDEA/AREA OF FOCUS

There are some important criteria you should keep in mind while identifying your general idea and subsequent area of focus (Creswell, 2005; Elliott, 1991; Sagor, 2000):

- The area of focus should involve teaching and learning and should focus on your own practice.
- The area of focus is something within your locus of control.
- The area of focus is something you feel passionate about.
- The area of focus is something you would like to change or improve.

Applying these criteria early in the process will keep you on track during the early stages of the action research process. They will also remind you of the vital and dynamic dimensions of action research—that it is important work done by teacher researchers for themselves and their students, the results of which will ultimately improve student outcomes. (See Research in Action Checklist 2–1.)

Reconnaissance

The next important step in the action research process is **reconnaissance**, or preliminary information gathering. More specifically, reconnaissance is taking time to reflect on your own beliefs and to understand the nature and context of your general idea. Doing reconnaissance takes three forms: self-reflection, description, and explanation.

GAINING INSIGHT INTO YOUR AREA OF FOCUS THROUGH SELF-REFLECTION

First, try to explore your own understanding of:

- The *theories* that impact your practice.
- The *educational values* you hold.
- How your work in schools fits into the *larger context* of schooling and society.
- The *historical* contexts of your *school* and *schooling* and how things got to be the way they are.
- The *historical* contexts of how you arrived at your *beliefs* about *teaching* and *learning* (Kemmis & McTaggart, 1988, 2000).

If your general idea for your action research inquiry is the question: How can I improve the integration and transfer of problem-solving skills in mathematics? You might think about the following:

- Based on my experience teaching mathematics and my reading of the subject, I have been influenced by Van de Walle's (2003) *theory* about teaching and learning mathematics developmentally. In particular, the goal of mathematics is *relational understanding*, which is the connection between *conceptual* and *procedural knowledge* in mathematics. This theory of mathematics directly affects the ways in which I think about teaching mathematics to my students.
- I hold the *educational value* that children ought to be able to transfer problem-solving skills to other areas of mathematics, as well as to life outside of school. That is, I am committed to relevancy of curriculum.
- I believe that mathematical problem solving, and problem solving in general, fits the *larger context* of schooling and society by providing children with critical lifelong learning skills that can be transferred to all aspects of their life.
- The *historical context* of mathematics teaching suggests a rote method of memorizing facts and algorithms. Although this approach to teaching mathematics worked for me (as a child and young teacher), it no longer suffices as a teaching method today.
- The historical context of how I came to *believe* in the importance of changing how I teach mathematics to children has grown out of my own frustration with knowing what to do to solve a problem, but not knowing *why* I need to use a particular approach or algorithm.
- Given this self-reflection on an area of focus related to the integration and transfer of problem-solving skills in mathematics, I can now better understand the problem before I implement an intervention that addresses my concern for how to best teach a *relevant* problem-solving curriculum.

This is part of the "mind work" or "mental gymnastics" of action research. It is not an activity that will immediately produce new and exciting curriculum and/or teaching materials—something that may follow later in the process when you become clearer about an intervention.

GAINING INSIGHT INTO YOUR AREA OF FOCUS THROUGH DESCRIPTIVE ACTIVITIES

Next, try to describe as fully as possible the situation you want to change or improve by focusing on *who, what, when, where,* and *how.* Grappling with these questions to clarify the focus area for your action research efforts will prevent moving ahead with an investigation that was too murky to begin with. For example, in this stage, you might answer these questions:

- What evidence do you have that this (the problem-solving skills of math students) is a problem?
- Which students are not able to transfer problem-solving skills to other mathematics tasks?
- How is problem solving presently taught?

- How often is problem solving taught?
- What is the ratio of time spent teaching problem solving to time spent teaching other mathematics skills?

GAINING INSIGHT INTO YOUR AREA OF FOCUS THROUGH EXPLANATORY ACTIVITIES

Once you've adequately described the situation you intend to investigate, try to explain it. Focus on the *why*. Can you account for the critical factors that have an impact on the general idea? In essence, this is the step in which you develop a hypothesis stating the expected relationships between variables in your study (Elliott, 1991).

In this case, you might hypothesize that students are struggling with the transfer of problem-solving skills to other mathematics tasks because they are not getting enough practice, they lack fundamental basic math skills, or the use of math manipulatives has been missing or not used to its full potential. Given these possible explanations for why children have not been successfully transferring problem-solving skills to other areas of mathematics, you might develop the following hypotheses:

- A relationship exists between the use of a mathematics curriculum that emphasizes the children's ability to know *what* to do and *why* to do it and children's abilities to transfer problem-solving skills.
- A relationship exists between the use of a mathematics curriculum that emphasizes the use of manipulatives (to help children create meaning) and children's abilities to transfer problem-solving skills.

These reconnaissance activities (self-reflection, description, and explanation) help teacher researchers clarify what they already know about the proposed focus of the study; what they believe to be true about the relationships of the factors, variables, and contexts that make up their work environment; and what they believe can improve the situation. Research in Action Checklist 2–2 summarizes the critical activities for reconnaissance that you should perform at this point in the action research process.

RESEARCH IN ACTION CHECKLIST 2–2

Critical Activities for Doing Reconnaissance

Self-Reflection:
____ Reflect on your area of focus in light of your values and beliefs; your understandings about the relationships among theory, practice, school, and society; how things got to be the way they are; and what you believe about teaching and learning.

Description:
____ Describe the situation you wish to change or improve.
____ Describe the evidence you have that the area of focus is a problem.
____ Identify the critical factors that affect your area of focus.

Explanation:
____ Explain the situation you intend to investigate by hypothesizing how and why the critical factors you've identified affect that situation.

Review of Related Literature

At this point you should make an initial foray into the professional literature, the formal record of other people's experiences, to try to better understand the problem on which you are focusing. The literature may suggest other ways of looking at your problem and help you to identify potential *promising practices* that you might use in your classroom to correct the problem. To borrow the words of Kemmis and McTaggart (1988), "Can existing research throw any light on your situation and help you see it more clearly?" (p. 55).

Some authors of action research books debate the importance of reviewing the literature as a strategy in the action research process. Most experts agree, however, that reviewing the literature is a valuable activity for action researchers. For example, Sagor (1992) writes: "I would encourage anyone interested in doing good research to review the literature immediately after engaging in the problem-formulation activities" (p. 76). Although reviewing the literature has long been a well-established component of dissertation and contract research and graduate research classes, its inclusion here signals the importance that teacher researchers have awarded the activity.

Reviewing the literature is a valuable contribution to the action research process that could actually save you time. Often, teacher researchers think that they know what their problem is but become stymied in the process because they weren't really sure what they were asking. Taking time to immerse yourself in the literature allows you to reflect on your own problems through someone else's lens. You can locate yourself within the research literature and find support for what you are doing or be challenged by what other researchers have done and how they have tackled a particular problem.

At the end of the process, you ought to be informed enough about the literature that you could talk to colleagues about the major themes that emerged. Similarly, you should be able to talk about "promising practices" that were discussed.

You might also view this activity as being analogous to the exercise most people undertake before making a major purchase for their family—they immerse themselves in the literature to see what other folks have learned about a particular product. For example, I recently purchased a new automobile. My wife and I discussed the kind of vehicle we wanted in light of our family needs (one child), recreational interests (skiing in the winter and camping in the summer) and, of course, budget (can we really afford a car payment?). In a sense, this activity was akin to selecting an area of focus. In our case, our area of focus was the purchase of a sport utility vehicle (SUV). This led me very naturally to review the related literature about SUVs in such sources as *Consumer Reports, Car and Driver, Edmund's Buying Guide* online, and the *Kelly Blue Book* for reviews and comparative pricing information.

This review of literature was an invaluable exercise for helping me see clearly the issues related to purchasing an SUV. For example: Did we really need all the extras included on a particular vehicle? What size engine did we need to tow our tent trailer? How did the safety and reliability of different vehicles compare? As in action research, immersion in the related literature helped to clarify all the issues that must be considered when undertaking the solving of problems.

This activity also helped me identify "promising practices" for purchasing a new vehicle. For example, given the "sticker price," how much should I really pay for the vehicle? Again, the literature identified purchasing strategies that had been used by experienced buyers. These strategies included determining the manufacturer's cost of the vehicle to the dealer; accounting for dealer incentive programs, dealer "holdbacks," and manufacturer-to-buyer "cashback" incentives; and, of course, calculating a "fair" price while still paying the dealer enough to cover advertising costs, commissions, and so on.

After reviewing this literature, I was prepared to implement a "promising practice" (buying strategy) for the SUV we had determined best met our needs and budget. And although the time spent immersing myself in the literature did not guarantee that my intervention would achieve my desired outcomes, I was better prepared to initiate my strategy and informed about how I would know if I achieved my goals—based on what other experts in the field had done in the past.

Sometimes, teacher researchers will claim that they cannot find any published research related to their area of focus. This invariably leads to questions of relevance and importance. After all, if nobody else has researched the problem, perhaps it is not worthy of investigation! Unlike the SUV example above, my illustration here is far more personal and serious. A few years ago my son, who was 3 years old at the time, inexplicably began to pass blood in his urine—a pretty scary sight for any parent. After many invasive medical tests over a 6-month period, we finally opted for a procedure that required general anesthesia in order to determine the cause of the blood. The surgeon emerged from the operating room and pronounced, "I have some good news, and I have some bad news!" The good news was that the surgeon was able to diagnose the cause of the internal bleeding—a rare, benign, and non–life-threatening condition called trigonitis. The bad news was that the surgeon was unable to tell us why our son had developed the condition or how to treat it! I was shocked at this revelation from the surgeon, a pediatric urology specialist. How could my son be bleeding internally and there not be a medical explanation? Simply, the surgeon responded, because the condition was rare, benign, and non–life-threatening it did not warrant research! My point here is not to be melodramatic but rather to make a case for the importance of your own research, regardless of whether it has been researched (and published) by other professionals. Just because your area of focus is unique to you does not make it any less important. It is your problem and you own it. Do not be disheartened if your review of the literature fails to provide you with helpful insights.

Action researchers rely on four main sources of literature to better prepare themselves to undertake research: online searching of the Educational Resources Information Center (ERIC) and similar online resources (for example, Education Index, PyscINFO, Dissertation Abstracts, Readers' Guide to Periodical Literature, and the Annual Review of Psychology), online searching of the Internet and the World Wide Web, membership in professional organizations, and visits to a university library.

SEARCHING ONLINE RESOURCES

Education Resources Information Center (ERIC)

Established in 1966 by the National Library of Education as part of the U.S. Department of Education's Office of Educational Research and Improvement, ERIC is the world's largest database on education. The online database provides information on subjects ranging from early childhood and elementary education to education for gifted children and rural and urban education. ERIC is used by more than 500,000 people each year, providing them with access to more than 1.1 million bibliographic citations and more than 107,000 full-text non-journal documents. In 2004, the ERIC system was restructured by the Department of Education. The new Web site, launched in September 2004, uses the most up-to-date retrieval methods to provide users access to the ERIC databases.

With its user-friendly features, ERIC is a quick, easy way to get access to the related literature. In addition, there is no charge associated with conducting an ERIC search online from your home or school computer and accessing full-text ERIC documents. The best starting point for your ERIC explorations is the ERIC home page at http://www.eric.ed.gov. (Internet addresses were checked for accuracy during the production of this text. Due to the rapidly changing nature of technology, some addresses and online procedures may be different at the time of your reading. The basic strategies for online searching, however, will remain the same.) This home page includes links to all other ERIC sites, most notably, ERIC Search.

You can conduct a search using ERIC online in several ways. The basic ERIC search prompts you to search using keywords, author only, title only, or ERIC document number. The advanced ERIC search offers the same prompts as the basic search but also allows you to search by ISBN number, journal name, source institution, sponsoring agency, publication types (e.g., book, review, dissertation), ERIC Thesaurus descriptor, publication date, and full-text availability.

The thesaurus search prompts you to search using your own descriptor, which is then matched to one or more ERIC descriptors (remember: garbage in, garbage out!). You must search ERIC using ERIC descriptors. For example, entering the term *achievement tests* results in a suggestion from ERIC to use a narrower search term such as *equivalency tests*, *mastery tests*, or *national competency tests*. You can browse the thesaurus alphabetically or look for descriptors in the 40-plus categories provided by ERIC. Once you have identified materials that you would like to examine, you need to access these materials. You may notice in your searches that documents are categorized with an ED or EJ designation. An ED designation is generally used for unpublished documents, such as reports, studies, and even lesson plans. ED references are available in university libraries through ERIC's microfiche collection or may be available as full-text online documents. An EJ designation is used for articles that have been published in professional journals. EJ articles are not available in full text from ERIC and must be tracked down in the periodicals collection of a library or purchased from article reprint companies.

Although ERIC is the largest computer database for searches of education literature, it is not the only source available. Other commonly used computer databases in education are described next.

Education Index

The Education Index is an electronic index of educational periodicals with abstracts since 1983. It provides bibliographic information and abstracts of sources (some libraries subscribe to a full-text feature) pertaining to the topic(s) that have been researched. A sample result of an Education Index search is shown in Figure 2–1. In addition to article abstracts, the database includes citations for yearbooks and monograph series, videotapes, motion picture and computer program reviews, and law cases.

Record 1 of 1 in Education Abstracts 6/83-6/01
TITLE: **Developing academic confidence** to build literacy: what teachers can do
AUTHOR(S): Colvin,-Carolyn; Schlosser,-Linda-Kramer
SOURCE: Journal of Adolescent and Adult Literacy v 41 Dec 1997/Jan 1998 p. 272–81
ABSTRACT: A study examined how the classroom literacy behaviors of middle school students relate to their academic success and reinforce students' evolving sense of self. The participants were at-risk students, academically successful students, and teachers from a middle school in southern California. It was found that when academically marginal students call on literacy strategies, these strategies are limited in scope and offer little help. However, more academically successful students seem well aware of the behaviors that are likely to result in a successful literacy experience. The characteristics of academically marginal and successful students are outlined, and suggestions for helping teachers create classrooms where students behave with greater efficacy are offered.
DESCRIPTORS: Attitudes-Middle-school-students; Middle-school-students-Psychology; Self-perception; Language-arts-Motivation

FIGURE 2–1 Results of an Education Index Search
Source: From Colvin, Carolyn, & Schlosser, Linda Kramer. (Dec 1997/Jan 1998). Developing academic confidence to build literacy: What teachers can do. *Journal of Adolescent & Adult Literacy, 41*(2), 272–281. Reprinted with permission of Carolyn Colvin and the International Reading Association. The International Reading Association makes no warranties as to the accuracy of this translation.

PsycINFO

The PsycINFO database is the online version of Psychological Abstracts, a print source that presents summaries of completed psychological research studies (see http://www.apa.org/psycinfo). Produced monthly, Psychological Abstracts contains summaries of journal articles, technical reports, book chapters, and books in psychology. It is organized by subject area according to the PsycINFO classification codes for easy browsing. The classification codes also serve as the table of contents for the Psychological Abstracts, which can be accessed at http://www.apa.org/psycinfo/training/tips-classcodes.html. These classification codes allow you to retrieve abstracts for studies in a specific category—for example, Developmental Disorders and Autism (3250) or Speech and Language Disorders (3270).

Dissertation Abstracts

Dissertation Abstracts contains bibliographic citations and abstracts from all subject areas for doctoral dissertations and master's theses completed at more than 1,000 accredited colleges and universities worldwide. The database dates back to 1861, with abstracts included from 1980 forward. If after reading an abstract you wish to obtain a copy of the complete dissertation, check to see if it is available in your library. If not, speak to a librarian about how to obtain a copy. The results of a Dissertation Abstracts search are shown in Figure 2–2.

Readers' Guide to Periodical Literature

Readers' Guide to Periodical Literature is an index similar in format to the Education Index. Instead of professional publications, however, it indexes articles in nearly 200 widely read magazines. Articles located through the Readers' Guide will generally be nontechnical, opinion-type references. These can be useful in documenting

Mark: ☑

Database: Dissertations

Title: **Learning community: An ethnographic study of popular education and homeless women in a shelter-based adult literacy program**

Author(s): Rivera, Lorna

Degree: Ph.D.

Year: 2001

Pages: 00264

Institution: Northeastern University; 0160

Advisor: Adviser Gordana Rabrenovic

Source: DAI, 61, no. 09A (2001): p. 3511

Standard No: ISBN: 0-599-95181-8

Abstract: This dissertation studies the impact of popular education approaches on the lives of fifty homeless and formerly homeless women who participated in the Adult Learners Program at a shelter located in one of Boston's poorest neighborhoods. Data were collected between January 1995 and June 1998. The guiding research questions are: How do poor women interpret the value of education? What poverty-related barriers interfere with their participation in popular education classes? How do the principles and practices of popular education build a sense of community and collective social action?

This ethnographic study utilizes multiple research methods to illustrate how popular education approaches make it possible for poor women to become empowered individually and collectively. Popular education is a methodology of teaching and learning through dialogue that directly links curriculum content to people's lived experience. It's roots are in critical social theory and the work of Paulo Freire. This research shows that poor women place a high value on education. They believe that a high school diploma will provide access to better economic opportunities and they struggle to complete their formal education within the context of homelessness and family violence.

It is argued that popular education's potential to build community is strengthened by the Adult Learners Program's participatory organization and the support services it offers to homeless families. Further, it is argued that popular education had a positive impact on the women's lives, as evidenced by: the women's increased levels of participation in their children's education; the women's participation in efforts to help other poor women in the community; the women's reported increase in self-confidence and group esteem; and, the women becoming stronger advocates for their basic legal rights related to welfare, housing, health, and education.

The research data suggest that the 1995 Massachusetts welfare reform legislation poses a significant barrier to adult literacy for welfare recipients. It is argued that limiting access to education through "work-first" welfare reform policies reproduces social inequalities. This dissertation about homeless women and popular education provides strong evidence in support of the social, political, and economic benefits of popular education programs for the poor.

SUBJECT(S)

Descriptor: EDUCATION, SOCIOLOGY OF
SOCIOLOGY, PUBLIC AND SOCIAL WELFARE
EDUCATION, ADULT AND CONTINUING

Accession No: AAI9988499

FIGURE 2–2   Results of a Dissertation Abstracts Search

Source: Screen capture retrieved from OCLC FirstSearch Web site: http://FirstSearch.oclc.org. FirstSearch electronic presentation and platform copyright © 1992–2001 by OCLC. Reprinted by permission. FirstSearch and WorldCat are registered trademarks of OCLC Online Computer Library Center, Inc.

the significance of your problem. The Readers' Guide lists bibliographic information for each entry. To obtain an article listed in the Readers' Guide, search your library's catalog for the magazine in which the article appears. If your library holds that magazine, it will be located in the periodicals department.

Annual Review of Psychology

The Annual Review of Psychology includes reviews of psychological research that are often relevant to educational research. It provides bibliographic information and abstracts for specific areas such as child development, educational administration, exceptional child education, and language teaching.

SEARCHING THE INTERNET AND THE WORLD WIDE WEB

The Internet and the World Wide Web provide information and resources on many educational topics. The World Wide Web is a service on the Internet that gives users access to text, graphics, and multimedia. You can access the Web using a computer with a modem that is hooked up to a telephone or cable line. Your computer will also need a browser (such as Netscape or Internet Explorer).

The resources you can find on the Web are almost limitless. With just a few clicks, you can access electronic educational journals that provide full-text articles, bibliographic information, and abstracts. You can also obtain up-to-the-minute research reports and information about educational research activities being undertaken at various research centers, and you can access education home pages that provide links to a range of education resources that other researchers have found especially valuable. But be warned—there is little quality control for much that is found on the Internet. At times, the sheer volume of information on the Web can be overwhelming. Be prepared to sift through piles of cyberspace junk to find the diamond in the rough. The best way to become adept at searching the Web efficiently is simply by surfing (browsing) it during your spare time. In this way, you will become familiar with maneuvering from site to site and implementing successful search strategies.

Following are some Web sites that are especially useful to action researchers. Their Internet addresses are in parentheses. In addition, you can access other electronic indexing and abstracting sources by using your computer's search engine (e.g., Lycos, Infoseek, Yahoo!, or Excite) to find some of your own addresses. Addresses containing *ed* or ending in *.edu* are related to educational institutions, and those ending in *.com* are related to commercial enterprises.

- **Uncover Periodical Index** (http://www.unm.edu/~brosen/uncover.htm). UnCover is a database with brief descriptive information about articles from more than 17,000 multidisciplinary journals. If you register (for a fee) with UnCover REVEAL, an automated alerting service, you will receive monthly tables of contents from your favorite periodicals. The service also allows you to create search strategies for your research topics.
- **NewJour** (http://gort.ucsd.edu/newjour/). This site provides an up-to-date list of journals and newsletters available on the Internet on any subject. Using NewJour's search option, you can do a title search to see if a specific journal is currently on the Web, or do a subject search to find out which journals in a particular subject are available on the Internet. Direct links are provided to available journals.
- **Education Week** (http://www.edweek.org/). Full-text articles from *Education Week*, a periodical devoted to education reform, schools, and policy, are available at the site. In addition to current and past articles, the site provides background data to enhance current news, resources for teachers, and recommended Web sites to investigate for other information.
- **CSTEEP: The Center for the Study of Testing, Evaluation, and Educational Policy** (http://www.csteep.bc.edu/). The Web site for this educational research organization contains information on testing, evaluation, and public

policy studies on school assessment practices and international comparative research.

- **National Center for Education Statistics** (http://www.nces.ed.gov/). This site contains statistical reports and other information on the condition of U.S. education. It also reports on education activities internationally.
- **Developing Educational Standards** (http://www.edstandards.org/Standards.html). This site contains a wealth of up-to-date information regarding educational standards and curriculum frameworks from national, state, local, and other sources. Information on standards and frameworks can be linked to by subject area, state, governmental agency, or organization. Entire standards and frameworks are available.
- **Internet Resources for Special Education** (http://specialed.miningco.com). This site provides links to a variety of topics, including teaching resources for regular and special education teachers; Web sites for students to visit; disability information, resources, and research; disability laws; special education laws; assistive technology; clearinghouses; and information about current topics of interest.
- **U.S. Department of Education** (http://www.ed.gov/). This site contains links to the U.S. government's education databases (including ERIC). It also makes available full-text reports on current findings on education. In addition, it provides links to research offices and organizations, as well as research publications and products. One Department of Education publication, *A Researcher's Guide to the Department of Education*, helps researchers access the various resources that the department has to offer.

You most likely will want to access information on the World Wide Web that is not available in the Web addresses just described. The easiest and quickest way to find interesting new sites is to use a search engine (such as Google, Yahoo!, Lycos, Excite, or Alta Vista) to look for Web pages containing keywords related to your topic. Once you have entered a keyword or keywords in the appropriate place on the search engine's home page, the search engine examines a selected large portion of the Internet (or a specific domain of the Internet, if you say so) for sites that contain your keyword(s).

BECOMING A MEMBER OF PROFESSIONAL ORGANIZATIONS

Another way to access current literature related to your research topic is through membership in professional organizations. The following list gives the names of a few U.S.-based professional organizations that could be valuable resources for research reports and curriculum materials. Countries other than the United States are likely to have similar organizations that could also be accessed through an Internet search. This list of professional organizations is not intended to be comprehensive, for there are as many professional organizations as there are content areas (reading, writing, mathematics, science, social studies, music, health, and physical education, to name a few) and special interest groups (Montessori education, for example). A search of the Internet will provide a listing of more Web sites than you will have the time or energy to visit!

- **Association for Supervision and Curriculum Development (ASCD)** (http://www.ascd.org). Boasting 160,000 members in more than 135 countries, ASCD is one of the largest educational organizations in the world. ASCD publishes books, newsletters, audiotapes, videotapes, and some excellent journals that are a valuable resource for teacher researchers, including *Educational Leadership* and the *Journal of Curriculum and Supervision*.
- **National Council of Teachers of Mathematics (NCTM)** (http://nctm.org). With 100,000 members, NCTM is dedicated to the teaching and learning of mathematics and offers vision and leadership for mathematics educators at all age levels. NCTM provides regional and national professional development opportunities and publishes the following journals: *Teaching Children Mathematics, Mathematics Teaching in the Middle School, Mathematics Teacher, Online Journal for School Mathematics*, and the *Journal for Research in Mathematics Education*.
- **National Council for the Social Studies (NCSS)** (http://www.ncss.org). The NCSS supports and advocates social studies education. Its resources for educators include the following journals: *Social Education* and *Social Studies and the Young Learner*.
- **National Science Teachers Association (NSTA)** (http://nsta.org). The NSTA, with 55,000 members, provides many valuable resources for science teachers. It develops the National Science Education Standards and publishes the following journals: *Science and Children, Science Scope, The Science Teacher*, and *Journal of College Science Teaching*.
- **International Reading Association (IRA)** (http://www.ira.org). The IRA provides resources to an international audience of reading teachers through its publication of the following journals: *The Reading Teacher, Journal of Adolescent and Adult Literacy*, and the *Reading Research Quarterly*.

Visiting a University Library

With all this talk about user-friendly resources, don't overlook the most valuable, user-friendly resource of all—your university librarian! Most university libraries (and public libraries, for that matter) have a librarian on duty to help with requests. My university has an "education" librarian who has experience in both K–12 and graduate education and is very skilled in helping folks who are intimidated at the thought of navigating around the "stacks." However, if a librarian is not available when you make your initial visit, you are likely to find the following important resources that will allow you to start your work:

- *Computers*. Instead of the card catalogues that many of us remember using in the "old days" (it's funny how those old days become an increasingly frequent frame of reference!), you will now find a computer terminal that provides you with access to the library's resources. You may even be able to access other libraries with whom your institution has reciprocal loan agreements if a particular reference is not available at your home library. These electronic databases are extremely user friendly and provide a good place to start your search for literature related to your area of focus.

- *ERIC on CD-ROM.* The same computers that contain the library's electronic database may also provide access to a CD-ROM version of ERIC. You will be able to use the same search strategies outlined in the earlier online discussion.
- *Browsing the stacks.* In all this discussion about electronic databases, we have not considered the old strategy of browsing the stacks. This is similar to the kind of activity you might undertake at a public library when looking for a new fiction book to read. If you can locate the area of the library with books related to your area of focus, it can be productive to browse and pull interesting books off the shelves. You may also find leads to related materials, not necessarily uncovered in your electronic search, by looking at any given book's reference list.

EVALUATING YOUR SOURCES

Once you have a source in hand, you will need to evaluate it. Obviously, the first thing to do is to determine whether it really applies to your research topic. If it does, you then need to evaluate the quality of the information. For example, does the information come from a scholarly journal or a popular magazine? Is the information someone's personal opinion or the result of a research study? Clearly, sources of different types merit different weight in your review.

An initial appraisal of a source includes looking closely at the date of publication and where the source was found. Look at the copyright date of books that you find and the dates on which articles were published. Appropriate research in topic areas of current interest and continuing development generally require recent, up-to-date references.

Next, identify where the source was found. For instance, did you find your source in a refereed or a nonrefereed journal? In a **refereed journal**, articles are reviewed by a panel of experts in the field and are thus seen as more scholarly and trustworthy than articles from nonrefereed or popular journals. Research articles in refereed journals are required to comply with strict guidelines regarding not only format but also research procedures.

You also need to verify that the information presented in a particular source is objective and impartial. Does the author present evidence to support the interpretations made? Does the content of the article consist mainly of an individual's opinion or does it contain appropriately collected and analyzed data? Finally, does the source add to the information you have already gathered about your topic? If the source adds to your growing knowledge of your topic, it is useful and worth paying attention to.

Special care and caution must be taken when evaluating World Wide Web sources, because anyone can post information on the Web. Just because an Internet search identifies a particular source does not mean that the source is accurate or credible. Sources from the World Wide Web must be closely examined for bias, subjectivity, intent, and accuracy.

Conducting effective library and Internet searches will yield an abundance of useful information about your topic. By using both search methods, you will collect information that is both up to date and comprehensive. As time goes on and you become more experienced, you will be able from the beginning to conduct more efficient searches that are focused appropriately on your topic.

ABSTRACTING

After you have identified the primary references related to your topic, you are ready to move on to the next phase of a review of related literature—abstracting the references. Basically, this involves creating abstracts by reviewing, summarizing, and classifying your references. Students sometimes ask why it is necessary to read and abstract original, complete articles (or reports, or whatever) if they already have perfectly good abstracts. There are two basic reasons. First, a provided abstract is not necessarily "perfectly good." It may not be a totally accurate summary of the article's contents. Second, there is a great deal of important information that you can obtain only by reading the complete article. (You'll see.)

To begin the abstracting process, arrange your articles and other sources in reverse chronological order. Beginning with the latest references is a good research strategy because the most recent research is likely to have profited from previous research. Also, recent references may cite preceding studies you may not have identified. For each reference, complete the following steps:

1. If the article has an abstract or a summary, which most do, read it to determine the article's relevancy to your problem.
2. Skim the entire article, making mental notes of the main points of the study.
3. On an index card or in a computer database, write a complete bibliographic reference for the work. (The word *reference* can mean either a reference work or a bibliographic reference—a note containing complete bibliographic information on a work.) Include the library call number on the card or in the database if the source work is a book. This is tedious but important. You will spend much more time trying to find the complete bibliographic information for an article or book you failed to abstract completely than you will abstracting it in the first place. If you know that your final report must follow a particular editorial style, such as that described in the *Publication Manual of the American Psychological Association* (APA), put your bibliographic reference in that form. For example, an APA-style reference for a journal article would look like this:

   > Snurd, B. J. (1995). The use of white versus yellow chalk in the teaching of advanced calculus. *Journal of Useless Findings, 11*, 1–99.

   In this example, 1995 is the date of publication, 11 is the volume number of the journal, and 1–99 are the page numbers. A style manual such as the APA's provides reference formats for all types of sources. Whatever format you use, use it consistently and be certain your bibliographic references are accurate. You never know when you might have to go back and get additional information from an article.
4. Classify and code the article according to some system, and then add the code to the database entry or index card (or a photocopy) in a conspicuous place, such as the upper right corner. The code should be one that can be easily accessed when you want to sort your notes into the categories you devise. Any coding system that makes sense to you will facilitate your task later when you have to sort, organize, analyze, synthesize, and write your review of the literature. Coding and keeping track of articles is key for organization. Useful

computer programs that simplify coding and subsequent data retrieval are HyperRESEARCH and EndNote.

5. Abstract, or summarize, the reference (source work) by typing or neatly writing (you're going to have to read your abstracts later) its essential points. If the work is an opinion article, write the main points of the author's position—for example, "Jones believes parent volunteers should be used because [list the reasons]." If it is a study, state the problem, the procedures (including a description of participants and instruments), and the major conclusions. Make special note of any particularly interesting or unique aspect of the study, such as use of a new measuring instrument. Double-check the reference to make sure you have not omitted any pertinent information. If the abstract provided at the beginning of an article contains all the essential information (and that is a big *if*), by all means use it.

6. Indicate any thoughts that come to your mind, such as points on which you disagree (mark them with an *X*, for example) or components that you do not understand (mark with a *?*). For example, if an author stated that he or she had used a double-blind procedure, and you were unfamiliar with that technique, you would put a question mark next to that statement in your database entry, on your index card, or on a photocopy of the page. Later, you could find out what it is.

7. Indicate any statements that are direct quotations or personal reactions: Plagiarism (intentional or not) is an absolute no-no, with the direst of consequences. If you do not put quotation marks around direct quotations on your card or database entry, for example, you might not remember later which statements are, and which are not, direct quotations. You must also record the exact page number of the quotation in case you use it later in your paper. Incidentally, direct quotations should be kept to a minimum in your research plan and report; both should be in *your* words, not those of other researchers. Occasionally, however, a direct quotation may be quite appropriate and useful. Be sure, however, that you record all bibliographic information required in your style manual. (You may choose to photocopy entries from other researchers' reference lists, but the main disadvantage of this is cost.)

Whatever approach you use, guard your notes with your life. Make a copy and put it away in a safe place. When you have completed your reviewing task, those notes will represent many hours of work. Students have been brought to tears because they left their notes "on the bus" or "on a table in the cafeteria" or, even worse, lost all their files to a computer virus! Beyond being sympathetic, your instructor can do little more than to tell you to start over. Also, when the research report is completed, the cards or computer information can be filed (photocopies can be placed in notebooks) and saved for future reference and future studies (nobody can do just one!).

ANALYZING, ORGANIZING, AND REPORTING THE LITERATURE

For beginning researchers, the hardest part of writing the literature review for a plan or report is thinking about how hard it is going to be to write the literature review. More time is spent worrying about doing it than actually doing it. This hesitancy stems mostly from a lack of previous experience writing a literature review.

- *Document facts and substantiate opinions.* Cite references to support your facts and opinions. Note that facts are usually based on empirical data, while opinions are not. In the hierarchy of persuasiveness, facts are more persuasive than opinions. Differentiate between facts and opinions in the review.
- *Define terms clearly, and be consistent in your use of terms.*
- *Organize content logically.*
- *Direct your writing to a particular audience.* Usually the literature review is aimed at a relatively naive reader, one who has some basic understanding of the topic but requires additional education to understand the topic or issue being studied. Do not assume your audience knows as much as you do about the topic and literature! They don't, so you have to write to educate them.

- *Follow an accepted manual of style.* The manual of style indicates the style in which chapter headings are set up, how tables must be constructed, how footnotes and bibliographies must be prepared, and the like. Commonly used manuals and their current editions are *Publication Manual of the American Psychological Association,* Fifth Edition, and *The Chicago Manual of Style,* Fifteenth Edition.
- *Evade affected verbiage and eschew obscuration of the obvious.* In other words, limit big words; avoid jargon.
- *Start each major section with a brief overview of the section.* The overview might begin like this: " In this section, three main issues are examined. The first is. . . ."
- *End each major section with a summary of the main ideas.*

FIGURE 2–3   Guidelines for Technical Writing

A literature review requires a technical form of writing that is unlike most of the writing we do. In technical writing, facts must be documented and opinions substantiated. For example, if you say that Ohio's high school dropout percentage has increased in the last 10 years, you must provide a source for this information. Technical writing is precise, requiring clarity of definitions and consistency in the use of terms. If the term *achievement* is important in your review, you must indicate what you mean by it and be consistent in using that meaning throughout the written review. Figure 2–3 summarizes these and other important technical writing guidelines useful in a literature review.

If you have efficiently abstracted the literature related to your problem, and if you approach the task in an equally systematic manner, then analyzing, organizing, and reporting the literature will be relatively painless. To get warmed up, you should read quickly through your notes. This will refresh your memory and help you identify references that no longer seem sufficiently related to your topic. Do not force references into your review that do not really fit; the review forms the background and rationale for your hypothesis and should contain only references that serve this purpose. The following guidelines—based on experience acquired the hard way—should be helpful to you:

- *Make an outline.* Don't groan; your eighth-grade teacher was right about the virtues of an outline. However you construct it, an outline will save you time and effort in the long run and will increase your probability of having an organized review. The outline does not have to be excessively detailed. Begin by identifying the main topics and the order in which they should be presented. For example, the outline of the review for the problem concerned with salaried paraprofessionals versus parent volunteers might begin with the headings: "Literature on Salaried Paraprofessionals," "Literature on Parent Volunteers," and "Literature Comparing the Two." Note that you can always add or remove topics in the outline as your work progresses. The next step is to differentiate each major heading into logical subheadings. The need for further differentiation will be determined by your topic; the more complex it is, the more subheadings you will require. When you have completed your outline, you will invariably need to rearrange, add, and delete topics. It is much easier, however, to reorganize an outline than it is to reorganize a document written in paragraph form.

- *Analyze each reference in terms of your outline.* In other words, determine the subheading under which each reference fits. Then sort your references into appropriate piles. If you end up with references without a home, there are three logical possibilities: (1) your outline is not correct, (2) the references do not belong in your review and should be discarded, or (3) the references do not belong in your review but do belong somewhere else in your research plan and report introduction. Opinion articles or reports of descriptive research often will be useful in the introduction, whereas formal research studies will be most useful in the review of related literature section.

- *Analyze the references under each subheading for similarities and differences.* If three references say essentially the same thing, you will not need to describe each one; it is much better to make one summary statement and cite the three sources, as in this example:

  Several studies have found white chalk to be more effective than yellow chalk in the teaching of advanced mathematics (Snurd, 1995; Trivia, 1994; Ziggy, 1984).

- *Give a meaningful overview of past research.* Don't present a series of abstracts or a mere list of findings (Jones found A, Smith found B, and Brown found C). Your task is to organize and summarize the references in a meaningful way. Do not ignore studies that are contradictory to most other studies or to your personal bias. Analyze and evaluate contradictory studies and try to determine a possible explanation. For example:

  Contrary to these studies is the work of Rottenstudee (1998), who found yellow chalk to be more effective than white chalk in the teaching of trigonometry. However, the size of the treatment groups (two students per group) and the duration of the study (one class period) may have seriously affected the results.

- *Discuss the references least related to your problem first and those most related to your problem just prior to the statement of the hypothesis.* Think of a big V. At the bottom of the V is your hypothesis; directly above your hypothesis are the studies most directly related to it, and so forth. The idea is to organize and present your literature in such a way that it leads logically to a tentative, testable conclusion, namely, your hypothesis. Highlight or summarize important aspects of the review to help readers identify them. If your problem has more than one major aspect, you may have two Vs or one V that logically leads to two tentative, testable conclusions.

- *Conclude the review with a brief summary of the literature and its implications.* The length of this summary depends on the length of the review. It should be detailed enough to clearly show the logic chain you have followed in arriving at your implications and tentative conclusions.

To assist with writing the literature review I suggest the following tools and strategies:

Literature Matrix

A helpful way to keep track of the literature you are reading is to record it on a matrix (see Figures 2–4 and 2–5). The matrix is a powerful organizer for when you are committing your thoughts to text. Along the Y-axis list the authors' names and year of publication. Along the X-axis list the kinds of variables/themes/issues addressed by the studies. The matrix will provide you with a mental map of what you are reading and what the studies share in common.

Thematic and Chronological Review

Attend to the themes that emerge from the matrix and use these as the subheadings for your written narrative. In this way you can construct a "compare and contrast" of the authors included in your literature review. Similarly, within each category organize the literature chronologically, that is, from the most dated to the most recent. Oftentimes this strategy will reveal the changing trends within the field you are investigating.

A Concluding Statement of the Review

The concluding statement serves a number of purposes that teacher researchers find useful. First, it provides a starting point for your own research in terms of what previous studies have found. Second, it provides support for the importance of your study and the potential your work has to contribute to the existing body of published

Author/s	Year	Variables Considered in the Study					

FIGURE 2–4   Literature Matrix

Variables Considered in the Study

Author/s	Year	Academic Achievement	Military Personnel	Social Adjustment	Attitude to Change	Discontinuous Education	Caravan Parks	S.E.S.	I.Q.	School Counsellors	Solutions Provided
Cramer, W., & Dorsey, S.	1970	●	●								
Bourke, S. F., & Naylor, D. R.	1971	●	●								
Collins, R. J., & Coulter, F.	1974	●	●	●							
Mackay L. D., & Spicer, B. J.	1975	●	●	●							
Lacey, C., & Blare, D.	1979	●				●					
Parker, L.	1979	●				●	●				
Parker, L.	1981	●		●			●	●			
Bell, D. P.	1962	●					●				
Smith, T. S., Husbands, L. T., & Street, D.	1969	●							●		
Whalen, T. C., & Fried, M. A.	1973	●						●	●		
Black, F. S., & Bargar, R. R.	1975	●									
Goodman, T. L.	1975	●									
Splete, H., & Rasmussen, J.	1977	●								●	●
de Noose, D. A., & Wells, R. M.	1981	●		●						●	●
Allan, J., & Bardsley, P.	1983	●						●		●	●
King, M.	1984	●									●
Thomas, B. D.	1978	●				●					●
Rahmani, Z.	1987		●								●
Mills, G. E.	1989	●		●		●					●

FIGURE 2–5 Sample Literature Matrix

Source: From "Transient Children," by G. E. Mills, 1985, Unpublished M. Ed. thesis. Perth, Australia: Western (Australian) Institute of Technology.

research. If you are applying for a grant to support your work, linking your area of focus to previous research is an important component. Third, it provides you with an opportunity to share what promising practices have emerged from the research that have the potential to have a positive impact on your own research.

For an example of a literature review, go to the Companion Website at www.prenhall.com/mills and read the Review of Literature on High Stakes Testing.

The Action Research Plan

Ideally, your investment of time and energy in the reconnaissance and literature review stages will be rewarded with a synthesis of the related literature that helps you to see your project more clearly. In addition, it may have helped you to identify promising practices that become an integral part of your ongoing action research efforts.

At this stage of the action research process, you should create an action plan. An action plan summarizes your action research thoughts in a plan that will guide you through your action research work and includes the following nine steps (adapted from Elliott, 1991; Kemmis & McTaggart, 1988):

1. Write an area-of-focus statement.
2. Define the variables.
3. Develop research questions.
4. Describe the intervention or innovations.
5. Describe the membership of the action research group.
6. Describe negotiations that need to be undertaken.
7. Develop a timeline.
8. Develop a statement of resources.
9. Develop data collection ideas.

Write an Area-of-Focus Statement

An area of focus identifies the purpose of your study. To start, write a statement that completes the following sentence: "The purpose of this study is to. . . ." For example:

- The purpose of this study is to describe the effects of an integrated problem-solving mathematics curriculum on student transfer of problem-solving skills and the retention of basic math facts and functions.
- The purpose of this study is to describe the impact of bringing audience members into an interactive relationship with teen theater productions on participants' abilities to identify issues and incorporate solutions to similar problems in their own lives.
- The purpose of this study is to describe the effects of student-led conferences on parent and student satisfaction with the conferencing process.

Define the Variables

As part of the area-of-focus statement construction process, write definitions of what you will focus on in the study. These definitions should accurately represent what the factors, contexts, and variables *mean to you*. A **variable** is a characteristic of your study that is subject to change. That is, it might be the way you are going to change how you teach, the curriculum you use, and student outcomes. Definitions may also emerge from the literature, but it is important that you own whatever you are defining and communicate that with others. In the preceding examples, the researchers would define what they mean by transfer of solutions to life's situations, an integrated problem-solving curriculum, transfer of problem-solving skills, the retention of math facts and functions, interactive participation in teen theater, student-led conferences, and parent and student satisfaction with the conferencing processes. If you are clear about what you are examining, it will be easy to determine how you will know it when you see it! That is, your data collection ideas will flow more freely and there will be no confusion when you communicate with your action research collaborators about your purpose.

DEVELOP RESEARCH QUESTIONS

Develop questions that breathe life into the area-of-focus statement and help provide a focus for your data collection plan. These questions will also help you validate that you have a workable way to proceed with your investigation. For example:

- What is the effect of teen theater audience participation strategies on audience comprehension of issues?
- How does the "Violence Improv" affect the audience's understanding of the issues of violence and harassment?
- What is the effect of incorporating math manipulatives into problem-solving activities on student performance on open-ended problem-solving tests?
- In what ways do students transfer problem-solving skills to other areas of mathematics?
- How do students incorporate problem-solving skills into other curriculum areas?
- How do students transfer problem-solving skills to their life outside of school?

DESCRIBE THE INTERVENTION OR INNOVATION

Describe what you are going to do to improve the situation you have described. For example, "I will implement a standards-based, integrated problem-solving mathematics curriculum," "I will include audience improvisation as part of the teen theater performances I direct," and "I will incorporate student participation in student-parent-teacher conferences." Remember, this is simply a statement about what you will do in your classroom or school to address the teaching/learning issue you have identified.

DESCRIBE THE MEMBERSHIP OF THE ACTION RESEARCH GROUP

Describe the membership of your action research group and discuss why its members are important. Will you be working with a site council team? A parent group? If so, what will be the roles and responsibilities of the group's participants? For example:

I will be working with seven other high school math teachers who are all members of the math department. Although we all have different teaching responsibilities within the department, as a group we have decided on problem solving as an area of focus for the department. Each of us will be responsible for implementing curriculum and teaching strategies that reflect the new emphasis on problem solving and for collecting the kinds of data that we decide will help us monitor the effects of our teaching. The department chair will be responsible for keeping the principal informed about our work and securing any necessary resources we need to complete the research. The chair will also write a description of our work to be included in the school newsletter (sent home to all parents), thus informing children and parents of our focus for the year.

DESCRIBE NEGOTIATIONS THAT NEED TO BE UNDERTAKEN

Describe any negotiations that you will have to undertake with others prior to implementing your plan. Do you need permission from an administrator? Parents? Students? Colleagues? All this assumes that you control the focus of the study and that you undertake the process of negotiation to head off any potential obstacles to implementation of the action plan. It's very frustrating to get immersed in the action research process only to have the project quashed by uncooperative colleagues or administrators.

DEVELOP A TIMELINE

In developing a timeline, you will need to decide who will be doing *what* and *when*. Although not part of a timeline in the strictest sense, you can also use this stage to anticipate *where* and *how* your inquiry will take place. For example:

- **Phase 1 (August–October)**. Identify area of focus, review related literature, develop research questions, reconnaissance.
- **Phase 2 (November–December)**. Collect initial data. Analyze videotapes of lessons, do first interviews with children, administer first problem-solving probe.
- **Phase 3 (January–May)**. Modify curriculum and instruction as necessary. Continue ongoing data collection. Schedule two team meetings to discuss early analysis of data.
- **Phase 4 (May–June)**. Review statewide assessment test data and complete analysis of all data. Develop presentation for faculty. Schedule team meeting to discuss and plan action based on the findings of the study. Assign tasks to be completed prior to year 2 of the study.

DEVELOP A STATEMENT OF RESOURCES

Briefly describe what resources you will need to enact your plan. This is akin to listing materials in a lesson plan—there is nothing worse than starting to teach and finding that you don't have all the manipulatives you need to achieve your objectives. For example, to participate in the study of math problem-solving skills, the team determines that it will need teacher release time for planning the project, reviewing related literature, and completing other tasks; funds to purchase classroom sets of manipulatives; and a small budget for copying and printing curriculum materials. After all, there is no sense developing a study that investigates the impact of a new math problem-solving curriculum if you don't have the financial resources to purchase the curriculum.

DEVELOP DATA COLLECTION IDEAS

Give a preliminary statement of the kinds of data that you think will provide evidence for your reflections on the general idea you are investigating. For example, brainstorm about the kind of intuitive, naturally occurring data that you find in your classroom or school, such as test scores, attendance records, portfolios, and anecdotal records. As we learn more about other types of data that can be collected, this list will grow, but in the early stages think about what you already have easy access to and then be prepared to supplement it with interviews, surveys, questionnaires, videotapes, audiotapes, maps, photos, and observations as the area of focus dictates.

These activities can be undertaken whether you are working individually, in a small group, or as part of a schoolwide action research effort. The resolution of these issues early in the action research process will ensure that you do not waste valuable time backtracking (or even apologizing) once you are well down the action research path. The process of developing an action plan is summarized in the Research in Action Checklist 2–3.

PUT THE ACTION PLAN INTO ACTION

Kemmis and McTaggart (1988) provide the following conclusion to the process of developing a plan:

> Your plan orients you for action, of course; but it is also a reference point for reflection later on, and it is something which you can modify and develop in later plans. Since you have done so much hard thinking to put your plan together, don't skimp when it comes to drafting and redrafting it before you go into action. It represents the fruits of one round of reconnaissance and thinking ahead—it provides you with a benchmark for later reflection and replanning. (p. 77)

RESEARCH IN ACTION CHECKLIST 2–3

Developing an Action Plan

_____ Write an area-of-focus statement.
_____ Define the variables.
_____ Develop research questions.
_____ Describe the intervention or innovation.
_____ Describe the membership of the action research group.
_____ Describe negotiations that need to be undertaken.
_____ Develop a timeline.
_____ Develop a statement of resources.
_____ Develop data collection ideas.

With the plan complete, it's time to determine what information (data) you can collect that will increase your understanding about your own practice and its impact on your students. You are now ready to decide how you will monitor the effects of the innovation or intervention you are going to implement and to develop your data collection techniques.

Summary

Defining an area of focus, or making explicit the question or problem to investigate, is a critical step in the action research process. The process of articulating a meaningful area of focus involves doing reconnaissance (self-reflection, description, and explanation) and reviewing the related literature. You can use online resources such as ERIC, search the World Wide Web, visit a university library, or review the publications issued by professional organizations for educators to define the context for your action research inquiry.

After defining your area of focus, doing reconnaissance, and reviewing the literature, the next step is to write an action plan to guide your action research efforts. The action plan should include the following nine steps: write an area-of-focus statement; define the variables; develop research questions; describe the intervention or innovation; describe the membership of the action research group; describe negotiations that need to be undertaken; develop a timeline; develop a statement of resources; and develop data collection ideas (adapted from Elliott, 1991; Kemmis & McTaggart, 1988).

For Further Thought

1. What general ideas do you have for action research?
2. What is your area of focus?
3. Complete the following statement: "The purpose of the study is to. . . ."
4. Conduct an initial search of the related literature using ERIC online.
5. Complete an action plan that includes an area-of-focus statement, definitions, research questions, a description of the intervention, membership of the action research group, negotiations to be undertaken, a timeline, the necessary resources for the project, and data collection ideas.

3 | Data Collection Techniques

This chapter introduces qualitative and quantitative data collection techniques that can be used to systematically investigate an area of focus. These techniques include using direct observation, interviews, questionnaires, attitude scales, new and existing records, artifacts, teacher-made tests, standardized tests, and school-generated report cards.

After reading this chapter you should be able to:
1. Identify multiple data collection techniques to be included for each research question.
2. Develop the research instruments needed to begin your research.

Reflection on Action Research

JAMES ROCKFORD

James Rockford is an elementary teacher in a rural school district in Oregon. James is primarily responsible for teaching music and computer keyboarding skills to young children and initially became involved with action research as part of a statewide action research initiative. As a result of his first attempt at doing action research and his effort to make it a standard part of his teaching, James has also worked as a mentor for other teachers in his region. James's story highlights the importance of collecting data from a variety of sources to fully understand the effects of an intervention on student outcomes.

It seemed to be a perfect match. I had charge of a new computer lab and a mandate to develop a program of instruction to match the curriculum guide, and I needed a "problem" for a collaborative action research class that began in the Spring of 1995.

The only software that came with the computers was a popular program to teach keyboarding and ClarisWorks. It didn't make any sense to spend several thousand dollars to teach keyboarding, so the problem became, "How does keyboarding instruction enhance students' ability to use word processing, database, spreadsheet, and draw functions?"

Looking at the literature proved to be a formidable problem because there wasn't a good academic library in the area. The local community college had one online computer to access ERIC (Educational Resources Information Center) through the World Wide Web if I gave search terms to the librarian. A little help came, but I preferred to do the search myself. Our school was not yet online, so I resorted to using my son's computer. A quick survey of the literature showed plenty of research on keyboarding, but not much focused on young children. Opinions ranged from "Start them as early as possible" to "Avoid bad habits" to "Don't bother

because they can hunt and peck as fast as they can type."

The problem proved to be a little overwhelming in that I had just started an instructional program to teach all the keyboarding skills, and it became obvious that results would be harder to get for database, spreadsheet, and draw functions. As a result, I decided to look initially only at the effect of teaching keyboarding on word processing for students in grades 4 through 6.

This was supposed to be a collaborative venture, so my first task was to enlist the help of the teachers in grades 4 through 6. We met after school one afternoon so I could explain the purpose of the project. They agreed to help gather data, but only one class actually got into the lab every day. This was disappointing, but it helped make the project more manageable since I would be handling data from only one class instead of three.

What variables might have an effect on students' success in learning to keyboard? I conducted a survey of teacher attitudes and a survey to assess whether students had any prior knowledge, how much time they spent on a computer at home and at school, and whether they had a computer at home. Records were kept for time on computers at school in instructional and free-choice situations.

51

A well-designed action research project should, as its name declares, lead to some kind of action. The purpose of my action research project was to determine if teaching keyboarding skills to sixth-grade students had enough of an impact on their word processing skills to warrant spending the time and money. It seemed rather obvious that it would, but several students had developed their own unique "hunt-and-peck" system and could already approach the district-mandated target of 20 words per minute. There are many variables that might affect word processing rates and that led to the following questions:

1. Do students have a computer at home? How much time do they spend at it per week?
2. What preexisting knowledge do students have about computers?
3. How much time do students spend at the computer when they're at school? How does it affect word processing rates?
4. What is the effect of the keyboarding software used in the lab at school?

The questions were then placed in a data matrix and triangulated as follows (Note: D.S. = data source):

Questions	D.S. 1	D.S. 2	D.S. 3
Preexisting knowledge?	Students' survey	Computer knowledge pretest	
Keyboarding speed?	Pretest	Posttest	Teacher help
Appropriate use (WP)?	Pretest software	Posttest software	Timed typing teacher constructed
Time on computers?	School lab records	Student survey	Parent survey

I collected data using surveys that I developed to measure the following areas:

- Student self-evaluation questionnaire.
- Teacher-constructed vocabulary/facts pretest of general computer knowledge.

- Teacher-constructed timed typing test rates.
- A classroom teacher survey of knowledge/attitudes about technology.
- A teacher observation record for the computer lab.
- Existing records of students' word processing rates with software.
- Parent survey of student computer use outside of school.

Data were compiled as follows:

- The three variables of time, prior knowledge, and use of keyboarding software were analyzed using a scatter plot graph to determine any correlation to word processing speed.
- Surveys were compiled to show tendencies.
- Keyboarding rates between October and May were compiled in graph form to show progress over time.

In general, the data indicated the following:

- Student time spent on computers out of school had no effect on word processing rate. (They love those computer games!)
- Time spent on computers at school was critical.
- In only 1 month, the class word processing rate mean had increased 300%.

As a result, it was apparent that the keyboarding software was effective, and on that basis I continued its use. Because time on task is critical, teachers were urged to take students to the lab every day and monitor keyboarding habits as well as install keyboarding software on classroom computers so that each student received a minimum of 10 minutes practice per day. Timed typing tests require greater and different skills than are called for on keyboarding software. In the future, timed typing tests will be given weekly to provide an authentic assessment of student progress, and a tracking system will be used to monitor the acquisition of skill development.

Any research worth its salt appears to generate more questions than it answers. At the completion of this project, I was left wondering if a student's

Student Self-Evaluation Survey

1. Do you have a computer that you use outside of school?

   (a) Yes   (b) No

2. How many hours a day do you spend at the computer outside of school?

   (a) 0   (b) 1 or less   (c) 1–2   (d) 2–3

3. How much time do you spend at the computer while you're at school?

   (a) 0   (b) 15 minutes   (c) 30 minutes   (d) more than 30 minutes

4. When you type on a keyboard, do you look at the

   (a) monitor   (b) keyboard   (c) rough draft   (d) your neighbor

5. I use the computer to   (circle all that apply)

   (a) play games   (b) write stories and reports
   (c) draw pictures   (d) collect information and store it
   (e) find information in the library

6. Learning to keyboard in the lab made my life with computers

   (a) easier   (b) more frustrating   (c) no different

7. If I had the chance to do more with computers, I would

   _____

8. The best thing about learning to keyboard is

   _____

9. Tho hardest thing about learning to keyboard is

   _____

learning style had any impact on the ability to learn word processing skills. Would keyboarding instruction improve students' use of database, spreadsheet, and draw/paint functions? Could other types of authentic assessment be used to determine skill/concept development? These are questions I will continue to investigate.

The project became a springboard to address issues in setting up a computer lab. Instead of being behind the eight ball, I was able to anticipate problems and find solutions. Collaboration was an important part of the process. But perhaps the most powerful part of the action research process was the extent to which I became more reflective about what

Teacher Survey

1. I take my class to the lab

    (a) once a week   (b) twice a week   (c) 3 times a week
    (d) 4 times a week   (e) every day   (f) only when Mr. Rockford
                                                   is there

2. I expect my students to (circle all that apply)

    (a) compose reports/stories   (b) revise reports from written copies
    (c) practice keyboarding   (d) other:_____

3. If I rated my comfort level with computers it would be

    Use it every   Don't want to be in the
    chance I get   same room as one

    5   4   3   2   1

4. I monitor my students' keyboarding technique

    (a) only during lab sessions   (b) any time they're at the computer
    (c) never

5. My students' abilities to use the computer have been enhanced by learning
    to keyboard

    They're experts!   They're still looking
                                                    for the on switch!

    5   4   3   2   1

6. I would like my students to be able to

    _____

I was doing in the computer lab. The lab at my school has received a lot of praise from administrators, board members, and teachers, and I believe that going through the action research process has had much to do with the continued success of the lab.

I don't look at classroom problems quite the same way now. For example, I also teach middle school choir and began to notice that the weeks on which I saw eighth graders on Mondays (we're on block scheduling), it was usually a difficult, if not unproductive rehearsal. Keeping some informal data about those days and reflecting about why they were so difficult led me to try some interventions that might help alleviate the problem. It may be a bit corny, but action research has changed my life . . . in the classroom anyway. Student learning is enhanced, I approach problems more systematically, I gather data more carefully and accurately, and my practice is more reflective.

The year following my word processing action research project, I had the good fortune to be a mentor for other teachers learning the action research process. Based on this experience, two observations come to mind. Problem formulation is a difficult process. Extra time spent in this phase of the action research cycle will prevent backtracking, headaches, and frustration down the road. When teachers do identify something that needs addressing, there appears to be a measurable difference between problems that are student centered and those that arise from a teacher complaint about a teaching situation. It appeared that the problems that are student centered are more likely to result in the improvement of instruction.

Making action research a natural part of the teaching process, in the classroom and the school, is critical to success. Traditionally, teachers are not researchers. The school routine isn't geared to provide teachers with the time and resources that research demands. Teachers are considered to be working only when they're in front of a class. On the other hand, teachers need to develop the attitude that improvement of the teaching/learning process can and should be addressed with data-based decision making formalized through action research.

T HE DECISION about what data are collected for an action research area of focus is largely determined by the nature of the problem. There is no one recipe for how to proceed with data collection efforts. Rather, the individual or group must determine what data will contribute to their understanding and resolution of a given problem. Hence, data collection associated with action research is largely an idiosyncratic approach fueled by the desire to understand one's practice and to collect data that is appropriate and accessible.

The emphasis in this chapter is on qualitative (experience-based) data collection techniques as compared with quantitative (number-based) techniques. The former includes data sources such as fieldnotes, journals, surveys, attitude scales, standardized test scores, maps, audiotapes, and videotapes, whereas the latter focuses on the collection of teacher-made tests (criterion-referenced tests), standardized tests (norm-referenced tests), school-generated report cards, and the results of student achievement reported on statewide assessment tests.

One approach is not *better* than the other. However, the literature on action research supports the assertion that qualitative methods are more appropriately applied to action research efforts compared with the application of an experimental pretest-posttest control group design in which the teacher researcher randomly assigns children to a control group or experimental group in order to receive a "treatment." Qualitative research is not the "easy" way out for teacher researchers who fear statistics (a.k.a. sadistics!). As you will see, the rigor of good qualitatively oriented action research equals the rigor of doing good quantitatively oriented action research. If your area of focus necessitates a more quantitative, experimental approach, then you should consult more quantitatively oriented references such as Gay, Mills, and Airasian (2006, Chapters 6, 7, 8, 9, and 10), or Creswell (2005).

Qualitative Data Collection Techniques

The receptivity among educators in general, and action researchers specifically, to a qualitative (descriptive) way of examining problems is reflected in the action research literature that emphasizes the following data collection techniques and sources:

- Existing archival sources within a school
- Tools for capturing everyday life
- Tools for questioning
- Conventional sources (surveys, questionnaires, etc.)
- Inventive sources (exhibits, portfolios, etc.)
- Interviews
- Oral history and narrative stories
- Rating scales
- Inventories
- Observation
- Mapping
- Visual recordings
- Photography
- Journals and diaries
  (Anderson, Herr, & Nihlen, 1994; Calhoun, 1994; Hendricks, 2006; Sagor, 2000; Stringer, 2004; Wells, 1994)

As you can see from these examples, the kinds of data you collect would be descriptive, narrative, and even nonwritten forms. In many cases, these data occur naturally and are regularly collected by teachers and administrators. In simple terms, we are engaging in an activity that seeks to answer the question: "What is going on here?" It is not a mysterious quest, but is quite simply an effort to collect data that increase our understanding of the phenomenon under investigation.

In the following sections we will look at the myriad of data collection techniques that can shed light on your area of focus. In research terms, this desire to use multiple sources of data is referred to as **triangulation**.

TRIANGULATION

It is generally accepted in action research circles that researchers should not rely on any single source of data, interview, observation, or instrument. Sagor (2000) has suggested that action researchers complete a "triangulation matrix—a simple grid that shows the various data sources that will be used to answer each research question" (pp. 19–20). In the James Rockford vignette that opened this chapter you can see how Rockford has laid out his triangulation matrix to address issues related to bias in the data collection. (See Figure 3–1 for an example of a triangulation matrix.) We will adopt a less prescriptive approach here, but we support the triangulation principle. That is, the strength of qualitative research lies in its triangulation, collecting information in many ways, rather than relying solely on one (Wolcott, 1988). Pelto and Pelto (1978) have described this as a "multi-instrument" approach (p. 122). For our purposes in doing action research, this suggests that the teacher is the research instrument who, in collecting data, utilizes a variety of techniques over an extended period of time, "ferreting out varying perspectives on complex issues and events" (Wolcott,

Research Questions	Data Source		
	1	2	3
1. Preexisting Knowledge?	Student Survey	Computer Knowledge Pretest	
2. Keyboarding Speed?	Pretest	Posttest	Teacher Help
3. Appropriate Use (WP)?	Pretest Software	Posttest Software	Timed Typing Teacher Constructed
4. Time on Computers?	School Lab Records	Student Survey	Parent Survey

FIGURE 3–1   Triangulation Matrix Example

1988, p. 192). As we begin to focus our data collection efforts, we must keep in mind the principle of triangulation and apply it to our regular data collection efforts.

The three primary fieldwork strategies we will discuss in this chapter are experiencing, "enquiring," and examining (Wolcott, 1992, p. 19). Each of these strategies will be discussed in the context of actual teacher researchers' experiences.

Experiencing Through Direct Observation

Teachers who undertake action research have countless opportunities to observe in their own classrooms. They observe as a normal component of their teaching, monitoring and adjusting instruction based on the verbal and nonverbal interactions in their classrooms. Therefore, using direct observation as a data collection strategy is familiar and not overly time consuming. As teachers we are constantly observing our environment and adjusting our teaching based on what we see. Action research gives us a systematic and rigorous way to view this process of observation as a qualitative data collection technique.

PARTICIPANT OBSERVATION

The action research vignettes shared at the beginnings of Chapters 1, 2, and 3 illustrate how teachers "experience" their teaching through observation. James Rockford observed the "hunt-and-peck" keyboarding strategies of his students as a natural part of his teaching. Cathy Mitchell observed audience reactions to the "Violence Improv" and recorded fieldnotes in her daily journal. Deborah South observed the interpersonal interactions of her "study skills" students and recorded her observations in a journal—observations that quickly confirmed the presence of major problems in the classroom. These experiences are all examples of participant observation.

If the researcher is "a genuine participant in the activity being studied," then the researcher is called a **participant observer** (McMillan, 1996, p. 245). According to Spradley (1980), participant observation is undertaken with at least two purposes in mind:

- To observe the activities, people, and physical aspects of a situation; and
- To engage in activities that are appropriate to a given situation that provide useful information.

Participant observation can be done to varying degrees depending on the situation being observed and the opportunities presented: A participant observer can be an *active participant observer*, a *privileged, active observer*, or a *passive observer* (Pelto & Pelto, 1978; Spradley, 1980; Wolcott, 1982, 1997). Depending on the problem, teachers have many opportunities to be active participants in the observation process as they go about their work. However, the tendency with observing is to try to see it all! A good rule of thumb here is to try to do less but do it better. That is, as you embark on some degree of participant observation, do not be overwhelmed with the task. It is not humanly possible to take in everything that you experience. Be content with furthering your understanding of your area of focus through *manageable* observations. Avoid trying to do too much and you will be happier with the outcomes.

Active Participant Observer

Teachers, by virtue of teaching, are active participant observers of their teaching practice. When they are actively engaged in teaching, teachers observe the outcomes of their teaching. Each time we teach we monitor the effects of our teaching and adjust our instruction accordingly. As an active participant observer of our own teaching practices, however, we may be so fully immersed in what we are doing that we don't have time to record our observations in a systematic way during the school day. Such recording is a necessary part of being an active participant observer.

In the action research vignettes from Chapters 1, 2, and 3, we saw teachers who were active participant observers of their own teaching. Deborah South observed the "off-task" behavior of her "unmotivated" students during the study skills lessons. Cathy Mitchell observed the nature of the audience participation while she directed the teen theater. James Rockford observed the "hunt-and-peck" strategies used by keyboarding students while he was teaching keyboarding skills. As researchers of our own teaching practices, active participant observation is likely to be the most common "experiencing" data collection technique that we use.

Privileged, Active Observer

Teachers may also have opportunities to observe in a more privileged, active role. That is, they may wish to observe their children during a time when they are not directly responsible for the teaching of a lesson, for example, during a "specialist's" time in music, library, or physical education. These times provide opportunities for teachers to work as a "teacher's aide" and at the same time they can withdraw, stand back, and watch what is happening during a particular teaching episode, moving in and out of the role of teacher, aide, and observer.

Many teachers comment on how valuable these experiences have been in allowing them time to observe the social interactions of students and the impact of a particular instructional strategy on those interactions. By necessity, these privileged, active observer opportunities require teachers to give up valuable time that is often dedicated to duties other than teaching, such as planning, attending team meetings, reading, visiting other classrooms, and relaxing (the all-important "downtime" during a day, if they are fortunate enough to have such a schedule). Taking time to observe one's class is a valuable use of nonteaching time that honors a teacher's effort to improve practice based, in part, on observational data.

Passive Observer

Teachers also have opportunities to be passive observers in classrooms and schools. When teachers take on the role of passive observer, they no longer assume the responsibilities of the teacher—they should be focused only on their data collection. A privileged, active observer could be transformed into a passive observer by making explicit to the students and a teaching colleague that the classroom teacher is present only to "see what's going on around here." Students will quickly learn that there are times when their teacher is not going to interact with them as the teacher normally does. The teacher might simply announce that today "I am going to watch and learn from what you are doing!" Taking a step back from the daily rigor of being "on stage" and performing can be refreshing and provide an insightful opportunity for teachers who are unaccustomed to watching their students in a different setting, through a different lens.

FIELDNOTES

The written records of participant observers are often referred to as **fieldnotes**. For teachers undertaking participant observation efforts in their classrooms, these fieldnotes may take the form of anecdotal records compiled as part of a more systematic authentic assessment or portfolio effort. So, what do you write down in these fieldnotes? Well, it depends on what you are looking for! I can offer only limited guidance to help quell your concerns about the "how-to" of writing fieldnotes. But first let me start with an example of how *not* to do fieldnotes!

During my graduate studies at the University of Oregon, I took a class on "Ethnographic Research in Education," and as part of learning how to do ethnography (qualitative research) I was required to conduct a "beginning ethnography" of something that was "culturally different" for me. As an Australian studying in the United States, I had a number of opportunities to study a culturally different phenomenon while at the same time having fun with the project. I chose to study a sorority. As part of this study I participated in one of the regular ceremonies that was part of the sorority members' lives—a formal dinner held each Monday night at which members were required to wear formals and male guests were expected to wear a jacket and tie.

During the course of the dinner, I frequently excused myself to visit the restroom, stopping along the way to take out my notebook so I could try to record quotes and reconstruct events as they were happening, as I tried to capture in great detail all that I was observing. Of course, the irony in this strategy was that I was missing a great deal of the dinner by removing myself from the setting in a futile effort to record everything. The ridiculousness of the situation became evident when one of my dinner hosts asked me if I was feeling well or if the meal was to my satisfaction. After all, why did I keep leaving the dinner table?!

The message here for teacher researchers who wish to use fieldnotes as part of their data collection efforts is clear: You can't physically record everything that is happening during an observational episode, nor should you try to. The following options for observing and recording fieldnotes are useful ways to proceed (adapted from Wolcott, 1994).

Observe and Record Everything You Possibly Can

If going into an observation you knew exactly what you wanted to observe, you would find this data collection process to be inefficient. Engaging in an effort to "record everything" will quickly attune you to what is of most interest to you. During these observational periods, you can start with a broad sweep of the classroom and gradually narrow your focus as you gain a clearer sense of what is most pressing. You can also decide on your strategies for recording observations. You might choose verbatim conversations, maps and illustrations, photographs, videotape or audiotape recordings, or even writing furiously in the fashion of a principal or university professor undertaking an evaluation. It is a very idiosyncratic activity, but follow one rule: Don't run off to the restroom every 5 minutes—you *will* miss something! Do try to maintain a running record of what is happening in a format that will be most helpful for you.

For example, in my study of a school district attempting multiple change efforts (see Mills, 1988), I attended the 37th Annual McKenzie School District Teacher Inservice Day. Part of my fieldnotes from this observation were as follows:

8:30 A.M.   An announcement is made over the public address system requesting that teachers move into the auditorium and take a seat in preparation for the inservice. As the teachers file into the auditorium, the pop song "The Greatest Love of All" is played.

8:41 A.M.   The Assistant Superintendent welcomes the teachers to the inservice with the conviction that it is also the "best district with the best teachers." The brief welcome is then followed by the Pledge of Allegiance and the introduction of the new Assistant Superintendent.

8:45 A.M.   The Assistant Superintendent introduces the Superintendent as "the Superintendent who cares about kids, cares about teachers, and cares about this district."

The next hour of the inservice is focused on introducing new teachers to the district (there were 60 new appointments) and the presentation of information about how a new focus for the district would be at-risk children.

10:00 A.M.   The Superintendent returns to the lyrics of "The Greatest Love of All" and suggests that the message from the song may be suitable as the district's charge: "Everyone is searching for a hero. People need someone to look up to. I never found anyone who fulfilled my needs. . . ." The Superintendent compels the teachers to be the heroes for their students and wishes them a successful school year before closing the inservice.

As you can see from this abbreviated example, there is nothing mystical about fieldnotes. They serve as a record of what an observer attended to during the course of an observation and help guide subsequent observations and interviews. This was the beginning of my year-long fieldwork in the McKenzie School District, and this initial observation helped me to frame questions that guided my efforts to understand how central office personnel, principals, and teachers manage and cope with multiple innovations.

Observe and Look for Nothing in Particular

Try to see the routine in new ways. If you can, try to look with "new eyes" and approach the scene as if you were an outsider. Wolcott (1994) offers helpful advice for teachers conducting observations in classrooms that are so familiar that everything seems ordinary and routine:

> Aware of being familiar with classroom routines, an experienced observer might initiate a new set of observations with the strategy that in yet another classroom one simply assumes "business as usual . . . ." The observer sets a sort of radar, scanning constantly for whatever it is that those in the setting are doing to keep the system operating smoothly. (p. 162)

Look for "Bumps" or Paradoxes

In this strategy, you consider the environment you are observing as if it were "flat"; nothing in particular stands out to you. It is an opportunity for observers to look for the "bumps" in the setting. In action research projects these "bumps" might be unexpected student responses to a new curriculum or teaching strategy or an unexpected response to a new classroom management plan, seating arrangement, monitoring strategy, or innovation.

For example, the "bumps" observed by a teacher concerned with gender inequity may become painfully evident when the "locus of control" in a classroom is on one or two boys. That is, by keeping a tally of who commanded most of the teacher's attention by answering and asking questions, it became clear that one or two dominant boys were the focus of the activity during a lesson.

This strategy also suggests that teacher researchers look for contradictions or paradoxes in their classrooms. In a sense, this is not dissimilar to the "looking for bumps" strategy, because a paradox will often stand out in an obvious way to the teacher who has taken the time to stand back and look at what is happening in the classroom. (See Key Concept Box 3–1 for a description of the components of effective observation.)

For example, teacher researchers often comment on the unintended consequences of a particular teaching strategy or a curriculum change that has become evident only when they have had an opportunity to stand back and observe the results of their actions. These consequences often present themselves in the form of a paradox—a contradiction in terms. For example, as one teacher researcher commented after attempting to incorporate manipulatives into her math instruction in a primary classroom, "I thought that the use of manipulatives in teaching mathematics would also lead to increased cooperation in group work. Instead, what I saw were my kids fighting over who got to use what and not wanting to share."

Enquiring: When the Researcher Asks

A second major category of data collection techniques can be grouped as data that are collected by the teacher through the asking of questions. Teacher researchers may ask questions of students, parents, and other teachers using **interviewing** and **questionnaire** techniques.

Components of Effective Observation	
PRINCIPAL COMPONENTS	
DEGREES OF PARTICIPATION	
Participant observer	Engage in activities Observe activities, people, and physical aspects
Privileged observer	A teacher's aide during specialists' time
Passive observer	Present only to observe what's going on
FIELDNOTES	
Observe and record everything	Attune to what you actually record through verbatim conversations, maps and illustrations, photos, and video and audio recordings
Observe and look for nothing	Try to see beyond the routine and look with a fresh perspective
Look for paradoxes	What are the unintended consequences of action?

As Agar (1980) suggests, information from interviews can serve as the "methodological core" against which observational data can be used to "feed" ongoing informal interviews. That is, observational data (collected through the "experiencing" techniques described earlier) can suggest questions that can be asked in subsequent interviews with children, parents, teachers—whomever the participants in the study might be. Participants in an interview may omit things. Pairing observation and interviewing provides a valuable way to gather complementary data. For example, Cathy Mitchell's Teen Theater Group (see Chapter 2) developed a group interview technique based on observations of audience reactions to performances. This technique involved three company members meeting with a small group of audience members for about 15 minutes following a performance so that they could gauge the audience response to the scenes about teen violence and harassment. One actor served as the interviewer, one as the scribe, and one kept a running tally of comments and responses.

INFORMAL ETHNOGRAPHIC INTERVIEW

The **informal ethnographic interview** is little more than a casual conversation that allows the teacher, in a conversational style, to inquire into something that has presented itself as an opportunity to learn about their practice. Agar (1980) suggests strategies that allow teacher researchers to have a ready set of questions to ask participants in a study, for example, the "5 Ws and H": *who, what, where, when, why,* and *how.* Using these prompts, teachers will never be at a loss for a question to add to their understanding of what is happening in their classrooms. For example, in considering the example of the teacher researching the impact of manipulatives on math performance,

Student Anecdotal Record Form

Name: _Mary Smith_____

Grade: _K_____

Date: _10/23___   Comments: _Writing table_____
observation. Mary appears unhappy during the time
she spends at the writing table. Her explanation:
"I don't have time to think about my story."

Date: _____   Comments: _____
_____
_____
_____

FIGURE 3–2   Student Anecdotal Record Form

and through observation recognizing the unanticipated consequence of poor sharing of manipulatives, the teacher might ask questions such as these:

- *Who* should be responsible for rotating the materials through the group?
- *What* was the cause of the problem?
- *Where* did the problem originate?
- *When* did the problem of sharing begin?
- *Why* don't you want to share the manipulatives with each other?
- *How* do you think we can solve this problem?

Following the episode, the teacher might briefly jot down in a plan book a summary of what the students had to say and refer back to it later as a valuable data source. Alternatively, the teacher researcher may keep anecdotal records on each student and simply make an entry on the student's file. An example of a student anecdotal record form is presented in Figure 3–2.

STRUCTURED FORMAL INTERVIEWS

Teacher researchers may also want to consider formally interviewing children, parents, or colleagues as part of their data collection efforts. Using a structured interview format allows the teacher to ask all the participants the same series of questions. However, a major challenge in constructing any interview is to phrase questions in such a way that they elicit the information you really want. Although this may seem obvious, teacher researchers often feel compelled by tradition and history to ask a lengthy set of questions of which only a part is really their focus. When planning interviews, consider the following options for ensuring the quality of your structured formal interviews:

- **Pilot questions on a similar group of respondents.** That is, if you have developed an interview schedule to use with the students in your classroom, try it out on some similarly aged students (not in your class) to see if it makes sense. Their feedback will quickly confirm, or challenge, the assumptions you have made about appropriate language. Using the feedback from the students, revise the questionnaire before administering it to your class.
- **Use questions that vary from convergent to divergent.** That is, use both "open-ended" and "closed" questions in a structured interview or questionnaire. For example, a closed (convergent) question allows for a brief response such as "Yes/No." Alternatively, an open-ended (divergent) question can conclude with an "Other comments" section, or a request for the interviewees to "add anything else" they would like to. In so doing, you will provide students with opportunities to elaborate on questions in ways that you had never anticipated. However, the information gathered through open-ended questions is often more difficult to make sense of. But it does allow the teacher researcher to obtain information that might otherwise be considered "outlying" or "discrepant."
- **Persevere with silence and "wait time" to elicit a response.** Otherwise it becomes too easy to answer your own question!
- **Consider using an audio tape recorder to capture the interview responses.** One way to ensure that you capture verbatim responses during an interview is to use a tape recorder. After all, you can't write down everything that is said and still maintain rapport with your interviewee. But be warned—this will add to the amount of time that it takes to "write up" your interview. You will need to listen to the tape and to transcribe the responses. Furthermore, I seem to suffer from Murphy's Law when it comes to the use of tape recorders! (That is, if something is going to break or malfunction it will develop a terminal illness on my shift!) I have also interviewed teachers, principals, and superintendents who are very uncomfortable with "being taped." After all, who else will listen to the tape?! Check the body language of whoever you are interviewing to determine if they are okay with the use of the tape recorder. You may find that your interviewees loosen up when the tape runs out!
- **Locate a private place to interview.** Whether you are conducting one-on-one or focus group interviews, be sure to conduct the interview in a private place where you are not likely to be interrupted and where you have the tools for the interview (tape recorder and notepad). You may choose to

use your classroom, another teacher's classroom, a study room in the library—anywhere will work as long as you have privacy and your interviewee feels comfortable in the environment. Alternatively, in an informal interview you may choose to talk to students outside during a recess and play a game of some sort. Some of your colleagues may be very comfortable being interviewed in a faculty lounge or lunch room. Take your cues from your interviewees as to where they are most comfortable being interviewed.

- **Carefully choose who you will interview**. Teacher researchers have considerable flexibility about how they will choose who they interview. The decision to interview will largely depend on the questions you are trying to answer and whether the interviewee is "information rich" (Patton, 1990, p. 169). This is perhaps a statement of the obvious—it doesn't make a lot of sense to interview folks who don't know anything about your area of focus! But at some point you will make a conscious decision about who you will interview. Will you interview all the children in your class/school? All the teachers? The answer is probably "No." Therefore, you will choose who to talk to based on a number of factors: knowledge and experience of the area of focus, verbal skills, and willingness to be interviewed. For most teacher researchers the choice will be fairly limited—the students in their classes will be the primary targets for interviews. Depending on the number of students in your classes, you may choose to conduct a combination of focus group and individual interviews in order to develop a comprehensive understanding of your area of focus.

- **Take notes during the interview**. Regardless of whether you use a tape recorder during an interview, be sure to take notes to capture the essence of the conversation. This is also an antidote for Murphy's Law! No matter how quickly you can write, you will not be able to capture everything that transpires during the interview. The notes taken during the interview will serve as a roadmap for you so that you can fill in the blanks as soon as possible after the actual interview. Your interviewees will also appreciate the rapport that you establish with them and not be distracted by your fervent scratching on a notepad! Note taking is largely an idiosyncratic activity. What works for one person may not work for another. I tend to use a combination of verbatim quotes (taken in longhand), abbreviations, and sketches (uses of arrows to link comments that are repeated, smiley faces to capture the interviewees body language, etc.) to enable me to reconstruct an interview. Given my increasing number of "senior moments," it also speaks to the importance of taking time **as soon as possible after the interview** to write up your fieldnotes for the interview! (The components of interviewing are listed in Key Concepts Box 3–2.)

FOCUS GROUPS

Another valuable interview technique is the use of focus groups with several individuals who can contribute to your understanding of your area of focus. One way to think of focus groups is as a group interview where you are trying to "collect shared understanding from several individuals as well as to get views from specific people"

Components of Interviewing	
Informal interviews	5 Ws and H: *who, what, where, when, why,* and *how?*
Structured formal interviews	Pilot the interview. Use a variety of question formats. Use divergent and convergent questions. Allow ample "wait time" to elicit a response. Consider using an audio tape recorder to capture the interview responses. Locate a private place to conduct the interview. Carefully choose who you will interview. Take notes during the interview.

(Creswell, 2005, p. 206). Focus groups are a particularly useful technique when the interaction between individuals will lead to a shared understanding of the questions being posed by the teacher researcher. For example, James Rockford may have conducted a focus group with the parents of students in his word processing classes to determine a collective view of computer use in the home.

When conducting focus groups it is important to ensure that all participants have their say and to nurture a group agreement to take turns, that is, participants understand that the focus group is a group-sharing activity and not something to be dominated by one or two participants. Using a structured or semistructured interview schedule, the teacher researcher can pose questions to the group and encourage all participants to respond. To use sporting metaphors, use a basketball versus a ping-pong questioning style. That is, ask the question, elicit a response, and pass it off to another participant (basketball) versus ask the question, accept the response, and ask another question. Get as much information out of each question as you possibly can and, in the process, ensure that all group participants have an opportunity to respond.

Ideally, the teacher researcher will use an interview to capture the responses from the focus group and to later transcribe the discussion. This is a time-consuming process—perhaps even more so than individual interviews, so be prepared to allocate time to ferreting out the nuances of the focus group interview and the shared understandings that emerge.

E-Mail Interviews

Another relatively new approach to interviewing that can be used effectively by teacher researchers is the use of e-mail interviews. With schools becoming increasingly networked, the use of e-mail to interview colleagues (and students) can easily be achieved. For busy teachers, it may be a far more effective use of time to engage in an ongoing conversation using e-mail. Busy professionals can respond to an e-mail either synchronously (during a "live" conversation) or asynchronously (at some other time when you are not sitting at your computer).

There are some pros and cons associated with the use of e-mail interviews. For example, one advantage of the e-mail interview is that the transcription of the interview has already been done for you by the respondent! That is, you don't have to transcribe a taped interview with a colleague or student. However, there are ethical issues associated with assuring your respondent that their text response will be confidential and anonymous. I am not an expert when it comes to technology, but I do not trust that once I have sent an e-mail to someone that it is not sitting on a server somewhere that is accessible to other curious folks! This paranoia is further enhanced by the amount of "spam" (junk e-mail) I receive that has been forwarded from someone else's computer.

In spite of these technical and ethical challenges associated with the use of e-mail interviews, such interviews may be a useful tool to use at your school. If your colleagues are like mine, it is difficult to find time during a day when we can sit down face-to-face to talk. The use of e-mail will allow your colleagues and students to respond on their own timeline—perhaps from the comfort of their home or the quiet of their classroom or library after school.

QUESTIONNAIRES

Perhaps the major difference between a structured interview schedule and a questionnaire is that the student or parent will write out the responses on the form provided. Clearly there are positives and negatives with each approach: Questionnaires allow the teacher researcher to collect large amounts of data in a relatively short amount of time (compared with interviewing the same number of students or parents), whereas interviews allow an opportunity for the teacher to intimately know how each student (and parent) feels about a particular issue, but in a time-consuming fashion that few teacher researchers feel is justified. A compromise is to use a questionnaire (when appropriate) and to conduct follow-up interviews with students who have provided written feedback that warrants further investigation. For example, in a conversational way, teachers as part of their regular teaching may ask, "Mary, in the questionnaire you returned you commented that.... Can you tell me a little more about that?" Similarly, as part of a parent-teacher conference the teacher may follow up with parents who have returned questionnaires

Clearly, one major assumption associated with the use of a questionnaire is that the student can read and write. Many teacher researchers exclude the use of a questionnaire on this basis alone, but also compromise the time it takes to interview all their students by interviewing only a "representative sample" in their class.

A solid data collection instrument will help to ensure useful responses. Consider the following guidelines for developing and presenting questionnaires:

1. **Carefully proofread questionnaires** (or better still have a "critical" friend read your questionnaire) before sending them out. Nothing will turn parents off more quickly than receiving a message from their child's teacher that is filled with errors. Alternatively, students may be thrilled by the chance to point out that there is an error in their teacher's written work.
2. **Avoid a sloppy presentation.** Make the survey attractive and consider using BIG print if necessary.

3. **Avoid a lengthy questionnaire.** Piloting the instrument will give you a realistic sense of how long it will take for your students (or parents) to complete the task. Remember, no matter how much they want to help you, if the questionnaire is too long, it will find its way into the "circular file" instead of back into your hands.

4. **Do not ask unnecessary questions.** This is akin to teachers developing tests that don't match what was taught—a common complaint directed toward the administration of standardized tests. Often, we feel compelled to ask a great deal of trivial information on a questionnaire that is tangential to our stated purpose.

5. **Use structured items with a variety of possible responses.** (See the discussion of Likert scales in this chapter.) Indicate what you mean by "often" and "frequently" and how they differ from each other. Otherwise, your respondents will interpret the meaning of the terms in quite different ways.

6. **Whenever possible, allow for an "Other Comments" section.** This provides respondents with an opportunity to respond openly to your questions. These comments also provide you with an excellent source of "discrepant" data ("I hadn't expected someone to say that!") and an opportunity to follow up with an informal interview to elicit more information from the respondent as your time, energy, and inquisitiveness allow. For example, "In your response to question 3 you stated that . . . . Can you tell me a little more about what you meant?"

7. **Decide whether you want respondents to put their names on the questionnaires or whether you will use a number to keep track of who has responded.** You should assure respondents (students, parents, colleagues) that their confidentiality will be protected throughout the process. However, you can protect respondents while also keeping track of who has responded and deciding whether they have made comments that you feel warrant a follow-up conversation. The key issue here is to assure the students, parents, and colleagues that they will not suffer any negative consequences for anything they might share with you. If we want respondents to be honest and forthright in their answers, we must assure them that they will not be persecuted if they tell us something we don't want to read or hear. (For further discussion of this matter, see the section on ethics in Chapter 4.) See Research in Action Checklist 3–1 for guidelines on devising a questionnaire.

Examining: Using and Making Records

This third category for data collection techniques suggests a catch-all term to describe everything else that a teacher researcher may collect. Again, many of these data sources are naturally occurring and require only that teachers locate them within their school setting.

Archival Documents

Like classrooms, schools are repositories for all sorts of records—student records, minutes of meetings (faculty, PTA, school board), newspaper clippings about significant events in the community, and so on. With permission, the teacher researcher

Guidelines on Devising Questionnaires

_____ Proofread the questionnaire carefully.
_____ Avoid a sloppy presentation.
_____ Avoid a lengthy questionnaire.
_____ Do not ask unnecessary questions.
_____ Use structured items with a variety of possible responses.
_____ Include an "Other Comments" section.
_____ Decide whether to use respondents' names.
_____ Pilot the questionnaire.
_____ Use a variety of question formats.

can use these sources of data to gain valuable historical insights, identify potential trends, and explain how things got to be the way they are. Clearly, there are many archival data sources that can be accessed by teacher researchers if indicated by their focus areas. Often, clerical assistants, school aides, and student teachers are happy to help with uncovering archival data and organizing them in a way that is most useful to the classroom teacher if they believe that it is contributing to the collective understanding of a pressing educational issue. Don't be bashful about asking for assistance with this task.

Calhoun (1994) lists several archival data sources that exist in schools:

- Attendance rates
- Retention rates
- Discipline referrals
- Dropout rates
- Suspension rates
- Attendance rates at parent-teacher conferences
- Disaggregated data by grade level for student performance on statewide assessments in math, reading, writing, etc.
- Standardized test scores
- Student participation rates in extracurricular activities

JOURNALS

Daily journals kept by both students and teachers are also a valuable data source. As Anderson, Herr, and Nihlen (1994) point out:

The journal acts as a narrative technique and records events, thoughts, and feelings that have importance for the writer. As a record kept by a student, it can inform the teacher researcher about changing thoughts and new ideas and the progression of learning. (p. 153)

Students' journals can provide teachers with a valuable window into the students' world (in much the same way that homework assignments provide parents with insights into their children's daily experiences). A daily journal kept by teachers can also be an opportunity to keep a narrative account of their perspectives of what is happening in their classrooms.

Cochran-Smith and Lytle (1993) have incorporated teachers' journals as a central part of their work with teacher researchers and offer a somewhat expanded definition of what journals might incorporate:

- Journals are records of classroom life in which teachers write observations, and reflect on their teaching over time.
- Journals are a collection of descriptions, analyses, and interpretations.
- Journals capture the essence of what is happening with students in classrooms and what this means for future teaching episodes.
- Journals provide teachers with a way to revisit, analyze, and evaluate their experiences over time.
- Journals provide windows on what goes on in school through teachers' eyes. (pp. 26–27)

Journals, conceptualized in this way, are more than a single data source—they are an ongoing attempt by teachers to systematically reflect on their practice by constructing a narrative that honors the unique and powerful voice of the teachers' language. Regardless of your specific area of focus, journaling is recommended as a way to keep track of not only observations but feelings associated with the action research process.

MAKING MAPS, VIDEOTAPES, AUDIOTAPES, PHOTOGRAPHS, FILM, AND ARTIFACTS

These nonwritten sources of data can also be extremely helpful for teacher researchers trying to monitor movements in a classroom—data that are not always easily recorded in a narrative form.

Construction of Maps

Teacher researchers find class maps and school maps useful for a number of reasons. They provide contextual insights for people who have not visited the school, and they provide the teacher researcher with a reflective tool—a way of rethinking the way things are in their classrooms. For example, why are the computers in the classroom placed in a "bank" along one wall, and what are the effects of the individual student computer time on other seat-work activities? A map can also record traffic flow in a classroom as well as teacher movement during instruction.

The school map may also prove useful for teams of teachers who are concerned about the movement and interactions of different grade levels of students and any problems that emerge from the traffic flow. Quite simply, maps are easy, useful tools that help teacher researchers and the people with whom they are sharing their research locate particular teaching episodes in the space of the teacher's classroom or school. For qualitatively oriented classroom researchers, context is everything! Figure 3–3 shows an example of a classroom map.

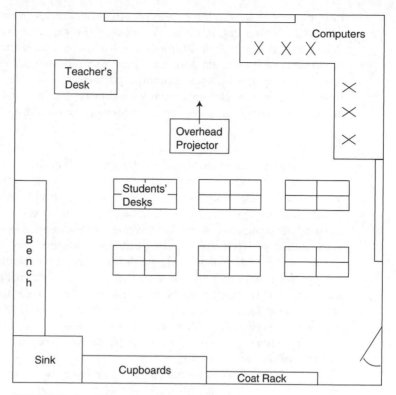

FIGURE 3–3 Classroom Map Example

Use of Videotape, Audiotape, Photographs, and Film

Videotapes and audiotapes provide teacher researchers with another data source when the teacher is fully engaged in teaching but still wants to capture classroom events and interactions. Of course, there are drawbacks to these techniques. For example, their presence may elicit the usual "funny faces" and bizarre comments that we normally associate with the presence of such technology in a classroom for the first time. One way of moving ahead with these efforts is to introduce them into a classroom early in an action research project and provide the illusion that the "camera is running" when, in fact, there is no film in the camera. Alternatively, be prepared to use a lot of videotapes and audiotapes and to record over them! However, with the move to outcome-based performance assessment and "capstone" experiences, children are often required to demonstrate knowledge and skills through presentations to peers or panels of teachers and parents. Videotape is an excellent way to capture these events and to provide an opportunity for teachers and students alike to reflect on content, skills, and attitudes demonstrated by the students. Similarly, I have seen teacher researchers effectively use still photographs (of the traditional 35mm kind and digital photos) to capture events in their classrooms that are central to their given area of focus. For example, James Rockford might have considered the use of photographs to capture the kinds of activities engaged in by students learning word processing.

Assuming there are no technical problems (and that is a pretty big assumption!), the use of audiotape and videotape also raises the serious issue of time—the time it takes to watch, listen, and record observations from these recorded sources. Although finding enough time is probably the number one challenge for teachers doing action research, it is important for us to weigh the potential benefits and drawbacks of these data sources. These techniques have the potential to be more time consuming and, thus, potentially threatening to the goodwill of any action research endeavor. However, many teacher researchers use these methods to great advantage—which only confirms the idiosyncratic nature of data collection efforts!

Artifacts

Classrooms are rich sources of what we might call **artifacts**—written or visual sources of data that contribute to our understanding of what is happening in our classrooms and schools. The category of artifact can include almost everything else that we haven't already discussed. For example, there has been a trend in schools to move toward "authentic assessment" techniques, including the use of student portfolios—a presentation of work that captures individual student's work samples over time and the relative growth of that work. Portfolios, although difficult to quantify, provide the teacher with valuable outcome data that get at the heart of the qualitatively different samples of work. Such artifacts are a valuable data source that teachers may use as a starting point for conversation with their students. For example, a teacher may ask students to explain the differences they see between the work they included in their portfolios earlier and later in the school year. Key Concepts Box 3–3 shows the components of using and making records.

Hence, we have gone full circle in looking at how teacher researchers could use the contents of student portfolios as the basis for an informal interview with their students as they search for greater understanding of the students' perspectives of their learning. For example, a teacher may ask a student to elaborate on the thinking behind a piece of creative writing, artwork, or explanation of an open-ended mathematics problem-solving solution. Utilize Agar's "5Ws and H" to informally engage students in conversation about their work—you'll be pleased with the outcome and

KEY CONCEPTS BOX 3–3

Components of Using and Making Records	
Archival sources	Minutes of meetings Attendance rates, retention rates, dropout rates, suspension rates Discipline referrals Statewide assessment scores Newspaper clippings
Journals	Daily observations and analysis Reflections Record keeping
Artifacts	Maps and seating charts Photographs, audiotapes, and videotapes Portfolios or less formal examples of student work

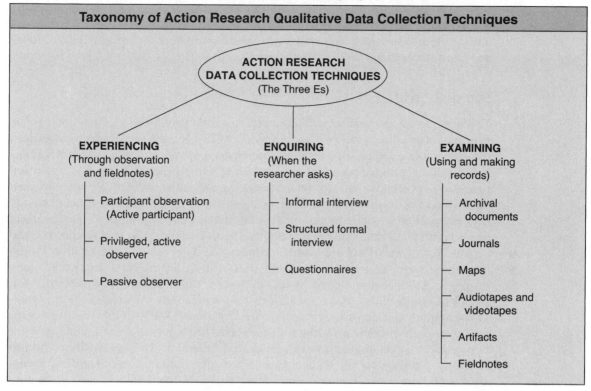

Taxonomy of Action Research Qualitative Data Collection Techniques

ACTION RESEARCH
DATA COLLECTION TECHNIQUES
(The Three Es)

EXPERIENCING
(Through observation
and fieldnotes)

- Participant observation
  (Active participant)
- Privileged, active
  observer
- Passive observer

ENQUIRING
(When the
researcher asks)

- Informal interview
- Structured formal
  interview
- Questionnaires

EXAMINING
(Using and making
records)

- Archival
  documents
- Journals
- Maps
- Audiotapes and
  videotapes
- Artifacts
- Fieldnotes

the return for your investment of time. Key Concepts Box 3–4 shows the taxonomy of action research qualitative data collection techniques.

Quantitative Data Collection Techniques

Many data collection techniques can be used by action researchers that represent common "evaluation" practices in schools and provide the teachers with data that can be reduced to numbers. Action researchers must not confuse the quantitative collection of data with the application of a quantitative research design. The tenets guiding the use of a quantitative research design are different from those guiding the use of qualitative research designs. In this chapter, I will focus on the kinds of quantitative data collection techniques that are commonly used by action researchers and that result in data that can be analyzed and interpreted using the descriptive statistical techniques described in Appendix B.

TEACHER-MADE TESTS

Perhaps one of the most common quantitative data collection techniques used by teachers to aid them in their ability to monitor and adjust instruction is the use of teacher-made tests. That is, teachers will not rely solely on the unit tests provided by textbook companies to determine whether their students have achieved mastery of specific goals and objectives. Oftentimes, teachers *adapt* rather than *adopt* commercial curriculum materials and therefore cannot rely on the unit test accompanying the curriculum to be a valid measure of student performance. Similarly, teachers are expert at developing innovative curriculum to address a particular area of focus and must make their own test from scratch.

STANDARDIZED TESTS

Teachers are all too familiar with the kind of standardized tests that have swept the nation as a result of No Child Left Behind (NCLB) legislation. These standardized tests are intended to provide teachers, principals, parents, and state and federal education officials with individual student achievement data. These data are often reported as percentile ranks or stanines (see Appendix B) and provide teachers with data about the relative performance of their students. That is, these data provide teachers with a snapshot of how their students are performing on a given subject test relative to all other students taking the test. These data are also aggregated to provide policy makers (for example, principals and superintendents) with information about whether groups of students and schools are meeting Adequate Yearly Progress (AYP). In the United States, AYP is a critical component of the federal NCLB act. Under this legislation, all states must establish student achievement targets that gradually increase over time so that by the 2013–14 school year all students in the state are proficient on state assessments. Schools that do not attain AYP for two or more years in a row receive state and federal sanctions (usually related to funding). Needless to say, teachers are increasingly finding these quantitative data sources to be a critical component of any action research data collection plan.

SCHOOL-GENERATED REPORT CARDS

As the parent of a middle-school-aged child, I have intimate knowledge of the kind of report cards provided to children and parents to map student progress. My son, Jonathan, is proud to display his report card on the front of our refrigerator along with all the other important family artifacts that are commonly found on the family fridge (e.g., pictures of family and friends, special vacation places, and of course the family dog, Jesse). Along with the teachers' comments (e.g., "Jonathan is an awesome writer." A chip off the old block I would say!) there are the all important credits earned and the even more important GRADE! At Jonathan's school, grades are reported as letters (A–F) that are ultimately translated into numbers (0–4) in order to calculate a grade point average (GPA). Students who earn a 3.5 GPA or higher, with a minimum of four credits, qualify for Honor Roll and their names appear in the local newspaper. Hence, school-generated report cards are a valuable data source for teachers (who can quantify student achievement) and for students and parents (who can interpret the data and set goals accordingly).

ATTITUDE SCALES

Many teacher researchers are curious about the impact of their work on students' attitudes. Scales that are often used to measure attitudes, such as Likert scales and semantic differentials, are useful tools for the action researcher. The use of attitude scales allows teacher researchers to determine "what an individual believes, perceives, or feels" (Gay, Mills, & Airasian, 2006, pp. 130–131). Nearly all of the action research vignettes in this book include examples of how teacher researchers wanted to know how children "felt" about something (a keyboarding software program, the violence and harassment scenes presented by the Teen Theater group, the absenteeism policy at the school, and the de-emphasis of grades). In some cases, these teacher researchers used an attitude scale, whereas others used open-ended questions, such as "How do you feel about the school's absenteeism policy?"

Likert Scales

A **Likert scale** asks students to respond to a series of statements indicating whether they strongly agree (SA), agree (A), are undecided (U), disagree (D), or strongly disagree (SD) with each statement. Each response corresponds with a point value and a score is determined by adding the point values for each statement. For example, the following point values might be assigned for positive responses: SA = 5, A = 4, U = 3, D = 2, SD = 1. As Gay and colleagues (2006) point out, "A high point value on a positively stated item would indicate a positive attitude and a high total score on the test would be indicative of a positive attitude" (p. 130).

Although these instruments provide teacher researchers with quantitative (numerical) data, these data can still be considered descriptive. The responses to such a survey can be reduced to numbers (for example, the average response was 4.2), but the data are still largely descriptive and analyzed using descriptive statistics, such as mean and standard deviation (see Appendix B) and an accompanying narrative. (For example, "the average response was 4.2 and was supported by the following comments. . . .")

To illustrate, students experiencing a new math curriculum that emphasizes problem-solving strategies may be asked to respond to the following item on a questionnaire:

Please respond to the following items by drawing a circle around the response that most closely reflects your opinion: strongly agree (SA), agree (A), undecided (U), disagree (D), or strongly disagree (SD).

1. I believe that the problem-solving skills I learn in class help me make good problem-solving decisions outside of school.

SA   A   U   D   SD

By assigning the following point values, SA = 5, A = 4, U = 3, D = 2, SD = 1, the teacher researcher would be able to infer whether the students felt positively or negatively about the effect of math problem-solving skills outside of the classroom.

Semantic Differential

A **semantic differential** asks a student (or parent) to give a quantitative rating to the subject of the rating scale on a number of bipolar adjectives. For example, following the implementation of a new math curriculum, students might be asked to rate the curriculum in terms of whether it was exciting or boring, relevant or irrelevant, or enjoyable or unenjoyable.

Quantitative Data Collection Techniques

- Teacher-made tests
- Standardized tests
- School-generated report cards
- Attitude scales
- Likert scales
- Semantic differential

Each location on the continuum between the bipolar words has an associated score:

Boring	__ __ __ __ __ __ __	Exciting
	−3 −2 −1 0 1 2 3	
Irrelevant	__ __ __ __ __ __ __	Relevant
	−3 −2 −1 0 1 2 3	
Unenjoyable	__ __ __ __ __ __ __	Enjoyable
	−3 −2 −1 0 1 2 3	

By totaling scores for all items on the semantic differential, the teacher researcher can determine whether a child's attitude is positive or negative. Semantic differential scales usually have five to seven intervals, with a neutral attitude being assigned a value of zero.

A child who checked the first interval on each of these items would be expressing a positive attitude toward mathematics (for further discussion of semantic differentials, see Gay, Mills, & Airasian, 2006; Pelto & Pelto, 1978).

Key Concepts Box 3–5 lists quantitative data collection techniques.

OTHER MEASUREMENT TECHNIQUES

Teacher researchers are often pressured or required to use standardized tests. It is not possible to list here all of the standardized tests that exist. We should acknowledge, however, that standardized test scores are another data source that contributes to our understanding of how teaching practices affect our students. A good source for teachers who are investigating standardized tests is the Mental Measurements Yearbook (MMY). The MMYs are published by the Buros Institute of Mental Measurements and are a major source of test information for educational researchers. The yearbooks, which can be found in most large libraries, provide information and reviews of published tests in various school subject areas (such as English, mathematics, and reading) as well as personality, intelligence, aptitude, speech and hearing, and vocational tests. The Web addresses for the Buros Institute and its catalogs are http://www.unl.edu/buros/ and http://www.unl.edu/buros/bimm/html/catalog.html.

Realign Your Area of Focus and Action Research Plan When Necessary

By this point in the action research process, teacher researchers have already articulated their area of focus in a problem statement and reviewed the literature based on that idea. However, once they start their data collection, many teacher researchers find themselves drawn into other directions that appear more interesting, relevant, or problematic. That is the very nature of action research; it is intimate, open-ended, and often serendipitous. Being clear about a problem is critical in the beginning, but once teacher researchers begin to systematically collect their data, the area of focus will become even clearer.

Be prepared to modify and adjust your action research plan if necessary. For example, a group of teachers started their action research project with an area of focus on the impact of early literacy development on problem-solving skills in mathematics. As their study evolved, it became clear to the participants that their real focus was not on the transfer of literacy to problem solving but rather on the effects of a phonemic skills curriculum on early literacy development. When this focus became clear after some initial data collection, the group decided to change their research questions to more accurately reflect the real nature of their work.

There is nothing wrong with realigning your inquiry midway through it. Remember, action research is done to benefit you and the students in your classroom. The process is a spiral. If you discover a question or a method that seems more fruitful than the one you are currently using, adjust your action research plan and continue on!

Summary

This chapter has examined how to identify and develop data collection techniques appropriate for an action research project. The concept of triangulation, or ensuring that teacher researchers do not rely on a single data source, was presented as a guiding principle when thinking about a "multi-instrument" approach to systematic action research.

Teacher researchers can become participant observers and gather fieldnotes, assuming different degrees of involvement in the class. They can use a variety of inquiry tools such as interviews, questionnaires, or attitude scales to gather data. Teacher researchers can also benefit from the exploration of new or existing school archives and student artifacts. Increasingly, teacher researchers are finding quantitative data collection techniques to be a critical data source that also connects their research to state and federal requirements such as Adequate Yearly Progress.

As you gather data, you may find a more interesting or fruitful line of inquiry. Do not be afraid to revise your action research plan midway to suit your needs.

For Further Thought

1. What data collection techniques will you use to answer each of your research questions?
2. What data collection instruments do you need to locate or develop?
3. Complete a triangulation matrix (Figure 3–4) for your proposed study. (Reminder: Don't force the issue of three data sources for each question. In some cases you may have more than three data sources that you wish to use, and in other cases it may not be possible to include more than one data source. For example, standardized test scores.)

Research Questions	Data Source		
	1	2	3
1.			
2.			
3.			
4.			
5.			

FIGURE 3–4   Triangulation Matrix Exercise

Data Collection Considerations: Validity, Reliability, and Generalizability

This chapter addresses the importance of validity, reliability, and generalizability as ways to ensure the quality of qualitatively oriented action research.

After reading this chapter you should be able to:
1. Understand the concepts of validity, reliability, and generalizability as they apply to action research.

Improving Student Understanding and Motivation of Multiplication Facts

Alyson Marland

Alyson Marland, a student teacher in a fourth-grade classroom, was a participant in an action research class. Like many elementary teachers, Alyson was challenged about how best to teach elementary students basic number facts, while at the same time keeping the children motivated to learn. Alyson's story illustrates the importance of using multiple data sources (qualitative and quantitative) to address issues of validity and reliability that ensured the quality, and robustness, of her action research findings.

This action research project focuses on promoting student understanding and motivation while teaching the basic multiplication facts (0–9). The study examined the effectiveness of teaching methods with an emphasis on rote memorization, compared to those focusing on problem solving. Research advocates the use of problem solving when introducing and teaching basic facts, and holding off on drill and practice methods until after they've developed an understanding. The participants in the study consist of thirty-five fourth-grade students. The students participated in lessons on arrays and multiplication games, and they discussed efficient versus inefficient counting strategies. Data were collected from their old timed tests, state math scores, interviews, and worksheets. The results of the study suggest a positive relationship between balancing conceptual understanding and procedural skills, and student success with basic facts. The results also show a positive relationship between playing games and student motivation for studying the basic facts.

Introduction

Research suggests that for every time you do something wrong, you have to do it right seventeen times before your brain gets used to doing it correctly.

These findings are startling when you consider the vast amount of drill and practice methods used in the classroom to teach students their basic math facts. The purpose of my action research project was to seek out and examine effective and efficient methods for teaching the basic facts. My second objective for this project was to develop effective strategies for increasing student motivation in terms of studying their multiplication facts. Students are often frustrated and bored studying things they don't understand, or when using tedious study methods.

Background

According to the 2004–2005 Oregon State Standards, by the end of fourth grade students are expected to have developed efficient strategies for solving multiplication problems. They should be fluent with these strategies and able to solve all basic fact problems mentally within three seconds. Unfortunately, researchers have found that an alarming number of eighth grade students still resort to finger counting and other inefficient strategies when solving simple problems (Isaacs, Carroll, & Bell, 2001). These strategies are inefficient because they take too much time and are not done mentally.

One promising practice is to reduce the use of drill and practice methods (Jones, 1995). These methods include timed tests, flash cards, and worksheets with rows of basic facts. One reason researchers advise educators to stay away from drill and practice methods is because they don't aid in students' conceptual understanding of multiplication. These methods provide students with procedural skills that they are taught to mimic. Teaching in this way makes it hard for students to apply multiplication concepts to word problems or real-life situations.

Effective strategies for teaching basic facts include balancing procedural skills and conceptual knowledge. Teaching with balance includes the use of word problems, arrays, and open-ended problem-solving assignments. Isaacs et al. (2001) recommend practicing multiplication in a variety of contexts and situations to increase the students' ability to transfer the skill/concept.

Other promising practices suggest three components to use when teaching basic facts. The first component is developing a strong understanding of the operations of number relationships. The second focuses on trading inefficient strategies for efficient ones, and the third component is providing students with drill and practice assignments. Van de Walle (2003) stresses the importance of not moving to step three until after the students have developed efficient strategies. If you introduce drill before the students have mastered one or more efficient strategies, the practice will only reinforce the inefficient strategies. Inefficient strategies include counting on fingers, adding the numbers instead of multiplying them, using manipulatives, drawing pictures, etc. Inefficient methods are inefficient because they take a long time and cannot be done mentally. Efficient methods include skip counting, simplifying the problem, and ultimately, memorization.

Intervention

My planned intervention to address students' understanding of, and motivation to learn, basic number facts included the following:

- Lessons focused on building students' conceptual understanding of the multiplication process.
- Teaching students efficient strategies for solving basic facts.
- Introducing students to fun games they could play while studying their basic number facts.

Data Collection

The data collection tools I used were:

1. Students' scores on state math tests
2. Results of timed tests
3. Informal interviews
4. Students' written work

Data Analysis

The data I collected from the students' state math test was surprising. I was shocked to find that eleven students (about thirty-five percent of the class) did not meet the state standards in math. The students who did not meet state standards were consistent with the students who were not passing their timed tests. I decided I would need to spend some extra time working with these eleven students.

The data I collected from students' timed tests were by far the most helpful in planning my intervention and understanding where students were having the most trouble. The data I collected from the timed tests focused on the types of errors students were making. Edelman, Abdit, and Valentin (1995) describe four types of errors humans make when multiplying; they include operand, table, operation, and non-table errors. Operand errors occur when the incorrect answer given is correct for another problem that shares an operand (e.g., $4 \times 2 = 16$, when 16 is the correct answer for 4×4). Table errors occur when the incorrect answer given does not share an operand with the correct answer, but the answer given does reside in the multiplication table (e.g., $6 \times 9 = 56$). Humans make operation errors when they perform a different operation, such as adding or subtracting, when solving a multiplication problem (e.g., $9 \times 0 = 9$). The final error is a non-table error, and it occurs when the incorrect answer is not an answer to any problem in the multiplication table (e.g., $5 \times 6 = 31$). Operand errors were by far the most common error made by the students. They accounted for fifty-five percent of the error total. This data told me that students were associating the incorrect answer with one of the operands, and the early emphasis on drill and practice has reinforced these wrong answers. Non-table errors accounted for twenty-three percent of the errors. I believe students are making a high amount of non-table errors, because they are miscounting on their fingers. Solving 6 × 7 on your fingers is both hard and confusing, so I assumed students who rely on their fingers make the majority of the table errors. Operation errors occur mostly in problems containing an operand of zero or one. The students often switch to addition and solve the problem by adding zero or one to the other number. This error occurs mostly when the zero or one is on the bottom. I didn't feel the error occurred consistently enough to be considered a problem, so I decided not to focus on it during my intervention.

I also used the students' timed tests to identify which multiplication facts they were having the most trouble with. The problems I found gave students the most trouble were 6 × 7, 7 × 6, 7 × 4, 7 × 7, 8 × 8, 8 × 7, 6 × 6, 8 × 6, and 6 × 8. In general, though, any problem including an operand of six, seven, eight, and/or nine was answered incorrectly by the majority of students. This data was especially helpful in adjusting my interventions, because it allowed me to focus on the problems with which students were having the most trouble.

The informal interviews provided me with insight into what the students thought about timed tests, what strategies they used to solve basic fact problems, and how well they could transfer their skills to real-world situations. I was surprised to find that every student answered "yes" to the question about whether or not they felt timed tests were helpful. The majority of students supported their answer stating that timed tests gave them a chance to practice their multiplication facts. The interviews also allowed me to discover which strategy each student relied on when solving multiplication facts.

Discussion

The purpose of my action research project was to seek out and examine effective and efficient methods for teaching basic math facts. Upon completion of my action research project, I feel confident that I will be able to effectively and efficiently teach basic facts to any grade, first through sixth. I am now aware of the common misconceptions regarding rote memorization and the premature use of timed tests.

My results tell me that timed tests can be beneficial when used as a form of practice. Students should be able to correct their own tests, allowing for immediate feedback on which problems they got wrong and what the correct answer should have been. Teachers should also consider not grading the tests so students can focus on improving their skills and not on a grade.

From my research, experience, and results I was also able to infer that effective teaching strategies center around balancing conceptual understanding and procedural skills. To provide this balance, educators should emphasize problem-solving strategies at an early age. Problem-solving methods provide students with flexibility in their learning, making it easier for them to transfer their knowledge to various math problems and real-life situations. Also, teachers should teach one concept at a time, and teach it to master before moving on.

To motivate their students, educators must first develop their understanding of the multiplication procedure and concept. This understanding will boost the students' self-esteem, giving them confidence and motivating them intrinsically. The second step in motivating students is introducing fun ways for them to learn, study, and memorize the basic facts. In my experience, students preferred competitive games, especially when playing against the teacher. The participants in my study were really excited about having a "multiplication bowl," where the two fourth-grade classes would face off in a multiplication competition. I am excited to continue to test these teaching strategies in the next cycle of my action research journey.

References

Edelman, B., Abdit, H., & Valentin, D. (1995). Multiplication number facts: Modeling human performance with connections networks. *Psychologica Belgica.* 1–23.

Isaacs, A., Carroll, W., & Bell, M. (2001). UCSMP everyday mathematics curriculum. *Everyday Mathematics.* 2–5.

Jones, S. C. (1995). Review of cognitive research. *Educational Memory Aids.* 57–60.

Van de Walle, J. A. (2003). Elementary and middle school mathematics: Teaching developmentally. *Pearson.* 156–176.

ATTENTION TO THE three important concepts of validity, reliability, and generalizability will help teacher researchers ensure the quality of their work. These concepts are also important for teacher researchers who are reviewing published and unpublished research. That is, to both do action research and measure the quality of the action research you're reading about, you need a basic understanding of the concepts of validity, reliability, and generalizability.

Qualitative researchers, action researchers, and quantitative researchers disagree about the value of applying these concepts of validity, reliability, and generalizability to qualitatively oriented action research. In part, this debate takes place because such concepts have their roots in traditional quantitative research—research that uses mostly numerical data and that has different purposes from action research (see Chapter 1).

However, teacher researchers must understand the meanings of these terms to be knowledgeable consumers of research, as well as producers of research that we hope will be trustworthy and persuasive in their own eyes and in the eyes of their audience.

Validity

The use of the word *validity* is common in our everyday professional language. For example, teachers will ask, "Are the results of the California Achievement Test really valid?" Or, my preservice teachers will often comment, "My students did poorly on the history test I gave them, but I'm not sure it's an accurate representation of what they really know." Recently, I have also heard teachers discuss whether open-ended assessment strategies really measure their students' ability. All these examples are questions about **validity**, or how we know that the data we collect (test scores, for example) accurately gauge what we are trying to measure (in this case, what it is that our children "know" about history). To put it technically, "validity refers to the degree to which scientific observations actually measure or record what they purport to measure" (Pelto & Pelto, 1978, p. 33).

Historically, validity was linked to numerically based research conducted in the positivistic tradition. For example, Cronbach and Meehl (1955) developed criteria for four different types of validity. These types of validity served to convince the researcher and the researchee that the "results" of the research were "right," "accurate," and could withstand scrutiny from other researchers.

However, as many types of qualitative research became more popular in classroom settings in the late 1970s and early 1980s, it became common for qualitative researchers to begin to justify and defend the validity of their studies according to the criteria that had previously been applied to quantitative studies. For example, as a graduate student completing a research-based master's thesis on the effects of high geographic mobility on the children of low-income families, I was required by my advisors to dedicate considerable time and effort to justifying and defending the accuracy of my account. They confronted me with the question, "How will your readers know that your case studies accurately portray the lives of these children?" (Mills, 1985).

In the early days of my career this seemed like an overwhelming task, because there was a paucity of literature that specifically dealt with the issue. Since then, individuals have been experimenting with a new vocabulary that captures the essence of the term *validity* in a way that applies specifically to the methods of qualitative research. Kincheloe (1991) asks "Is *trustworthiness* a more appropriate word to use?" (p. 135), whereas Wolcott (1994) suggests *"understanding* seems to encapsulate the idea as well as any other everyday term" (p. 367). Greenwood and Levin (2000) argue that because action researchers do not make claims to context-free knowledge (that is, by its very nature action research is based in the context of our own classrooms and schools), issues of credibility, validity, and reliability in action research are measured by the willingness of teacher researchers (and the stakeholders in our studies) "to act on the results of the action research, thereby risking their welfare on the 'validity' of their ideas and the degree to which the outcomes meet their expectations" (p. 98). In short, the validity of our action research depends on whether the actual solution to a problem (our planned intervention) actually solves our problem!

Let's look at two systems for measuring the quality of qualitative research based on these two terms: trustworthiness and understanding.

GUBA'S CRITERIA FOR VALIDITY OF QUALITATIVE RESEARCH

Guba's article "Criteria for Assessing the Trustworthiness of Naturalistic Inquiries" (1981) speaks directly to qualitative researchers. Guba argued that the **trustworthiness** of qualitative inquiry could be established by addressing the following characteristics of a study: *credibility, transferability, dependability,* and *confirmability.*

Credibility

The **credibility** of the study refers to the researcher's ability to take into account the complexities that present themselves in a study and to deal with patterns that are not easily explained. To do this, Guba (1981) suggested that the following methods be used:

- *Do prolonged participation at the study site* to overcome distortions produced by the presence of researchers and to provide researchers with the opportunity to test biases and perceptions. By virtue of studying your own school, classroom, and students, you will be immersed in the setting and spend a prolonged amount of time at the site—probably close to 180 days per year!
- *Do persistent observation* to identify pervasive qualities as well as atypical characteristics.
- *Do peer debriefing* to provide researchers with the opportunity to test their growing insights through interactions with other professionals. For example, most of us will be able to identify a "critical friend," a colleague, "significant other"—somebody who is willing and able to help us reflect on our own situations by listening, prompting, and recording our insights throughout the process.
- *Practice triangulation* (discussed in Chapter 3) to compare a variety of data sources and different methods with one another in order to cross-check data.
- *Collect documents, films, videotapes, audio recordings, artifacts, and other "raw" or "slice-of-life" data items.*

- *Do member checks* to test the overall report with the study's participants before sharing it in final form (pp. 84–86).
- *Establish structural corroboration or coherence* to ensure that there are no internal conflicts or contradictions.
- *Establish referential adequacy*, that is, test analyses and interpretations against documents, recordings, films, and the like that were collected as part of the study.

Transferability

Guba's (1981) second criteria of **transferability** refers to qualitative researchers' beliefs that everything they study is context bound and that the goal of their work is not to develop "truth" statements that can be generalized to larger groups of people. To facilitate the development of descriptive, context-relevant statements, Guba proposed that the researcher should:

- *Collect detailed descriptive data* that will permit comparison of a given context (classroom/school) to other possible contexts to which transfer might be contemplated.
- *Develop detailed descriptions of the context* to make judgments about fittingness with other contexts possible.

The transferability of an action research account depends largely on whether the consumer of the research can identify with the setting. Include as much detail as possible to allow the recipients of your work to "see" the setting for themselves.

Dependability

According to Guba (1981), **dependability** refers to the stability of the data. To address issues related to the dependability of the data we collect, Guba recommended the following steps:

- *Overlap methods* (similar to a triangulation process). Use two or more methods in such a way that the weakness of one is compensated by the strength of another. For example, interviews with students may be used to contribute to your understanding of what you observed happening during a lesson.
- *Establish an "audit trail."* This process makes it possible for an external "auditor" (maybe a critical friend, principal, or graduate student) to examine the processes of data collection, analysis, and interpretation. This audit trail may take the form of a written description of each process and perhaps even access to original fieldnotes, artifacts, videotapes, pictures, archival data, and so on.

Confirmability

The final characteristic that Guba (1981) addresses is the **confirmability** of the data, or the neutrality or objectivity of the data that has been collected. Guba argues that the following two steps can be taken to address this issue:

- *Practice triangulation* (discussed in Chapter 3), whereby a variety of data sources and different methods are compared with one another to cross-check data.
- *Practice reflexivity*, that is, to intentionally reveal underlying assumptions or biases that cause the researcher to formulate a set of questions in a particular

way and to present findings in a particular way. One technique for doing this is to keep a journal in which reflections/musings are recorded on a regular basis. Key Concepts Box 4–1 lists Guba's criteria for validity of qualitative research.

MAXWELL'S CRITERIA FOR VALIDITY OF QUALITATIVE RESEARCH

More recently, Maxwell (1992) has adopted a stance more consistent with that of Wolcott (1990), that is, "that **understanding** is a more fundamental concept for qualitative research than validity" (p. 281). Maxwell's typology based on understanding includes *descriptive validity, interpretive validity, theoretical validity, generalizability*, and *evaluative validity*.

Descriptive Validity

Maxwell (1992) proposes that **descriptive validity**, or factual accuracy, is fundamental to any qualitative, descriptive account:

> The first concern of most qualitative researchers is with the factual accuracy of their account—that is, that they are not making up or distorting things they saw and heard. If you report that an informant made a particular statement in an interview, is this correct? (pp. 285–286)

KEY CONCEPTS BOX 4–1

Guba's Criteria for Validity of Qualitative Research		
CRITERIA	DEFINITION	STRATEGIES
Credibility	The researcher's ability to take into account the complexities that present themselves in a study and to deal with patterns that are not easily explained.	Do prolonged participation at study site. Do persistent observation. Do peer debriefing. Practice triangulation. Collect "slice-of-life" data items. Do member checks. Establish structural corroboration or coherence. Establish referential adequacy.
Transferability	The researcher's belief that everything is context-bound.	Collect detailed descriptive data. Develop detailed descriptions of the context.
Dependability	The stability of the data.	Overlap methods. Establish an "audit trail."
Confirmability	The neutrality or objectivity of the data collected.	Practice triangulation. Practice reflexivity.

Source: Adapted from "Criteria for assessing the trustworthiness of naturalistic inquiries," by E. G. Guba, 1981, *Educational Communication and Technology, 2* (1), pp. 75–91.

According to this criteria, any matters related to descriptive validity could be validated by checking with the informant, or the tape-recorded or videotaped account of the interview, that the quote that has been reproduced in the account is correct.

For example, in a study I was working on related to documenting the implementation of the National Council of Teachers of Mathematics (NCTM) Standards, I conducted interviews with teachers, principals, students, and district superintendents throughout the United States and Canada. At one of these sites, the superintendent responded to a question about how best to change the way high school teachers teach math in the following way: "I think that the only way to change the way high school math teachers teach math is to line them up and shoot them!" In a case study I wrote about the site, I used the quote to illustrate the frustration the superintendent felt toward the implementation of the NCTM Standards in high schools in the district. When the account was shared with the participants in the study to check the accuracy of the story, the superintendent had a violent reaction to the quote. He responded to me that he never said such a thing and that the account bordered on "tabloid journalism."

To check the descriptive validity of the account, I returned to the taped interview, the transcript of the interview, and to my fieldnotes and the fieldnotes of my co-researcher who was present at the interview. Sure enough, the quote was accurate, and I felt justified in incorporating it into the account. The project director, however, was more concerned about the "potential harm" of the quote, and in a subsequent draft of the case study the account was "paraphrased." Nevertheless, I had established the descriptive validity of a questionable section of the account by returning to data sources to double-check the accuracy of what was said by whom.

Interpretive Validity

Maxwell (1992) describes **interpretive validity** as the concern researchers have with the meaning attributed to behaviors by the people who have been studied, that is, it is concern for what is commonly called the "participants' perspective":

> Interpretive accounts are grounded in the language of the people studied and rely as much as possible on their own words and concepts. The issue, again, is not the appropriateness of these concepts for the account, but their accuracy as applied to the perspective of the individuals included in the account. (p. 289)

To return to the story of the superintendent who was upset with my use of the "shoot the math teachers" quote, the issue was also related to interpretive validity. How might someone at the site reading the account interpret the language of "line them up and shoot them"? For example, a high school math teacher in the district might interpret the remark as an indication that all high school math teachers in the district will be fired—literally! Indeed, this was not the superintendent's intent and that alone was a good enough reason to change the account and forgo the use of the quote.

Theoretical Validity

Theoretical validity refers to the ability of the research report to explain the phenomenon that has been studied and described:

> Theoretical validity thus refers to an account's validity as a theory of some phenomenon. Any theory has two components: the concepts or categories that the theory employs, and the relationships that are thought to exist among the concepts. (Maxwell, 1992, p. 291)

For example, to return to my superintendent's story, the language used by the superintendent to describe the difficult nature of changing high school math teaching might be labeled as an act that perpetuates the traditional power relationships that exist in school districts and the intractability of educational reform efforts in general. For this interpretation to be theoretically valid, the reader of the account would need to apply a theoretical construct to the description and, based on that theory, extrapolate to other aspects of the school community.

Generalizability

According to Maxwell, there are two aspects of **generalizability**: generalizability within the community that has been studied (internal generalizability) and generalizability to settings that were not studied by the researcher (external generalizability). Internal generalizability is more important than external generalizability because qualitative researchers (and action researchers) rarely make claims about the external generalizability of their research (Maxwell, 1992).

For example, my reliance on the data I had collected through an interview with the superintendent may have had descriptive and interpretive validity, but I may have missed other aspects of the superintendent's perspective that were not evident during the interview. In this case, the internal generalizability of the account was threatened by the interpretation of the interview. However, by inviting the superintendent to respond to the account, I was able to add to the superintendent's perspective in his own words and to increase the internal generalizability of the account.

The relevance of generalizability will be discussed in greater detail later in this chapter.

Evaluative Validity

Evaluative validity has to do with whether the researcher was objective enough to report the data in as unbiased a way as possible, rather than making judgments and evaluations of the data. No account is immune to questions of whether the teacher researcher was focusing on being evaluative instead of being concerned with describing and understanding the phenomenon that was studied. Clearly, the superintendent thought that I had fabricated the "shoot them" quote to make an evaluative statement about the superintendent and the district. I, on the other hand, maintained that my purpose in doing the research was to increase our understanding of the phenomenon under investigation—not to evaluate the mathematics programs in the district. Key Concepts Box 4–2 shows Maxwell's criteria for validity of qualitative research.

Maxwell's Criteria for Validity of Qualitative Research	
CRITERIA	DEFINITION
Descriptive validity	Factual accuracy.
Interpretive validity	Concern for the participants' perspective.
Theoretical validity	The ability of the research report to explain the phenomenon that has been studied and described.
Generalizability	*Internal generalizability:* Generalizability within the community that has been studied. *External generalizability:* Generalizability to settings that were not studied by the researcher.
Evaluative validity	Whether the researcher was able to present the data without being evaluative or judgmental.

Source: Adapted from "Understanding and validity in qualitative research," by J. A. Maxwell, 1992, *Harvard Educational Review, 62* (3), pp. 279–300.

ANDERSON, HERR, AND NIHLEN'S CRITERIA FOR VALIDITY IN ACTION RESEARCH

For most qualitative researchers, it is helpful to apply words such as *trustworthiness* and *understanding* to indicate the validity of our research. Using these criteria provides us with an opportunity (and challenge) to ensure that our research satisfies professional standards. However, Anderson, Herr, and Nihlen (1994) argued that action researchers need a system for judging the quality of their inquiries that is specifically tailored to their classroom-based research projects:

> If practitioner researchers are to be accepted in a larger dialogue about education, they must develop some inquiry criteria for their research. This is not to say that they need to justify themselves by the same inquiry criteria as academic research, but rather that they must make the case for a different conception of validity. This conception of validity should respond to the purposes and conditions of practitioner research and the uniqueness of its contribution to the dialogue. (p. 29)

To this end, Anderson and colleagues (1994) offered the following criteria for the validity of action research: *democratic validity, outcome validity, process validity, catalytic validity*, and *dialogic validity*.

Democratic Validity

Democratic validity requires that the multiple perspectives of all the participants in the study (teachers, principals, parents, and students) have been accurately represented. The question for teacher researchers will be how to ensure that participants' multiple perspectives are captured. One way to ensure that there is democratic validity to an action research study will be to involve teachers and administrators in a collaborative effort with participants representing the group being studied. Make sure "the problems emerge from a particular context and solutions are appropriate to that context" (Cunningham, 1983, p. 30).

Outcome Validity

Outcome validity requires that the action emerging from a particular study leads to the successful resolution of the problem that was being studied, that is, your study can be considered valid if you learn something that can be applied to the subsequent research cycle. For example, Jack Reston's study of Eastview's absenteeism policy (see Chapter 7) led to a number of "findings" that affected the development of a new policy. These findings included a need to address:

- The "respectfulness of students";
- Issues related to "feeling safe" in a school;
- The reteaching of conflict management skills;
- The feeling of children in the upper grades that school rules were unfair;
- Student perception that absenteeism added to the image of being "bad"; and
- The fact that 75 percent of the general school population and students with excessive absenteeism have attended the school for more than 2 years.

All of these outcomes led to action that has helped to address the school's absenteeism problems.

Process Validity

Process validity requires that a study has been conducted in a "dependable" and "competent" manner. It is possible in any study to find support for any feasible perspective. However, we engage in research processes that help us combat the tendency to present our studies as only glowing validations of existing exemplary practices! One way to address this issue is to be vigilant in reflecting on the suitability of your data collection techniques and to modify your strategies if the data you are collecting are not answering your questions.

Catalytic Validity

The criteria of **catalytic validity** require that the participants in a study are moved to take action on the basis of their heightened understanding of the subject of the study. The results of your study should serve as a "catalyst" for action! According to this schema, your action research effort is valid if it moves you and others involved to action (see Chapter 7, Action Planning for Educational Change).

Dialogic Validity

Dialogic comes from the word *dialogue*, to have a conversation. Thus, **dialogic validity** involves having a critical conversation with others about your research findings and practices. Dialogic validity requires that the "goodness" of the research is established by application of a peer review process (similar to what already exists in traditional publication circles). For example, the teacher researchers with whom I work use an electronic bulletin board as a venue to share their research with the wider (cyberspace) professional community.

See Key Concepts Box 4–3 for Anderson's criteria for validity of action research.

Anderson's Criteria for Validity of Action Research	
CRITERIA	TEST QUESTION
Democratic validity	Have the multiple perspectives of all of the individuals in the study been accurately represented?
Outcome validity	Did the action emerging from the study lead to the successful resolution of the problem?
Process validity	Was the study conducted in a dependable and competent manner?
Catalytic validity	Were the results of the study a catalyst for action?
Dialogic validity	Was the study reviewed by peers?

WOLCOTT'S STRATEGIES FOR ENSURING THE VALIDITY OF ACTION RESEARCH

Given this book's focus on qualitatively oriented action research, teacher researchers should pay close attention to the following strategies. Taken in concert with the previous discussion about validity criteria, they provide qualitatively oriented teacher researchers with practical options for making sure their research is the best it can be (adapted from Wolcott, 1994).

Talk Little; Listen a Lot

This strategy suggests that teacher researchers who are conducting interviews, asking questions, or engaging children, parents, and colleagues in discussions about the problem being studied ought to carefully monitor the ratio of listening to talking. For example, interviewing children can be difficult work—our best thought-out questions elicit painfully brief replies, and we are left wondering what to do next. As teachers we are in the business of talking for a living, so it comes quite naturally to us to jump in with our own answer for the child. The trustworthiness of our inquiries will be enhanced if we can bite our tongue, think of some other probing questions, and wait patiently (one thousand . . . two thousand . . . three thousand . . . !). As a teacher I have never been very comfortable with silence in my classroom, particularly when I thought that I had asked an engaging question. My advice is to be patient and allow the respondents time to respond. Avoid being your own best informant.

Record Observations Accurately

When conducting classroom research, recording observations while you are teaching is nearly impossible. However, you should record observations as soon as possible following a teaching episode to accurately capture the essence of what transpired. Although audio and video recordings can assist with our efforts to record accurately, there will still be many occasions when, as participant observers, we have to rely on our fieldnotes, our journals, or our memories. And for me, relying on my memory is becoming an increasingly scary thing!

Begin Writing Early

In a work day that is already crunched by the pressures of time, finding time to write in journals is often difficult. However, if we rely solely on our memories of what has been happening in our classrooms over an extended period of time, we are likely to fall victim to writing romanticized versions of classroom and school life. Make time to write down your reflections. The act of writing down your recollections of a teaching episode or observation will make evident to you what blanks need to be filled in, for example, what questions need to be asked the next day or what should be the focus of your observations.

Let Readers "See" for Themselves

Include primary data in any account to let the readers of your action research accounts (colleagues, principals, university professors) see the data for themselves. As Wolcott (1994) suggests, "In striking the delicate balance between providing too much detail and too little, I would rather err on the side of too much; conversely, between overanalyzing and underanalyzing data, I would rather say too little" (p. 350). This is particularly true in a schoolwide action research effort in which you are seeking support for possible change based on the provocative and persuasive data that are presented to teaching colleagues who may not have had a central role in the conduct of the study. When sharing your research reports with colleagues, let them see the data. This may mean using charts, graphs, photographs, film— whatever you have collected. In doing so, you will bring the recipient of your work along in the process and perhaps earn their buy-in to the next action research cycle. Showing can be more persuasive than telling.

Report Fully

In our quest to find neat answers and solutions to our problems, it is often easy to avoid keeping track of discrepant events and data. Just when we think we know the answer, some data come along to shatter the illusion of having neatly resolved the problem! We do not need to be fearful of discrepant data. After all, it is all grist for the research mill, and although we do not need to report everything, it is helpful to keep track of the discrepant data and to seek further explanation to understand what is happening in our classrooms/schools.

Be Candid

Teacher researchers should be candid about their work, and if writing a narrative that they hope to publish or share with a broader audience, they should make explicit any biases that they may have about the inquiry they have undertaken. Teacher researchers should also make explicit the things about which they have made judgments, because it is easy to slip into a narrative that seeks to validate one's position. Being candid may also provide an opportunity to be explicit about events that occurred during the study and that may have affected the outcomes. For example, high student turnover rates may provide an explanation for fluctuating test scores.

Seek Feedback

It is always a good idea to seek feedback from colleagues (and perhaps even students, parents, volunteers, and administrators) on your written study. Other readers will help raise questions about what you as the writer will have taken for granted. They will raise questions about the accuracy of the account and help you to go back to your classroom in your quest to get the story right (or at least, not all wrong).

Write Accurately

Once you have written a description of your action research, it is a good idea to read the account aloud or solicit the assistance of a close colleague in a careful reading of the account to look for contradictions in the text. Often we are too close to the investigation to really see the contradictions that may be blatantly obvious to an outsider. Although we are assuming in this discussion that teacher researchers will generate a written account of their action research efforts, we will see in Chapter 7 some alternative formats that can be used for sharing the outcomes of an action research effort. Nevertheless, the accuracy of the account (whether written or "performed") is critical to the validity of the study. (For further discussion of these points and a discussion of "When It Really Matters, Does Validity Really Matter?" see Wolcott, 1994, pp. 348–370.) See Research in Action Checklist 4–1 for Wolcott's strategies for ensuring the validity of qualitative action research.

Reliability

In everyday English, reliability means dependability or trustworthiness. The term means essentially the same thing with respect to measurement. Basically, **reliability** is the degree to which a test consistently measures whatever it measures. The more reliable a test is, the more confidence we can have that the scores obtained from the administration of the test are essentially the same scores that would be obtained if the test were re-administered. An unreliable test is essentially useless; if a test is unreliable, then scores for a given sample would be expected to be different every time the test was administered. If an intelligence test was unreliable, for example, then a student scoring an IQ of 120 today might score an IQ of 140 tomorrow, and a 95 the day after tomorrow. If the test was reliable, and if the student's IQ was 110, then we would not expect his or her score to fluctuate too greatly from testing to testing; a score of 105 would not be unusual, but a score of 145 would be very unlikely. If you have ever administered standardized tests to students, you will be familiar with the reliability coefficients that are presented in the administration manuals. The numbers are meant to convey to the test user the peace of mind that, if the test were administered on a future occasion, individual students would score roughly the same.

Reliability is expressed numerically, usually as a coefficient; a high coefficient indicates high reliability. If a test were perfectly reliable, the coefficient would be 1.00; this would mean that a student's score perfectly reflected her or his true status with respect to the variable being measured. However, no test is perfectly reliable. Scores are invariably affected by errors of measurement resulting from a variety of

Wolcott's Strategies for Ensuring the Validity of Action Research

____ Talk little; listen a lot.

____ Record accurately.

____ Begin writing early.

____ Let readers "see" for themselves.

____ Report fully.

____ Be candid.

____ Seek feedback.

____ Write accurately.

Source: Adapted from Wolcott, H. F. (1994). *Transforming Qualitative Data*, pp. 348–370.

causes. High reliability indicates minimum error variance; if a test has high reliability, then the effect of errors of measurement has been reduced. Errors of measurement affect scores in a random fashion; some scores may be increased while others are decreased. Errors of measurement can be caused by characteristics of the test itself (ambiguous test items, for example, that some students just happen to interpret correctly), by conditions of administration (directions not properly followed, for example), by the current status of the persons taking the test (some may be tired, others unmotivated), or by a combination of any of the above. High reliability indicates that these sources of error have been eliminated as much as possible.

Errors of measurement that affect reliability are random errors; systematic or constant errors affect validity. If an achievement test was too difficult for a given group of students, all scores would be systematically lowered; the test would have low validity for that group (remember "valid for whom"). The test might, however, yield consistent scores (i.e., might be reliable): in other words, the scores might be systematically lowered in the same way every time. A given student whose "true" achievement score was 80 and who scored 60 on the test (invalidity) might score 60 every time he took the test (reliability). This illustrates an interesting relationship between validity and reliability; a valid test is always reliable but a reliable test is not necessarily valid. In other words, if a test is measuring what it is supposed to be measuring, it will be reliable and do so every time, but a reliable test can consistently measure the wrong thing and be invalid!

For qualitatively oriented action researchers the message is simple: As you think about the results of your inquiry, consider whether you think that your data would be consistently collected if the same techniques were utilized over time. Or if you are working as a member of a team that is collecting data, work out how to resolve any differences among observers so you can agree on the descriptive accuracy of an account.

THE DIFFERENCE BETWEEN RELIABILITY AND VALIDITY

To review, reliability "is the degree to which a test consistently measures whatever it is measuring" (Gay et al., 2006, p. 139). And validity is "the degree to which a test measures what it is supposed to measure" (Gay et al., 2006, p. 134). Reliability, however, is not the same thing as validity. Remember, a valid test that measures what it purports to measure will do so consistently over time. A reliable test may consistently measure the wrong thing!

Generalizability

Historically, research in education concerned itself with **generalizability**, a term that refers to the applicability of findings to settings and contexts different from the one in which they were obtained, that is, based on the behavior of a small group of individuals, researchers try to explain the behavior of a wider group of people. This view of generalizability, however, is not directly applicable to teacher action research—even though there is still a mindset among some teachers, administrators, and policy makers that the findings of action research studies should be transferable. Many of these people believe that we should be able to generalize from the outcomes of a study in one classroom, one school, and one district to all similar classrooms in the state or country. This is not the nature of the research in which we are engaged.

The goal of action research is to understand what is happening in your school or classroom and to determine what might improve things in that context (Sagor, 1992). Therefore, action researchers don't need to worry about the generalizability of data because they are not seeking to define ultimate truths. However, one of the reviewers for this book had the following reaction to this dismissal of generalizability:

> I fear, however, that this approach lends credence to many of my colleagues' beliefs that action research is unscientific, biased, and not generalizable. Some go so far as to call it "garbage research." The question that they often pose is what good is research that is not generalizable? (Anonymous reviewer)

Indeed, action research has faced a self-esteem problem among many "academics" who question the worthiness of the activity as "scientific" inquiry. Confronted with a similar argument, Stringer (1996) offered the following response:

> Whether or not action research is accepted as "scientific" depends on the way in which science is defined. Certainly it is, in one sense, rigorously empirical, insofar as it requires people to define clearly and observe the phenomenon under investigation. What is also evident, however, is that action research does not follow the carefully prescribed procedures that have become inscribed as scientific method. (p. 145)

Stringer goes on to argue that in spite of the success of the scientific method in advancing our knowledge in the "hard sciences," the applicability of this method to inquiries of human behavior has met with little success in increasing the predictability of human behavior. Other textbooks on educational research agree that action research is a different type of inquiry entirely and as such should not be focused on generalizability. For example, Vockell and Asher (1996) state:

> Action research refers to the practical application of the scientific method or other forms of disciplined inquiry to the process of dealing with everyday problems. It is particularly focused on teachers and other educators doing action research in order to make their particular educational activities more productive. It is more

concerned with specific classes and programs and less concerned with generalized conclusions about other classes and programs. (p. 10)

Action research is not "garbage research" at the classroom/school level. As teacher researchers we are challenging the experimental researcher's view that the only credible research is that which can be generalized to a larger population. Many examples of teacher research are generalizable to other classroom settings, but the power of action research is not in its generalizability. It is in the relevance of the findings to the researcher or the audience of the research.

Personal Bias in the Conduct of Action Research

Related to the issue of generalizability of research is the issue of personal bias. If we conduct our research in a systematic, disciplined manner, we will go a long way toward minimizing personal bias in our findings. However, in an intimate activity such as action research, it is a challenge to remain "objective" and open, to look into the mirror of our findings and reflect on what we see. It is relatively easy in any research, should we so choose, to collect data that simply validates our existing practices, to maintain the status quo, to pat ourselves on our collective backs, and to ignore discrepant data or discredit research results. The same can be said for reviewing related literature—we may choose to review only the literature that supports a particular thesis that we wish to promote. None of these are acceptable approaches for reconciling the biased collection of data.

PROPOSITIONS

One way for teacher researchers to get in touch with their biases about the subject they are investigating is to develop a list of propositions about what they think they will find during the course of their investigations. These propositions provide a window into the belief system and personal biases that can, and often do, creep into the investigation. These statements also provide a good starting point for examining teacher researchers' theories about teaching and learning and where they came from. For example, a teacher who wishes to investigate the effects of manipulatives on student achievement in mathematics may generate propositions such as:

1. The use of manipulatives when teaching mathematics will increase students' conceptual knowledge of mathematics.
2. The use of manipulatives will help overcome math anxiety because the children will have more fun doing math.
3. The use of manipulatives will improve students' basic number facts skills.

A closer examination of these propositions is a useful activity for exploring what the teacher researchers believe they will find before they start their investigations and what they might do to ensure that they remain vigilant in the fidelity with which they collect their data (thus addressing the concerns of researcher bias). Similarly, this activity helps to clarify teacher researchers' conceptual frameworks for their investigations by making explicit the theories that affect what they do before, during, and after the research.

Summary

This chapter has examined validity, reliability, and generalizability and how they affect the conduct of action research. **Validity** is a test of whether the data we collect accurately gauge what we are trying to measure. Reviewing the criteria for validity proposed by Anderson et al. (1994), Guba (1981), Maxwell (1992), and Wolcott (1994) will help ensure that valid action research is the outcome of the data collection phase of the action research process.

      Reliability is a measure of the consistency with which our data measure what we are attempting to measure over time. **Generalizability** refers to the applicability of research findings to settings and contexts different from the one in which they were obtained. In its strictest sense, however, generalizability is not directly applicable to teacher action research because of its highly contextualized nature.

For Further Thought

1. How have you addressed the issues of validity, reliability, and generalizability in your action research inquiry?
2. Specifically, how will you know that your planned intervention actually solves your problem?
3. How will you communicate this information to your colleagues?

Ethics

This chapter describes the ethical issues that confront teacher researchers and suggests a series of ethical guidelines to help ensure that your research is conducted in an ethical manner.

After reading this chapter you should be able to:
1. Clarify ethical issues involved in conducting action research.

The Use of Technology to Enhance Mathematics Achievement

Clem Annice

Children learn at an early age the concept of light refraction. Peering into fishbowls, children see that the fish, rocks, plants, and toys appear larger than life, their movement, shape, and size distorted by the refraction of light. We have all been puzzled at some time in our lives by this illusion and the contradiction between what we see and what we get as we attempt to reach in and touch the inhabitants of the fishbowl. Can the same be said for the use of technology in mathematics reform? Is what we see in classrooms really what we get? Are students and teachers developing a functional and appropriate use of the technology, or are they just playing at the computer? Are teachers and students making connections between the use of technology for presenting models and the concepts that the models represent? How is the use of technology to enhance curriculum and instruction in mathematics affecting student outcomes in mathematics? It is this final question that drove the schoolwide action research project at Billabong Elementary School.

Billabong Elementary School is a large K–7 school that has embraced the use of technology as a key component of its mathematics curriculum reform efforts. Visitors to the school—and there are many—are given tours. The teachers at Billabong Elementary consider that they "teach in a fishbowl," constantly on display to the outside world. In many ways, the school looks different from traditional schools, and visitors to the school are invited to look into classrooms through the large windows that provide them with snapshots into the inner sanctum of our classrooms.

The principal of Billabong Elementary is described by his teachers as a "visionary leader," and the school has a large collection of computer hardware and software because of the principal's grantwriting efforts. One key component of the principal's vision has been the introduction of technology to the school. In large part, this technology has been made possible through school-business partnerships that he has forged. The principal is committed to the use of technology at Billabong because of what he sees as the gap between the "real world" and the "school world"; he thinks that one way to bridge this gap is to embrace technology in an effort to prepare children for the 21st century.

As a site council responsible for guiding staff development efforts in the school, we decided to focus on the impact of our extensive investment in technology on student achievement in mathematics. In particular, we wanted to know:

1. If our use of technology was successfully meeting the National Council of Teachers of Mathematics (NCTM) Standards; and
2. How those Standards were being interpreted into classroom practice and student outcomes.

Our action research team decided that we would collect data by observing in each other's classrooms, interviewing teachers and children, analyzing mathematics test data, and comparing the mathematics curriculum taught in the school with the NCTM Standards. When we presented our project to the faculty, all of the teachers and the principal appeared to want to cooperate with the research team's requests for access to classrooms, curriculum materials, and so on. Our hope was to learn more about our technology intervention and how we might continue to evolve as a faculty in this area.

As you move through the halls at Billabong, there is a great deal to be seen—classrooms are open for the inquiring eye. Kindergarten through third-grade classrooms characteristically have six computers, as well as scanners, color printers, and networking with the school's library (thus having access to the extensive CD-ROM collection). The fourth- through seventh-grade classrooms have all of these resources and another six computers per classroom. In one class, all of the children are given an individual laptop computer to use for the year. Children can be seen using computers as part of their class assignments, busying themselves with creating HyperCard stacks for creative writing, "playing" math games, and so on. Math learning centers are evident, and each child is given varied opportunities to interact with a number of different math manipulatives: base 10 blocks, place value charts, construction materials, colored chips, tangrams, and geo-boards, to name a few.

However, what we saw from the inside of each other's classrooms was distinctly different from what we had seen from the outside "looking in." For example, in many of the classrooms children could be seen busily engaged with the computers playing math mazes. For the most part, however, children were engaged in low-level activities, and the purpose of the tasks was lost. Many of the children were engaged in "drill-and-kill" activities that had little relevance to their math learning. The computers had taken on the role of an electronic work sheet to keep children busy once they had completed other assigned math tasks.

Interviews with children were revealing. When we interviewed the children, we did so with a guarantee that their responses would be confidential and asked that they be honest with us—after all, our goal was to provide the best possible mathematics learning environment for them that we possibly could. Some children were brutally honest, telling in great detail the kinds of math activities some teachers used on the computers. Some activities were singled out by children as being a "waste of time," and others described some teachers as "not having a clue" about how the computers were really being used. Indeed, some of this information was confirmed by our own observations of classrooms where children had become proficient at "scribbling"

on the computer screen using the mouse and a graphics program and quickly returning to the "drill-and-kill" screen when the teacher approached.

While the computers were being heavily used, the appropriateness of their use was questionable. This was no more evident than in classrooms where the calculator function had been removed from the computers. As one teacher explained, "The children are unable to mentally compute, and their basic skills have deteriorated . . . so we can't have them using calculators until they master the basic skills!" There appeared to be consensus among the teachers that there was a direct relationship between providing children with access to computers and children's lack of ability to recall basic math facts.

The interviews with teachers revealed other problems. Many of the teachers knew very little about the NCTM Standards and continued to use their old "tried and proven" curriculum, in spite of a new textbook adoption promoted by the principal. In fact, some teachers were very unhappy about the textbook adoption because no teachers had been consulted in the process—the textbook had been selected by the principal who was a good friend of the author. In return for piloting the curriculum materials in the school, the principal secured free copies of the textbook.

Compared to other schools in the district, our children appeared to be doing below average on statewide assessments. This came as quite a surprise to some teachers who felt that their children were doing well in most math strands with the exception of open-ended problem-solving and algebraic relationships. In these teachers' views the problem was with the appropriateness of the tests, not the use of technology to enhance teaching and learning.

The findings of our schoolwide action research effort raised some difficult ethical dilemmas for the action research team:

1. What do we do with the data that provided a negative picture of individual teachers in the school? Do we share data on an individual basis with teachers who were singled out by students? What risks do we run in sharing this information? How can we promote professional development without hurting anyone?
2. What do we do with the data that indicated a great deal of dissatisfaction with how the

principal had mandated the choice of curriculum? Do we risk alienating the teachers from the administration? Could some teachers be hurt professionally by action the principal might take?

3. How can we improve student achievement through the use of technology without hurting teachers (and the principal) in the process?

The action research team decided to adopt a "hold harmless" approach to dealing with the findings of the study. We shared the general findings of the study with teachers at a faculty meeting and invited teachers, on a voluntary basis, to meet with us to discuss the data for their classrooms. Similarly, we invited the principal to meet with us to discuss implications of the findings for future professional development opportunities.

THIS VIGNETTE PROVIDES an excellent illustration of the unpredictable events that can occur during the conduct of educational research. This vignette is not intended to frighten action researchers, but rather to provide an example of the kinds of challenges teacher researchers can face in conducting research in their own classroom and school. This chapter will help action researchers develop their own list of ethical guidelines so that they will act appropriately if and when confronted with a difficult ethical question.

The Ethics of Research

Ethical considerations are included in all research studies. Therefore, all researchers must be aware of and attend to the ethical considerations related to their studies. In research, the ends do not justify the means, and researchers must not put their need to carry out their study above their responsibility to maintain the well-being of the study participants. Research studies are built on trust between the researcher and the participants, and researchers have a responsibility to maintain that trust, just as they expect participants to maintain it in the data they provide.

Many professional organizations have developed codes of ethical conduct for their members. Figure 5–1 presents the general principles of the American Psychological Association for the ethical conduct of researchers. Note that additional and much more specific ethical standards are grouped into the following eight categories: (1) general standards; (2) evaluation, assessment, or intervention; (3) advertising and other public statements; (4) therapy; (5) privacy and confidentiality; (6) teaching, training, supervision, research, and publishing; (7) forensic activities; and (8) resolving ethical issues. You may read the full text online at the American Psychological Association's Web site (http://www.apa.org/ethics/code.html). Most other professional organizations, such as the American Educational Research Association and the American Sociological Society, have similar codes for ethical research.

In 1974, the U.S. Congress put the force of law behind codes of ethical research. The need for legal restrictions was graphically illustrated by a number of studies in which researchers lied to or put research participants in harm's way in order to carry out their studies. For example, in a study on the effects of group pressure (conducted some years ago) researchers lied to participants while they participated in and

PRINCIPLE A: BENEFICENCE AND NONMALEFICENCE

Psychologists strive to benefit those with whom they work and take care to do no harm. In their professional actions, psychologists seek to safeguard the welfare and rights of those with whom they interact professionally and other affected persons, and the welfare of animal subjects of research. When conflicts occur among psychologists' obligations or concerns, they attempt to resolve these conflicts in a responsible fashion that avoids or minimizes harm. Because psychologists' scientific and professional judgments and actions may affect the lives of others, they are alert to and guard against personal, financial, social, organizational, or political factors that might lead to misuse of their influence. Psychologists strive to be aware of the possible effect of their own physical and mental health on their ability to help those with whom they work.

PRINCIPLE B: FIDELITY AND RESPONSIBILITY

Psychologists establish relationships of trust with those with whom they work. They are aware of their professional and scientific responsibilities to society and to the specific communities in which they work. Psychologists uphold professional standards of conduct, clarify their professional roles and obligations, accept appropriate responsibility for their behavior, and seek to manage conflicts of interest that could lead to exploitation or harm. Psychologists consult with, refer to, or cooperate with other professionals and institutions to the extent needed to serve the best interests of those with whom they work. They are concerned about the ethical compliance of their colleagues' scientific and professional conduct. Psychologists strive to contribute a portion of their professional time for little or no compensation or personal advantage.

PRINCIPLE C: INTEGRITY

Psychologists seek to promote accuracy, honesty, and truthfulness in the science, teaching, and practice of psychology. In these activities psychologists do not steal, cheat, or engage in fraud, subterfuge, or intentional misrepresentation of fact. Psychologists strive to keep their promises and to avoid unwise or unclear commitments. In situations in which deception may be ethically justifiable to maximize benefits and minimize harm, psychologists have a serious obligation to consider the need for, the possible consequences of, and their responsibility to correct any resulting mistrust or other harmful effects that arise from the use of such techniques.

PRINCIPLE D: JUSTICE

Psychologists recognize that fairness and justice entitle all persons to access to and benefit from the contributions of psychology and to equal quality in the processes, procedures, and services being conducted by psychologists. Psychologists exercise reasonable judgment and take precautions to ensure that their potential biases, the boundaries of their competence, and the limitations of their expertise do not lead to or condone unjust practices.

PRINCIPLE E: RESPECT FOR PEOPLE'S RIGHTS AND DIGNITY

Psychologists respect the dignity and worth of all people, and the rights of individuals to privacy, confidentiality, and self-determination. Psychologists are aware that special safeguards may be necessary to protect the rights and welfare of persons or communities whose vulnerabilities impair autonomous decision making. Psychologists are aware of and respect cultural, individual, and role differences, including those based on age, gender, gender identity, race, ethnicity, culture, national origin, religion, sexual orientation, disability, language, and socioeconomic status and consider these factors when working with members of such groups. Psychologists try to eliminate the effect on their work of biases based on those factors, and they do not knowingly participate in or condone activities of others based upon such prejudices.

FIGURE 5–1   General Ethical Principles

Source: From "Ethical Principles of Psychologists and Code of Conduct," by American Psychological Association, 2002, *American Psychologist, 57*, pp. 1060–1073. Copyright © 2002 by the American Psychological Association. Reprinted with permission.

watched what they thought was actual electric shocking of other participants (Milgram, 1964). In another study, men known to be infected with syphilis were not treated for their illness because they were part of a control group in a comparative study (Jones, 1998). Studies such as these prompted governmental regulations regarding research studies.

INFORMED CONSENT AND PROTECTION FROM HARM

Perhaps the most basic and important ethical issues in research are concerned with participants' informed consent and freedom from harm. Informed consent ensures that research participants enter the research of their free will and with an understanding of the study and any possible dangers that may arise. It is intended to reduce the likelihood that participants will be exploited by a researcher persuading them to participate without fully knowing the study's requirements. Freedom from harm is focused on not exposing students to risks. It involves issues of confidentiality (to protect students from embarrassment or ridicule) and issues related to personal privacy. Collecting information on participants or observing them without their knowledge or without appropriate permission is not ethical. Furthermore, any information or data that are collected, either from or about a person, should be strictly confidential, especially if it is at all personal. Access to data should be limited to persons directly involved in conducting the research. An individual participant's performance should not be reported or made public using the participant's name, even for an innocuous measure such as an arithmetic test. For example, individuals identified as members of a group that performed poorly on a research instrument might be subjected to ridicule, censure by parents, or lowered teacher expectations.

The use of confidentiality or anonymity to avoid privacy invasion and potential harm is common. **Anonymity** means that the researcher does not know the identities of the participants in the study. It does not mean, as many think, that the researcher knows the identities of participants but promises not to release them to anyone else. This is **confidentiality**. If the researcher knows participants' identities, there can be confidentiality, but no anonymity. Removing names or coding records is one commonly used way to maintain anonymity. When planning your study you must indicate to participants whether you will provide confidentiality (you'll know but won't tell) or anonymity (you will not know the participants' names) and be sure they know the difference. Sometimes researchers seek access to data from a prior study to examine new questions based on the old data. In such cases, the original researcher has the responsibility to maintain the confidentiality or anonymity promised the participants of the original study.

Two major pieces of legislation affecting educational research are the National Research Act of 1974 and the Family Educational Rights and Privacy Act (FERPA) of 1974. The National Research Act requires that, to ensure protection of participants, proposed research activities involving human participants be reviewed and approved by an authorized group prior to the execution of the research. Protection of participants is broadly defined and requires that they not be harmed in any way (physically or mentally) and that they participate only if they freely agree to do so (informed consent). If participants are not of age, informed consent must be given by parents or legal guardian.

Most colleges and universities have a review group, usually called the Human Subjects Review Board or the IRB (Institutional Review Board). By law, this board must consist of at least five members, not all of one gender, include one nonscientist, and include one (or more) member who is mainly concerned with the welfare of the participants. Persons who might have a conflict of interest are excluded.

Typically, the researcher submits a proposal to the chair of the board, who distributes copies to all the members. They review the proposal in terms of proposed treatment of participants. If there is any question as to whether participants might be harmed in any way, the researcher is usually asked to meet with the review group to answer questions and clarify proposed procedures. When the review group is satisfied that the participants will not be placed at risk (or that potential risk is minimal compared to the potential benefits of the study), the committee members sign the approval forms. Members' signatures on the approval forms signify that the proposal is acceptable with respect to participant protection.

The Privacy Act of 1974, usually referred to as the Buckley Amendment, was designed to protect the privacy of students' educational records. Among its provisions is the specification that data that actually identify students may not be made available unless written permission is acquired from the students' (if of age), or a parent or legal guardian. The consent must indicate what data may be disclosed, for what purposes, and to whom. If part of your study required obtaining information from individual elementary students' record files, you would need to obtain written permission from each student's parent or guardian, not a blanket approval from the school principal or classroom teacher. Note that if you are interested in using only class averages (in which no individual student is identified), individual consent from the principal would likely suffice. However, if you calculate the class average from individual student records, individual permission would be necessary because you have access to individual records.

There are some exceptions that may not require written consent. For example, school personnel with a "legitimate educational interest" in a student would not need written consent to examine student records. In other cases, the researcher could request that a teacher or guidance counselor either remove names from students' records completely or replace them with a coded number or letter. The researcher can then use the records without knowing the names of the individual students.

DECEPTION

Another ethical dilemma occurs when a researcher poses a topic that, if given complete information to potential participants, would likely influence or change their responses. For example, studies concerned with participants' racial, gender, cultural, or medical orientation or attitudes are especially susceptible to such influences, so researchers often hide the true nature of the topic of study. Or a researcher might want to study how teachers interact with high- and low-achieving students. If the researcher tells the teachers what the aim of the study is, it is likely that they will change their normal behaviors more than if the researcher tells them that the study is about how high- and low-achieving students perform on oral questioning. Lying about the real focus is intended to deceive study participants. Research that plans to deceive participants must be seriously considered and should not be carried out. It is recommended that you not do your action research studies using a topic that requires deception. Your advisor and the Human Subjects Review or IRB Committee at your institution will provide suggestions about ethical ways to carry out your research plan. Note that as the teacher researcher in an action research study it is your responsibility to maintain ethical standards in the research.

The sources and advice noted in this chapter will help you conceive and conduct ethical studies. The suggestions provided do not cover all the ethical issues you are likely to encounter in your research. Perhaps the fundamental ethical rule is that participants should not be harmed in any way, real or possible, in the name of science. Respect and concern for your own integrity and for your participants' dignity and welfare are the bottom lines of ethical research.

Doing the Right Thing: The Role of Ethics in Action Research

Simply stated, the role of ethics in action research can be considered in terms of how each of us treats the individuals with whom we interact at our school setting: students, parents, volunteers, administrators, and teaching colleagues. As Smith (1990) stated, "At a commonsense level, caring, fairness, openness, and truth seem to be the important values undergirding the relationships and the activity of inquiring" (p. 260). However, values such as these invariably take on a different meaning for different people with whom we interact. Nevertheless, the success of your action research project depends on a clear understanding of the intimate nature of the research process and on not harming participants in the name of research.

The vignette of Billabong Elementary School that opened this chapter is a good reminder of why it is important to think about ethical dilemmas before they occur. And although I have seen few instances of where ethical dilemmas have threatened to stall a collaborative action research effort, the very nature of the enterprise provides the potential for conflict and harm. Considering the ethics of action research before commencing the work is one way to ensure that you are prepared to respond in an ethical, caring manner to difficult situations that may arise.

The issue of ethics in qualitative research and action-oriented research has received considerable attention in recent years (c.f., Christians, 2000; Creswell, 2002; Eisner, 1991; Flinders, 1992; Gay, Mills, & Airasian, 2006; Smith, 1990; Soltis, 1990; Wolcott, 1990). Most of this literature describes mistakes made in the research process and how the ethics of the situation were addressed. What makes the subject of ethics particularly challenging for teacher researchers is the intimate and open-ended nature of action research.

Action research is intimate because there is little distance between teacher researchers and their subjects, the students in their classrooms and schools. Qualitatively oriented action research is open ended because the direction of the research often unfolds during the course of the study. This significantly complicates the ability of teacher researchers to obtain participants' "fully informed consent" to participate in the research process. **Informed consent** is central to research ethics. It is the principle that seeks to ensure that all human subjects retain autonomy and the ability to judge for themselves what risks are worth taking for the purpose of furthering scientific knowledge.

In action research the key participants in a study are often the students in our classrooms. How does the concept of informed consent apply to them? Do we need to obtain written permission from parents/guardians before collecting naturally occurring data such as test scores, observations, work samples, and so on? Probably not. But as you will see in the following discussion, it is important that you develop your own criteria for what is considered to be ethical behavior.

ETHICAL GUIDELINES

The following commonsense ethical guidelines may help teacher researchers respond appropriately when faced with ethical decisions before, during, and after an action research inquiry (adapted from Christians, 2000; Smith, 1990).

Ethical Perspective

Researchers Should Have an Ethical Perspective That Is Very Close to Their Personal Ethical Position. This may seem like a statement of the obvious except for this caveat: As teacher researchers, we may find ourselves in situations that are foreign to us. For example, in a collaborative action research project focused on the effects of a new math problem-solving curriculum on student achievement and attitude, teachers are asked to administer a student attitude survey. The surveys are then analyzed by a team of teacher researchers representing different grades or benchmark levels in the school. During the analysis, it becomes clear that one group of students is very unhappy with their math instruction and have supported their assertions with negative comments about the teacher. What will you do with the data? Should they be shared in an unedited form with the teacher? Who might be hurt in the process? What potential good can come from sharing the data? Or, perhaps the principal hears that there is a problem with one teacher and asks for access to the data so that the teacher can be placed on a "plan of assistance." How should the research team respond? What assurances of confidentiality were given to the participants prior to collecting the data? How will you respond to the principal when you are stopped in the hallway and asked for your opinion?

This scenario is not meant to scare you away from doing action research. However, these are the unexpected outcomes that occasionally face teacher researchers who have been made privy to information about their own teaching and that of their colleagues. Smith's (1990) lesson is an important one: You will potentially avoid such awkward situations if you have clarified your own ethical perspectives at the outset. This might take the form of a values clarification activity that can be undertaken individually or collectively. The point is this—be prepared to respond in a manner that is comfortable and natural for you. When you are placed in the "hot seat," there may not be time to give a well-thought out, rational response. This situation will be easier if you can respond in a personal manner.

Informed Consent

Informed Consent Should Take the Form of a Dialogue That Mutually Shapes the Research and the Results. Be clear about whether you need to seek permission from participants in the study. This may be determined by discussing the action research project with an administrator or central office person who can describe instances that necessitate written permission. For example, if you are using photographs or videotapes as data collection techniques and intend to use these artifacts in a public forum, such as a presentation at a conference, make sure that you have checked whether written permission is necessary. The answer may vary from district to district depending on how the materials are to be used.

Similarly, consider how to inform students that they are subjects in a study. For example, you may decide to interview a small group to determine how a problem-solving curriculum is being implemented in different classrooms as a follow-up to a survey or an observation. How will you ensure the anonymity of the respondents to protect their privacy? How will you protect the confidentiality of participants? According to Flinders (1992), confidentiality is important for the following reasons:

- Confidentiality is intended to protect research informants from stress, embarrassment, or unwanted publicity.
- Confidentiality protects participants in situations where the information they reveal to a researcher can be used against them by others.

Confidentiality usually involves the use of pseudonyms to conceal identities. However, protecting confidentiality in a qualitatively oriented action research effort is sometimes more problematic than just assigning pseudonyms. For example, a team of teacher researchers who are responsible for driving a schoolwide action research effort will likely be made privy to the intimate details of their colleagues' classrooms. It will be their challenge to make sure that they protect their colleagues from stress, embarrassment, or unwanted publicity that may come from sharing the action research findings. And, of course, all of this must be balanced against their commitment to improve the learning experiences of the students in their school.

Figure 5–2 presents a cover letter written by a principal in support of a doctoral student's proposed study. Note that the student secured not only the principal's permission, but also his strong support and cooperation, by sharing the potential benefits of the study with the principal's students. Figure 5–3 presents the parental consent form that accompanied the cover letter. It addresses many of the ethical and legal concerns discussed in this chapter.

Clearly, human relations are an important factor in conducting research in applied settings. That you should be your usual charming self goes without saying. But you should keep in mind that you are dealing with sincere, concerned educators who may not have your level of research expertise. Therefore, you must make a special effort to discuss your study in plain English (it is possible!) and to never give the impression that you are talking down to them. Also, your task is not over once the study begins. The feelings of involved persons must be monitored and responded to throughout the duration of the study if the initial level of cooperation is to be maintained.

Social Principles

You Should be Able to Identify Broader Social Principles That Are an Integral Part of Who You Are as a Teacher and a Contributing Member of the Community in Which You Live. These broader social principles should dictate your ethical stance. For example, democratic processes, social justice, equality, and emancipation may be the principles that guide your ethical behavior in a given situation.

Deception

There Is No Room for Deception in Action Research (or any other research for that matter). For example, if during an interview a colleague, parent, or student confides in you "off the record," then the substance of the conversation should remain off the record. Regardless of how meaningful the comments, you have a responsibility to act with integrity and to honor your interviewees' requests for

SCHOOL OF EDUCATION

BOSTON COLLEGE

January 17, 2005

Mr. Dennis Yacubian
Vice-Principal
Westside High School
Westside, MA 00001

Dear Mr. Yacubian,

The Department of Measurement and Evaluation at Boston College is interested in determining the types of testing, evaluation, research, and statistical needs high school administrators in Massachusetts have. Our intent is to develop a master's level program that provides graduates who can meet the methodological needs of high school administrators. The enclosed questionnaire is designed to obtain information about your needs in the areas of testing, evaluation, research, and statistics. Your responses will be anonymous and seriously considered in developing the planned program. We will also provide you a summary of the results of the survey so that you can examine the responses of other high school administrators. This study has been approved by the university's Human Subjects Review Committee.

We would appreciate your completion of the questionnaire by January 31. We have provided a stamped, addressed envelope for you to use in returning the questionnaire. You do not need to put your name on the questionnaire, but we request that you sign your name on the enclosed postcard and mail it separately from the questionnaire. That way we will know you have replied and will not have to bother you with follow-up letters.

We realize that your schedule is busy and your time is valuable. However, we hope that the 15 minutes it will take you to complete the questionnaire will help lead to a program that will provide a useful service to school administrators.

Thank you in advance for your participation. If you have questions about the study, you can contact me at 555-555-4444.

Yours truly,

James Jones
Department Chair

FIGURE 5–2 Sample Cover Letter

confidentiality. Similarly, there is no place for hidden microphones in order to capture interviewees "on tape." If you wish to tape a conversation, seek verbal and/or written permission.

Accuracy

Ensuring the Accuracy of Your Data Is a Central Concern of Action Research. It is unethical and unscientific to fabricate data in order to substantiate a personal belief or value. For example, your study may have focused on the effectiveness

PARENTAL CONSENT FORM

The information provided on this form and the accompanying cover letter is presented to you in order to fulfill legal and ethical requirements for Northwest Eaton College (the institution sponsoring this doctoral dissertation study) and the Department of Health and Human Services (HHS) regulations for the Protection of Human Research Subjects as amended on March 26, 1989. The wording used in this form is utilized for all types of studies and should not be misinterpreted for this particular study.

The dissertation committee at Northern University and the Research Review Committee of Knox County Public Schools have both given approval to conduct this study, "The Relationships Between the Modality Preferences of Elementary Students and Selected Instructional Styles of CAI as They Affect Verbal Learning of Facts." The purpose of this study is to determine the effect on achievement scores when the identified learning styles (visual, audio, tactile/kinesthetic) of elementary students in grades 3 and 5 are matched or mismatched to the instructional methods of specifically selected computer assisted instruction (CAI).

Your child will be involved in this study by way of the following:

1. Pretest on animal facts.
2. Posttest on animal facts.
3. Test on learning styles.
4. Interaction with computer-assisted instruction (CAI-software on the computer)—visual, audio, tactile CAI matching the student's own learning style.

All of these activities should not take more than two hours per student. There are no foreseeable risks to the students involved. In addition, the parent or researcher may remove the student from the study at any time with just cause. Specific information about individual students will be kept *strictly confidential* and will be obtainable from the school principal if desired. The results that are published publicly will not reference any individual students since the study will only analyze relationships among groups of data.

The purpose of this form is to allow your child to participate in the study, and to allow the researcher to use the information already available at the school or information obtained from the actual study to analyze the outcomes of the study. Parental consent for this research study is strictly voluntary without undue influence or penalty. The parent signature below also assumes that the child understands and agrees to participate cooperatively.

If you have additional questions regarding the study, the rights of subjects, or potential problems, please call the principal, Ms. Gwen Gregory, or the researcher, Ms. Joleen Levine (Director of Computer Education, Northern University, 555-5554).

_____

Student's Name

_____

Signature of Parent/Guardian   Date

FIGURE 5–3 Parental Consent Form for a Proposed Research Study

of a newly adopted reading program. Although you personally like the program, the data suggest that it is not effective in improving test scores. You must be able to accept the findings of the study despite your bias toward the reading program. Any attempt to manipulate the data to support a personal position is unethical.

FLINDERS'S CONCEPTUAL FRAMEWORK FOR ETHICS IN QUALITATIVE RESEARCH

Flinders (1992) offers a useful conceptual framework for guiding ethical conduct in qualitative research, a framework that is worth consideration by teacher researchers. Flinders provides the following conceptual framework: *utilitarian, deontological, relational,* and *ecological ethics.* In your efforts to clarify values, consider the issues raised by these four perspectives and how resolving these issues can contribute to your personal/professional ethical stance.

Utilitarian Ethics

The central tenet of **utilitarian ethics** is the notion of the greatest good for the greatest number or whether more good than harm is likely to be produced by a given decision. This principle of utility can be applied by teacher researchers who must struggle with whether the findings of their study have the potential to significantly improve the experiences of children while at the same time conforming to the concepts of informed consent, confidentiality, and avoidance of harm. We have already discussed informed consent and confidentiality, but this last concept can be a challenge to rationalize.

Avoidance of harm morally binds teacher researchers to conduct their inquiries in a manner that minimizes potential harm to those involved in the study—students, teachers, parents, administrators, and volunteers. This concept is obvious in the medical profession wherein participants' physical well-being may be placed at risk by virtue of being a subject in an experimental study and receiving a radical treatment (for example, a new HIV/AIDS vaccine). This concept, however, is less obvious in an educational setting. A broader view of this concept suggests that teacher researchers need to convey with confidence to action research participants that they will not suffer harm as the result of their involvement in the research effort.

Teacher researchers must remain sensitive to their colleagues' fears of participating in an action research effort and remain vigilant in their efforts to protect participants from harm. Similarly, they must assure parents that their children are not being used as laboratory rats in some poorly conceived clinical experiment that could potentially harm them. As teachers, we typically do not administer "treatments" or "experimental interventions" to children. However, as a result of focusing on a particular problem and immersing ourselves in the relevant literature, we may design an instructional or curriculum intervention to address a perceived need.

Deontological Ethics

Simply stated, **deontological ethics** can be seen as the ethics of "duty and obligation." From this perspective, an action may bring about good results but it is not deontologically correct unless that action also conforms to ethical standards such as honesty and justice. Thus, acting ethically may be viewed in terms of "doing unto others as you would have them do unto you." For example, it would clearly be unethical to deceive participants in an action research study or to simply treat them as research pawns or a means to an end.

As you begin to clarify your personal, ethical perspective, you should reflect on how you would want to be treated as a participant in a research study. How would you feel if you were deceived by the researchers? What action would you take? How can you prevent research participants from feeling exploited? Again, there are no simple answers to these ethical questions.

Relational Ethics

Flinders (1992) writes that "a proponent of **relational ethics** would readily accept that moral behavior often upholds utilitarian standards by leading to good consequences for individuals, communities, or society at large" (p. 106). In this view, collaboration in an action research effort would necessitate that the team members work out mutually beneficial agreements for everyone who participates in the inquiry. This would include working, talking, and debating together to help each person achieve individual and collective goals. However, the members of an action research team do not have to unconditionally accept an individual participant's teaching performance as "best practice." From this perspective, you may be faced with making a nonjudgmental assessment of colleagues' teaching and the possibility that friends and colleagues do not agree with the portrayal and interpretation of test results, surveys, interviews, and observation data, for example.

Ecological Ethics

Proponents of **ecological ethics** are culturally sensitive to the taken-for-granted aspects of our social and professional lives. From this perspective, the teacher researcher must remain attentive to the relationships between the researcher and the participants, a relationship that is determined by "roles, status, language, and cultural norms" (Flinders, 1992, p. 108). The lesson for teacher researchers who are proponents of this perspective is to pay attention to the research processes of giving information, reciprocity, and collaboration and to be sensitive to how these processes are viewed by other participants in the action research cycle. Again, this perspective forces us to confront the socially responsive characteristics of our research efforts as being democratic, equitable, liberating, and life enhancing.

The purpose of this discussion on ethics in action research has been to prepare you to think about a whole range of issues that face any researcher. Carefully consider how you will respond when confronted with difficult questions from colleagues, parents, students, and administrators. Taking time to clarify your values and ethical perspectives will help you to respond in a professional, personal, and caring fashion.

As you embark on your action research journey and data collection efforts, remember that you are ultimately condemned to freedom in matters of ethics (Eisner, 1991). There are few absolutes. Working with colleagues through issues related to confidentiality, anonymity, informed consent, and rational judgment in matters of ethics will ensure that you avoid potentially difficult situations that may arise in implementing your action research effort. Gay, Mills, and Airasian (2006) summarize ethical issues as follows:

> Perhaps the fundamental rule of ethics is that participants should not be harmed in any way, real or possible, in the name of science. Respect and concern for your own integrity and for your participants' dignity and welfare are the bottom lines of ethical research. (pp. 100–101)

Ethical Guidelines for Teacher Researchers

____ Develop an ethical perspective that is close to your personal, ethical position.

____ Seek your action research participants' informed consent.

____ Determine the broader social principles that affect your ethical stance.

____ Consider the principles of utilitarian, deontological, relational, and ecological ethics in developing your ethical position.

____ Consider confidentiality and anonymity and avoid harm.

____ There is no room for deception!

____ Ensure that you accurately record data.

Remember, you will be undertaking your action research in your own classroom and school—this is the place where you will continue to conduct your professional and personal life long after you have changed your current area of focus. Attention to the fundamental ethical guidelines presented in this chapter will help ensure that, regardless of your area of focus, life in school will not be adversely affected by your quest for excellence. (See Research in Action Checklist 5–1 for ethical guidelines for teacher researchers.)

Summary

Teacher researchers should, to the best of their ability, recognize their own personal biases and develop an ethical perspective that ensures they will do the right thing when confronted with a difficult ethical dilemma.

For Further Thought

1. Revisit the Billabong Elementary School vignette at the beginning of this chapter. Consider the questions that faced the action research team including:
   a. What do we do with the data that provided a negative picture of individual teachers in the school? Do we share data on an individual basis with teachers who were singled out by students? What risks do we run in sharing this information? How can we promote professional development without hurting anyone?
   b. What do we do with the data that indicated a great deal of dissatisfaction with how the principal had mandated the choice of curriculum? Do we risk alienating the teachers from the administration? Could some teachers be hurt professionally by action the principal might take?
   c. How can we improve student achievement through the use of technology without hurting teachers (and the principal) in the process? Be prepared to justify and defend your ethical positions in light of the ethical guidelines (ethical perspective, informed consent, social principles) and conceptual frameworks (utilitarian, deontological, relational, and ecological) presented in this chapter.
2. How would you characterize your ethical stance? What is your ethical perspective, your approach to informed consent, and your sense of the broader social principles that dictate your actions?

6 Data Analysis and Interpretation

After collecting your data, the next steps in the action research process are to review what you have learned and to draw conclusions about what you think your data mean. This chapter provides guidelines and techniques for data analysis (the attempt to fully and accurately summarize and represent the data that has been collected) and data interpretation (the attempt to find meaning in that data, to answer the question "So what?").

After reading this chapter you should be able to:
1. Define data analysis and data interpretation.
2. Identify appropriate data analysis techniques for your action research project.
3. Identify appropriate data interpretation techniques for your action research project.

Emphasizing Learning by Deemphasizing Grades

Lauren Fagel, Paul Swanson, John Gorleski, and Joe Senese, Highland Park High School

Lauren Fagel, Paul Swanson, John Gorleski, and Joe Senese are all members of the Action Research Laboratory (ARL) at Highland Park High School (HPHS) near Chicago, Illinois. This project provides a good example of a team approach to collaborative action research and the kinds of analysis and interpretations that can flow from various data sources.

The scene is a common one for teachers: Papers are returned to students who immediately search for the grade, sigh, take out calculators, tabulate quarter grades, and then compare grades with their neighbors! The rich comments and constructive feedback on the papers usually go unheeded—the all-important grade is the prime focus of the students' gazes!

This study was conducted at Highland Park High School, one of two large public high schools in Township District 113. Our student population consists of 1509 students with an ethnic makeup of 3% Asian American, 2% African American, 13% Hispanic American, and 82% White. Ninety-two percent of the student body is college-bound, and the parent community strongly encourages high student achievement. Many students enroll in Advanced Placement (AP) classes, strive to become members of the Highland Park Honor Society, and compete to become senior class valedictorian or salutatorian. This ARL group, which included an English teacher, a health teacher, and a history teacher, was concerned about the immense amount of pressure placed on students to receive good grades. We questioned the number system teachers use to assign grades, and we wondered whether grades actually represent what students have learned. We discussed the role of the teacher as assessor, questioning whether we act as true evaluators of student work or simply as "sorters" of students. We lamented the all-encompassing role grades play in the HPHS academic environment. We decided to conduct research in this area, investigating how a deemphasis of grades could, in turn, emphasize learning in the classroom. The research questions were as follows:

1. How does an elimination of number and letter grades throughout the year (with the exception of quarter and semester grades) affect student attitudes toward learning?
2. How does an elimination of number and letter grades throughout the year (with the exception of quarter and semester grades) affect our teaching styles, use of assessments, and choice of curriculum materials?
3. How does an extensive use of student self-assessment affect student growth, improvement, and achievement over the course of a school year?
4. How does deemphasizing grades allow us to enrich our teaching?

We began the year by informing students of our involvement in the ARL and presenting a rationale for deemphasizing grades and emphasizing learning. Teachers were still required to assign a grade at the end of each quarter, and students were curious about how their final grade would be determined. We explained how the system would work and followed up by asking students to write down what they thought they would like about the system, what they thought they would not like, and what they did not understand. A letter was also sent home to parents explaining the system and encouraging them to contact us with any questions, concerns, or comments.

Approximately once a month, we met as a team for an entire day of reflection, discussion, brainstorming, and future planning. We quickly found out that certain aspects of our system were working, while others needed refining, and still others needed to be eliminated or replaced.

With the exception of one major project during third quarter, we returned all student work without a number or letter grade. Instead, we used several different types of markings to indicate to students how well they performed on a particular assessment. On homework assignments, including journal entries, we wrote comments and then assigned a u, u1, or u2. On long-term projects, we either assessed different aspects of the final product on a scale of 1 to 5 and wrote one or two sentences to the student, or we did not use any scale and instead wrote extensive comments. On tests and quizzes we marked objective items wrong when appropriate, assigned a u, u1, or u2 to short-answer and other types of subjective questions, and wrote general comments throughout the test or quiz. Most students were able to tell how well they performed on a particular assessment, and only a very few students persisted by asking us how our comments would translate into a letter grade. In these cases, we found that students were less argumentative than our students had been in the previous year (prior to deemphasizing grades). This year we found ourselves more open to criticism about the way test questions were written and exams were formatted because students seemed to be more genuine in their questioning. They were not arguing for points because there were no points! This created a more community-like setting in the classroom, with all of us aiming for the same goal—learning.

Self-Assessment Worksheet

After some modification during the first semester, we adopted a self-assessment worksheet that encouraged students to reflect on their progress periodically throughout the year. The worksheet included the following headings: Content Mastery, Skill Mastery, Completion of Work, and In-Class Activity. This worksheet evolved into an end of quarter self-evaluation that asked students to select a grade they felt they deserved and then to provide evidence by referring to specific assignments, tests, quizzes, and projects. Finally, by the end of the school year, we were using an end-of-quarter evaluation sheet that listed the student's mid-quarter grade range, the marks they received on specific homework assignments completed since the previous student-teacher-parent conference, and a general comment for each major test, quiz, and project they had completed since mid-quarter. Students' grades were then assigned without holding an end-of-quarter conference.

Another important part of this project was that students accepted responsibility for their grades and participated in developing criteria that would be used to assess the quality of work. The following criteria are an example of what evolved from involving students in the decision-making process:

"A" Criteria

> Participates actively in class
> Shows a great deal of effort
> Does all homework
> Does well on tests
> Is on time for class
> Shows respect and works well with others
> Is always prepared

"B" Criteria

> Shows good participation
> Misses no more than 1 to 2 assignments
> Has 1 to 2 tardies
> Shows good knowledge of material
> Has no unauthorized absences
> Shows some effort
> Demonstrates respect for others

"C" Criteria
   Demonstrates some knowledge of material and
      passes all tests
   Work is frequently late or not turned in
   Rarely participates in class
   Shows little effort
   Has several tardies
   Has unauthorized absences
   Is frequently not prepared

"D" Criteria
   Doesn't show knowledge of material and per-
      forms poorly on tests
   Has large number of assignments not turned in
   Shows no effort or participation
   Shows little respect for others
   Has several unauthorized absences
   Is disruptive in class
   Is often tardy

By using this rubric, students had guidelines they could use as a reference to accurately assess their performance. The onus on defending a grade now became the students' responsibility and not the teachers'. If students could justify their self-evaluation grade, based on the criteria we had agreed to, that was the grade they received. As a result of this ownership, students had few complaints regarding their grades.

Student-Teacher Conferences

Students appeared to have a difficult time assigning and defending their grades during student-teacher conferences. For many years, students had been conditioned to accept the grades given to them by a teacher without question. They had rarely been asked to participate actively in assigning their own grade. The most valuable part of these conferences was the opportunity to speak with all students and to get a sense of how they were feeling about the class in general. Often the discussion of grade came at the end of the conference and was the shortest part of the conversation. Students were asked to suggest a grade (before the teacher), but there was a sense that a guessing game was in progress as we tried to balance the teacher's expectations with those of individual students.

The data collected from surveys, observations, and interviews with children suggest that the majority of students were either happy with the grading system or neutral about it. A majority of students indicated that the alternative grading system did affect their academic preparation and performance in class (in a positive way), and that they had a more positive attitude toward the class.

Grades

As we reflected on grade distributions, comparing this year to the previous year, there appeared to be a significant increase in the number of students whose grades fell in the A/A minus range (55% this year compared with 27% last year). There is no way of knowing exactly what accounted for the increase of As and A minuses; however, we believe that students' involvement in deciding their own grade, as well as the less objective nature of the way grades were assigned (that is, not entirely based on the percentages scored on tests), had something to do with the outcomes. We believe that the increased focus on personal learning, growth, and improvement that evolved from deemphasizing grades made it less likely for students to fail and more likely for students to accept responsibility for their learning and to provide the evidence that they had learned.

The end-of-year survey revealed that 71% of students agreed with the following statement: "I feel that the grading practices used in this course helped me to focus more on my learning than on my grade." Seventy-four percent agreed that "they would recommend that this teacher continue using these grading practices because they help students learn better." We believe that these kinds of statements indicate student support for our deemphasized grading practices and that learning can occur in an environment where the pressure to earn grades is reduced. Students made supporting comments such as these:

   "I felt I could concentrate on education."
   "It helped me concentrate on improving myself."
   "It helps you focus more on information and less
      on what the teacher wants."
   "It relieved a lot of stress and I was able to work
      at my ability without the competition of grades."
   "In comparison to the traditional grading system,
      this system is the most effective way of
      assessing my level of performance."

"This method helps me perform best because it's personal to my needs."

It was very reassuring to us to see the pride that students showed and the importance they placed on giving accurate self-evaluation grades. The following two comments illustrate the integrity with which the majority of students approached this responsibility:

"I knew I had to be honest with myself."

"Integrity defines you, and if you die tomorrow, people won't remember your grades or your statistics; they remember how true and real you were with yourself."

We learned a tremendous amount through this research, but like any research we were left with more questions than we answered. For example:

- Is the total elimination of letter and number grades (with the exception of quarter and semester grades) the best way to deemphasize grades?
- Is there a way to deemphasize grades that requires less paperwork on the teacher's part? (After all, one of the things we learned through the implementation of this intervention is that grades are expedient and convenient for a harried teacher!)
- What is an appropriate role for students to play in determining their own grades?

- How can we deemphasize grades and still maintain very specific criteria/outcomes for students?

By far the most rewarding part of working on an action research team was the opportunity to learn and grow with a small group of teacher colleagues. This experience of mutual commitment provided a wonderful staff development experience; by working with these colleagues consistently throughout the year, we were able to explore new ideas and take risks in the classroom with a type of "safety net" in place. For that reason alone, as well as our desire to explore the new questions and challenges raised by our research, we will continue to conduct action research into the effectiveness of our teaching and grading practices.

Giving up grading practices and beliefs that we have held for years can be a very scary proposition. It is not always easy to turn over some of our control to others. Perhaps our first action research steps need to be "baby steps." This action research project freed us from the grading merry-go-round and provided a new way to address assessment issues. By taking these steps, we were able to devote less time to pencil pushing and calculator crunching and to spend more time with our most important job: helping our students reach their full potential as we strive to reach our full potential as teachers.

P ERHAPS THE MOST difficult part of action research is the process of trying to make sense of the mountains of data collected over the course of the study. This task is often daunting for action researchers who, while engaged in the regular, ongoing collection of data, must change their focus and adopt a more analytical and interpretive lens. They must move beyond the description of the phenomenon they have studied and make sense of what they have learned.

The Highland Park High School example richly illustrates how a team of teachers worked together to increase their understanding of how deemphasizing grades could help reemphasize student learning. In so doing, the teachers were able to encapsulate the "findings" of their research into "sound bites" that could be shared with other teachers and participants.

Considering how to best proceed with data analysis and data interpretation is critical before, during, and after the action research process. It is important to think about "How am I going to make sense of this data?" prior to conducting the study to avoid collecting data that is not important or data that comes in a form that cannot be understood. Similarly, during the study, teacher researchers should reflect on what they are finding and how it can inform their ongoing data collection efforts. Finally, as the systematic collection of data concludes, teacher researchers should determine what they want to "celebrate" and share in their findings.

Ongoing Analysis and Reflection

Action research studies provide teacher researchers with data that can be used formatively and summatively, that is, much of the qualitative data collected during the study can be used to positively affect teaching throughout the study. For example, teachers have always reflected on their teaching before, during, and after a particular teaching episode—it's part of our professional disposition. Action research is no different. We can and should take time to analyze our data during the study to decide if what we are learning is what we had hoped to learn. For example, the HPHS team discovered early in their research that some aspects of their deemphasized grading system were working, whereas others needed to be refined or eliminated. Pausing to analyze and reflect during the action research process is essential.

Anderson and colleagues (1994) maintained that "it is very important to recognize that at various intervals you must stop gathering data and reflect on what you have thus far" (p. 155). For example, these authors suggested that teacher researchers answer two questions to guide their work and reflections:

1. Is your research question still answerable and worth answering?
2. Are your data collection techniques catching the kind of data you wanted and filtering out the data that you don't? (p. 155)

Similarly, Hendricks (2006) discusses the importance of *interim analysis*, a step in the action research process that allows the researcher to make changes to data collection strategies during the research based on the kinds of questions and issues that arise during the ongoing data analysis process. Consciously "pausing" during the investigation will allow you to reflect on what you are attending to and what you are leaving out. Such a reflective stance will continue to guide your efforts (in process) as well as to allow for early "hunches" about what you are seeing so far. As Anderson and colleagues (1994) suggested:

> Stopping periodically in the data collection process also allows you to see if you have any gaps in the data, holes where you need data to answer the questions. Seeing this early on in the research allows you to develop the correct techniques for a complete study. (p. 156)

Another way to think of this is in terms of Lewin's original action research model and the attention given to rethinking, reflecting, discussing, replanning, understanding, and learning during the action research process.

AVOID PREMATURE ACTION

Although ongoing analysis and reflection is a natural part of the action research process, you should avoid premature actions based on early analysis and interpretation of data. Action researchers—especially those who are inexperienced—often make rash or impulsive decisions based on limited or no data. Neophyte teacher researchers engaged in the first systematic study of their own teaching tend to zealously collect, analyze, and interpret data in a rapid-fire fashion. Their efforts go awry as they become their own best informants and jump to hasty conclusions and impulsive actions.

The action research process takes time. Teacher researchers must be wary of the lure of quick-fix strategies and patient enough to avoid the pitfalls of basing actions on premature analysis. Rarely will a few days of observation provide enough insight to enact a quick-fix strategy! Although it is much easier to start a study with a preconceived notion about what you will find, it's a far greater test of patience, endurance, and integrity to let the action research inquiry slowly unfold over the course of a semester or two.

The Role of Analysis and Interpretation

You will reach a point in the research process where you will want to summarize what you have learned and what you think it means for your students. You will want to share your findings without having to share all of your data and use these findings to identify what will happen next in the action research process. This critical component of the action research process is called data analysis and interpretation, and it needs to be carefully thought out.

Data analysis is an attempt by the teacher researcher to summarize collected data in a dependable and accurate manner. The type of data you collect will determine the data analysis techniques you will use. For example, if you collect narrative, descriptive, and nonnumerical data, such as fieldnotes from observations or interviews, questionnaires, or pictures, qualitative data analysis will be best suited for your needs. It is not possible to "number crunch" and quickly reduce this type of data to a manageable form, as is the case in quantitative data analysis. However, at times quantitative data analysis will be the most appropriate way to summarize your findings, such as when you need to summarize test scores. In action research, most of the data you collect will be narrative and nonnumerical so we will focus on qualitative data analysis in this chapter. Quantitative data analysis and interpretation are discussed in more detail in Appendix B.

After analyzing your data, you will be faced with the task of trying to understand it. Data interpretation is an attempt by the researcher to find meaning in the data, to answer the "So what?" question in terms of the implications of the study's findings. Put simply, analysis involves summarizing what's in the data, whereas interpretation involves making sense of—finding meaning in—that data.

Data analysis and interpretation are critical stages in the action research process that require the teacher researcher to both know and understand the data. When analyzing and interpreting data, challenge yourself to explore every possible angle and try to find patterns and seek out new understandings among the data. Remember Deborah South from the Chapter 1 vignette on "How to motivate unmotivated students"? At first, she was convinced that the only feasible interpretation of her data was that her class and her teaching were the causes of the dramatic drop in students' scores. After all, it was the only experience these 18 students had in common during the term! However, as Deborah revisited her data and her fellow action researchers pushed her to examine other possibilities, it became clear that the homogeneous grouping of "low-achieving" and "unmotivated" students contributed to a "critical mass of negativity" in the classroom. As a result of her commitment to quality data analysis and interpretation, Deborah was able to use her action research findings to make a persuasive argument for the school principal to investigate other "interventions" that might more effectively address the problems of the "unmotivated" student.

Data Analysis Techniques

Picture this: After weeks (months, years) of data collection using a variety of qualitative data collection techniques (observations, interviews, surveys, audiotapes, and the like), you sit in your living room (classroom, faculty lounge) with colleagues (or by yourself perhaps being observed by a curious significant other!) surrounded by files (boxes) of stuff (data in all shapes and forms)! This less-than-romantic image of the teacher researcher is a common one. Having immersed themselves in the systematic study of a significant problem, teachers (individually and collectively) are confronted with the somewhat daunting task of data analysis, engaging in analysis that will represent the mountains of descriptive data in a "correct," "accurate," "reliable," and "right" way. There is no easy way to do this work: It is difficult, time consuming, and challenging. And yet, it is potentially the most important step in the action research process as we try to understand what we have learned through our investigations.

The techniques outlined in the following sections will serve as guideposts and prompts to move you through your analysis as efficiently as possible. There is no substitute for taking time to fully immerse yourself in your data. Literally bury yourself in what you have. Read and reread, listen and relisten, watch and rewatch. Get to know intimately what you have collected. Struggle with the nuances and caveats, the subtleties, the persuasive, the incomplete. Avoid premature judgment and action and try to remain aware of what will ultimately improve the lives of the children in your care. These are lofty goals, but they are at the heart of what we are trying to achieve.

IDENTIFYING THEMES

One place to start your analysis is to work inductively as you begin to analyze the data: Consider the big picture and start to list "themes" that you have seen emerge in your literature review and in the data collection. Are there patterns that emerge, such as events that keep repeating themselves, key phrases that participants use to describe their feelings, or survey responses that seem to "match" one another? Consider the Highland Park High School action research team in the opening vignette of this chapter. As they gathered their data, they realized that they were dealing with many recurrent themes in their efforts to deemphasize grades—the stress on students created by grades, the satisfaction gained from the renewed focus on learning, the amount of time it took for teachers to assess student work not using traditional grades, and the issues of honesty and integrity, for example.

CODING SURVEYS, INTERVIEWS, AND QUESTIONNAIRES

One of the most frequent data analysis activities undertaken by action researchers is **coding**, the process of trying to find patterns and meaning in data collected through the use of surveys, interviews, and questionnaires. Working with these types of data is common because surveys, interviews, and questionnaires are generally accepted as part of the school culture, and they provide a great deal of information in a relatively short amount of time.

As you analyze your data, you may need to reduce that data to a manageable form. One way to proceed when working with fieldnotes, transcripts of taped interviews, pictures, maps, charts, and so on is to try to record data on 3″ × 5″ index cards so your data will be manageable and allow for sorting. As you read and reread through your data (possibly now reduced to fit on your cards), compile your data in categories or themes. Although there is nothing magical about this process, it does take time and a willingness to check that the mountains of descriptive data have been analyzed in a "correct," "accurate," "reliable," and "right" way.

If you can imagine playing a game of cards and not knowing what the symbols on the cards mean, the following analogy might work: You have a deck of cards each of which contains data. The order of the cards is random. As you initially scan the cards, you have an intuitive sense that the data on some of the cards look similar to other cards. You finish carefully looking at all of the cards and reshuffle the deck. Again you look through the deck, but this time you group together the cards (data) that look alike. You end up with 13 collections of 4 cards that have some kind of trait in common (the number or face value of the card). Again, you reshuffle the cards. This time as you start to sort through the cards, you notice a different theme (the suit of the card) and end up with 4 piles of 13 cards. This is puzzling. Not to be thwarted in your efforts, you again reshuffle the deck and attempt to settle on an organizing theme. You group together cards (data) that have sufficient common characteristics that you feel confident that your analysis of the data is undeniably accurate. But there is just one problem: What do you do with the Joker that found its way into the pack?! And what about that wildcard?! Where did they come from and where do they fit?! Just when you thought you had it all worked out, in crept something that challenges the themes you have used to organize and represent the data you have collected. The shuffling and sorting continues.

A few commonsense guidelines may make this somewhat overwhelming activity of coding mountains of data more manageable:

1. Read through all the data and attach working labels to blocks of text. These labels ought to have meaning for you—a kind of shorthand that will serve as a reference point when you return to the text later in the process.
2. Literally cut and paste the blocks of text onto 3″ × 5″ cards (similar to the card-playing analogy earlier) so that your data are in a manageable form. Use some kind of numbering system so that you can track the block of text back to the original context in which it appeared. For example, noting date and time (1/26/02 10:15) will help you to locate the reference in your journal or fieldnotes. Remember: Context is important and you will want to check that you have correctly labeled the text you are trying to funnel into a category with similar text. Trying to shuffle reams of paper can be a difficult task, so cards are beneficial.

3. Start to group together cards that contain the same or similar labels.
4. Revisit each pile of cards and see if, in fact, the label still fits or whether similar labels actually warrant their own category. This process is not dissimilar to brainstorming and seeking categories that will encapsulate similar thoughts and ideas.

For example, in my study of school district change (Mills, 1988), I found myself with a large pile of 3″ × 5″ cards that included some of the following notations:

Card 1. Assistant superintendent urges principals not to reinvent the wheel but to share ideas with each other as they attempt to deal with an identified problem. (In this case the problem was low test scores on the California Achievement Test [CAT].) The assistant superintendent states to the principals, "I don't want any of you to think that you are alone out there."

Card 2. One of the principals at the meeting comments, "Clearly, the CAT does not test what we teach in our schools. The test was designed for California, not Oregon."

Card 3. The next meeting of principals following the release of the CAT scores and the directive from the superintendent that "all schools will develop action plans to address areas of weakness identified by the test scores" does not include any discussion of action plan development.

Card 4. A principal sums up his feelings about standardized testing as follows, "The district makes us go through a whole lot of garbage for little outcome or benefit to the teachers and the students."

Card 5. Principals' meeting 3 months following the release of test scores and action plan mandate. Action plans were due to the Curriculum Director 7 weeks ago. Principals are instructed that they can have another 2 weeks to complete the plans.

Card 6. The assistant superintendent announces that he will be meeting with principals on an individual basis to discuss how action plans for school improvement will be implemented. It is 4 weeks before the end of the school year, and 16 weeks since the initial directive to develop school improvement action plans.

Card 7. One principal commented on the development of the action plan/school improvement plan, "Do I write plans of improvement just to let the central office know that it has been done so that they are satisfied and can get on with doing whatever it is that they do with all the paper work? I admit that I have written plans and never followed up on them because I'm too busy getting on with the real business of school."

By following the four commonsense guidelines presented earlier, the first step of "attaching working labels" to blocks of text that are then "cut and pasted" onto cards resulted in the following grouping of cards: Cards 1, 3, and 5 were labeled "Statement of school district approach to school change." Cards 2 and 4 were labeled "Principals' challenges to school district approach." And cards 6 and 7 were labeled "Inaction of school district approach."

These cards are indicative of the comments that were captured during interviews with individual principals and observations of principals' meetings and which collectively provided the context and understanding for the analysis that resulted in a statement of a theme titled "inaction." In writing about school change as it related to the McKenzie School District, my data analysis included a "Taxonomy of Managing and Coping Strategies for Educational Change" with themes such as "inaction" that emerged to describe the change process; that is, one of the ways that the McKenzie School District personnel managed and coped with educational change was to do nothing! Although the story of the change process was fascinating, I have included this example to demonstrate how a theme emerges from the data you collect. I chose the term "inaction" as a theme because it was descriptive (to me) of what was occurring in the district. The same will be true for your own analysis—as you code your data and reduce them to a manageable form, a label will emerge that describes a pattern of behavior. You will be well on your way to making sense of your data!

ANALYZING AN INTERVIEW

Another common form of qualitative data analyzed by action researchers is interview data, most commonly in the form of a transcript from the audio tape of the interview. What follows is an annotated interview between a researcher and a bilingual education teacher as an example of the researcher's analysis of the themes that emerged from the interview.

As this example illustrates, the process of analyzing an interview transcript involves a careful reading of the transcript to identify broad themes that emerge from the data that will help answer your research questions. This in-depth, intimate knowledge and examination of the data allows teacher researchers to categorize themes and ideas that will contribute to their understanding of the phenomenon under investigation. In this bilingual education teacher example, fear of change is a pervasive, recurring theme that contributes to the researcher's understanding of the phenomenon and possibly provides an answer to a research question.

ASKING KEY QUESTIONS

Another approach to data analysis involves the use of key questions. According to Stringer (1996), working through a series of questions can enable action researchers to "extend their understanding of the problems and contexts" (p. 87) they have investigated. These key questions may be the very questions with which you began your action research inquiry, the questions mentioned in Chapter 2 that involve the who, what, where, when, why, and how of the educational process. For example: Who is centrally involved? Who has resources? Which ones? What major activities, events, or issues are relevant to the problem? How do acts, activities, and events happen? When does this problem occur? and so on. Although not all these questions will be applicable to any single situation, they may provide a starting point for teacher researchers who are engaged individually or collectively in analysis.

To illustrate, the Highland Park High School team raised questions such as: What is an appropriate role for students to play in determining their own grades?

Coding from a Sample Interview Transcript

Codes

Culture

Themes (and Other Ideas)

Fear
Fear of change
Job stability
Fear of new job

Q: Why do you think that English-only teachers fear bilingual education?

A: I think the [fear factor] is on a real gut-level and personal level. Teachers feel it's kind of a one-way system in that the teachers who are in the all-English program are [fearful] at a real basic visceral level that their jobs and their livelihood are at risk. Not to mention their culture, their society, and their known world is at risk by this other language coming into the schools and being acknowledged in the schools. And the teacher might say, "Oh well, because I don't have Spanish that means I am going to be out of a job. Am I going to be replaced by a bilingual teacher? If you have this program in my school that means you're going to need bilingual teachers. I am not bilingual so my job is at risk."

Q: Do you think that there is resistance towards expecting all children to learn English?

Nativistic movements
Patriotic

A: I think that's an interpretation that comes out of a model like a 90/10. When the child needs to come into the first year and has 90% in Spanish and 10% in English, it's easily perceived that we are [withholding English] from the child. That is a perception. A 50/50 model is a little more amenable to that because it's obvious that 50% of the time the child isn't getting English.

Q: There is the old adage that teachers who oppose bilingual education say "My ancestors never received bilingual education services in public schools and they did just fine." How do you respond to that kind of attitude toward bilingual education?

A: I say that's old thinking. I think that what your parents or your grandparents had to do when they came here from Italy or Norway, or wherever they came from, to learn another language, the language demand was less than it is today. Employment was easier to obtain, let's say a hundred years ago on a manual labor kind of thing. So a person could come here and speak 80% Scottish and 20% English and still be able to get a job because he could manage to do the labor that was required with that little bit of English. It wasn't an academic level of English that he needed, or that my grandfather needed, coming here speaking Norwegian.

Q: What about the attitude, "Well they are in the United States and we speak English here so they can learn English. That's all there is to it." How would you respond to this attitude?

A: That's a big one. That's huge. I think that's a whole cultural, you know, it's based again in fear. Based again in the fact that the United States is a very isolated island in that we are closed in by two oceans and we have never had the habit of stretching out beyond our borders much, or valuing much of what is beyond our borders. We are xenophobic in that sense. So we haven't traditionally learned other languages, or been interested in other languages. "Why bother, we're America, the biggest, the toughest, so why would we value anybody else's culture or language?" And I think that's an old thinking as well. It's an old habit.

Fear

Fear

Q: Do you think that this attitude is changing?

Nativistic movement Patriotic

A: Well, I'm not sure. With September 11th and Homeland Security and all that, I think we have had a big reversal. I think we were going to be able to look at a global perspective and we were on the track of maybe reaching out and saying, "Oh, yea, this is interesting. Wow, this is great. Look at what we are getting from South America. Look at what we are learning from the Greeks. Look at what we are learning from folks traveling in Africa or traveling in Asia. We are gaining so much. We are taking in so much, it's been great." And then September 11th kind of closed that down and kind of put us back in our cave again and made us a little more fearful. I think the other phenomenon is, and I can speak from the point of view of my father, a good old Idaho boy, you know. Like, "If those folks are coming into our culture and they don't learn English. And they don't learn about Thanksgiving and the 4th of July and how we celebrate Valentine's Day and do it the same way we do, then they are going to change our culture. My culture. And if they change my culture then I won't know how to act. And it's my culture in the first place so if they want to be here they need to accept that."

Fear

Fear

Q: I hear in my class all the time, "If I go to Mexico they aren't going to speak English. They are going to expect me to speak Spanish and adhere to their culture." Why are we different? Why should we be more open?
A: Why should we be? Well, there is a big difference between a tourist going to Mexico and somebody coming here for two weeks, or somebody coming here to spend a lifetime and raise their children. That's a really big different set of elements that we are dealing with. So, one of the things about the United States is that we have always said we are a pluralistic culture. You can come here, settle, raise your family, bring your poor, humble, weak, and we will be collectively a nation. So it starts with

the idea, the salad bowl idea, that we can all be individuals but we are going to make a collective nation. And the contradiction of that is that we want to all be on the same page because we need to be united. I think the fear that we are not united is seen in the commonly held belief that the word "multicultural" is a nasty word. It's an eight letter word or whatever it is, because it means that we are separating out into our little ghettos, into our little cultures, and we've got Latinos over here and Russians over here, and we've got the Afghani's over here and we've got the Vietnamese here in San Francisco, and they are going to be separated and not be pulling together in one United States. So that goes for elections and social security and achieving resources and services that are federally provided. Schools for example. The thinking would be "why would we want all those really diverse thinkers? Like maybe we've got a whole bunch of people who are adhering to Islam and they want to come into the public schools and we should educate them? But Islam is apparently against the Anglo-Protestant way of the United States? Why would we let them access our services?" So that is from my father's point of view. Not from mine. But that is from that conservative, older generation in this country.

Fear

How can grades be deemphasized while teachers maintain specific criteria/outcomes for students? Answers to these and other questions will help extend the team's understanding of the problems associated with deemphasizing grades while emphasizing the importance of learning.

DOING AN ORGANIZATIONAL REVIEW

Another approach Stringer (1996) suggested is undertaking an organizational review that focuses on the following features of the organization (in this case, a school): vision and mission, goals and objectives, structure of the organization, operation, and problems, issues, and concerns (p. 90). Stringer noted: "As participants work through these issues, they will extend their understanding of the organization and aspects of its operation that are relevant to their problems, issues, and concerns" (pp. 90–91). A review of the school, with these features in mind, may provide insight into the data you have collected.

For example, in the Highland Park High School example that opened this chapter, an organizational review of the school's grading policies and communication policies with students and parents would include seeking answers to questions such as:

What is the school's mission and vision?

What is the school's policy on grading?

How is the school organized to provide effective communication with students and parents?

What issues arise when a change in grading policy is put in to effect?

Answers to these questions would provide the teacher researchers at Highland Park High School with additional insights into the data they collected. However, the questions asked by teacher researchers as part of an organizational review will depend on the organization and the area of focus.

DEVELOPING A CONCEPT MAP

Stringer (1996) suggested that concept maps are another useful strategy that helps action research participants to visualize the major influences that have affected the study. For example, what were the perspectives of the students? Parents? Teachers? Administrators? A concept map gives participants an opportunity to display their analysis of the problem and to determine consistencies and inconsistencies that may exist between the disparate groups. The steps for developing a concept map include the following:

1. List the major influences that have affected the study of your area of focus.
2. Develop a visual representation of the major influences (factors) connecting the influences with relationships you know exist (using solid lines), and influences you have a "hunch" about (using dotted lines).
3. Review the concept map to determine any consistencies or inconsistencies that exist between the influences. This forces you back to your data to see "what's missing."

For example, Jack Reston at Eastview Elementary School (see Chapter 7) concluded that the following factors were major influences on the success of the school's absenteeism policy: respectfulness, safety, conflict management, discipline, school rules, behavior, getting along, self-esteem, and academics. Further, Jack believed that some relationships (real and perceived) existed between these factors (see Figure 6–1).

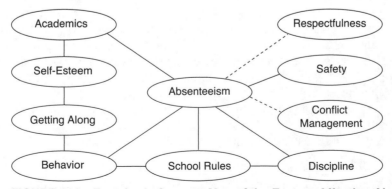

FIGURE 6–1 Eastview's Concept Map of the Factors Affecting Absenteeism

ANALYZING ANTECEDENTS AND CONSEQUENCES

Stringer (1996) also suggested a process of mapping antecedents (causes) and consequences (effects) to help action researchers identify the major elements of their analysis. Using this framework provides a visual representation of the causal relationships that you, the teacher researcher, now believe exist. It is also helpful to revisit the causal relationships uncovered in your review of the literature to determine challenges and support for your analysis and interpretations.

The steps for analyzing antecedents and consequences are:

1. List the influences that emerged from the analysis for which there appears to be a causal relationship.
2. Revisit the review of literature to determine whether the analysis of the study supports, or is challenged by, the findings of previous studies.
3. Revisit your data to determine if anything is missing and suggest how your findings may influence the next action research cycle.

As an example, in the Eastview Elementary School study, the concept map (see Figure 6–1) could be expanded to include a mapping of antecedents (causes) and consequences (effects) as an outcome of the analysis. In this example, Jack Reston clearly identified (based on his analysis) that a causal relationship existed between absenteeism and academics (student performance), and absenteeism and discipline (student behavior). Based on these relationships, Jack Reston revisited his review of literature to determine if his data analysis challenged or supported the findings of previous studies. Furthermore, Reston could use these reflections to help formulate the next action research cycle focused on another planned intervention that addresses absenteeism at Eastview Elementary school.

DISPLAYING FINDINGS

The information you have collected should be summarized in an appropriate and meaningful format that you can share with interested colleagues. To do this, teacher researchers should "think display" as they consider how to convey their findings to interested colleagues. You might use matrices, charts, concept maps, graphs, and figures—whatever works as a practical way to encapsulate the findings of your study. I have also witnessed teacher researchers who have made excellent use of other audiovisual media, such as videotape and computer multimedia presentations (incorporating text, charts, matrices, audio, and video), to represent their findings. These visual displays of data serve an important function for teachers who wish to share findings and celebrate their insights in a public forum (see Chapter 7 for further discussion). Putting your data into a visual format might also help you "see" new aspects of your data! (See Appendix C for examples of visual displays of data.)

STATING WHAT'S MISSING

Finally, as part of your full reporting, flag for the consumers of your research what pieces of the puzzle are still missing and identify what questions remain for which you have not been able to provide answers. Often we find ourselves wanting and needing to provide answers, to move beyond our data with unwarranted assertions that may, in some cases, ultimately lead to embarrassing questions about what we actually did! In keeping with the theme of avoiding premature judgment (arriving at answers to problems without systematic inquiry), the data analysis technique of stating what's missing allows you to hint at what might/should be done next in your quest to better understand the findings of your study. (See Research in Action Checklist 6–1 for a list of data analysis techniques.)

Using Computer Software to Assist with Data Analysis

Increasingly, computer software is being developed to assist with the analysis of qualitative, narrative data. The key word in this sentence is "assist." This software will not do the analysis for you! Novice researchers need to remember that computers alone do not analyze or even code data. They are designed only to help expedite these operations when researchers are working with large bodies of text and other kinds of data. The process of coding, retrieving, and subsequently mulling over and making sense of data remains a laborious process completely controlled by researchers. Even if a computer is used, researchers still must go through the process of punching each code into the data on the computer as they read through their interviews, fieldnotes, and audio- and videotapes. Computers are merely handy and extremely fast labeling and retrieval tools. Researchers also must remember that they alone can tell or program the computer to retrieve and count data in specific ways; the machines do not do these tasks automatically. Although computers can enhance and broaden qualitative research analysis, if you are not connected in some way with a research university it is unlikely that you will have access to the software and the expertise of someone to teach you how to use the software.

To help you with your decision about whether to proceed with locating and learning a qualitative data analysis software package, let's review some of the factors that might affect the decision:

- Are you analyzing large amounts (for example, more than 500 pages of field-notes and transcripts)?

RESEARCH IN ACTION CHECKLIST 6–1

Data Analysis Techniques

_____ Identify themes.
_____ Code surveys, interviews, and questionnaires.
_____ Analyze an interview.
_____ Ask key questions: who, what, where, when, why, and how?
_____ Do an organizational review of the school.
_____ Develop a concept map.
_____ Analyze antecedents and consequences.
_____ Display findings.
_____ State what is missing.

- Are you adequately trained in the use of the programs and in using computers in general?
- Do you have the resources to purchase a program or do you know someone who has the program?
- Do you need to be able to capture specific quotes from a large database? (Adapted from Creswell, 2005, p. 234.)

Four of the more common and popular qualitative analysis software packages are NVivo 2.0, The Ethnograph, HyperRESEARCH, and NUD*IST 6.

- NVivo is designed for qualitative researchers who need to work complex data (especially multimedia data). More information on NVivo can be found on the QSR International Web site at http://www.datasense.org.
- The Ethnograph is a program designed to help qualitative researchers work with text files (in any format) and search for, and code, segments of interest to the researcher. More information about The Ethnograph can be found on the Qualis Research Web site at http://www.qualisresearch.com.
- HyperRESEARCH is a more advanced software program that allows the qualitative researcher to work with text, graphics, audio, and video sources, and to code and retrieve data. More information about HyperRESEARCH can be found on the ResearchWare Web site at http://www.researchware.com.
- NUD*IST 6 (N6), the latest version of the original NUD*IST, is a powerful program for teams of qualitative researchers working with large amounts of data. More information about N6 can be found on the QSR International Web site at http://www.qsrecommerce.com/us/acatalog/ and the DataSense site at http://www.datasense.org.

Let's look more closely at one of these programs, N6, to see how it can help with your data analysis efforts. QSR NUD*IST (*n*onnumerical *u*nstructured *d*ata *i*ndex *s*earching and *t*heorizing) series, including N6, provides qualitative researchers with a system for storing, coding, and searching large amounts of word processed data, such as fieldnotes, interviews, and open-ended survey responses. Table 6–1 lists various data analysis elements, their manual tasks (writing objectives), and corresponding procedures that may be carried out or assisted by using NUD*IST.

Once the text is coded, N6 allows you to pose questions that involve the retrieval of one or more categories of responses. The computer program collates the coded "text units," but again it is the qualitative researcher who must construct meaning from the search results, to look for patterns and contradictions, and to decide how best to proceed with the analysis. It is at this point that qualitative researchers often rethink their initial preconceptions or research questions and may even decide to revise or recode their data. It is also at this point that you may be glad your massive amount of data is stored, manipulatable, and responsive to new lines of questioning.

As an illustration of a researcher's thought processes while coding and recoding data, let's consider a study by William Greene on the ethnic identity among adolescents in Hawaii (Greene, 2002). The study involved transcripts of 40 interviews and close to 400 pages of text. Each of the interview transcripts was initially coded by thematic categories. If a student's response related to more than one category, all related categories were coded with the corresponding portion of the response. For instance, this was common when the question asked for students' perceptions of ethnic relations

TABLE 6–1 Data Analysis Elements, Writing Objectives, and NUD*IST Procedures

Data Analysis Element	Writing Objective	NUD*IST Procedure
Create a template for analysis	Develop a visual of data analysis plan	Create a tree of steps in analysis into which data segments are placed
Create headings in the manuscript for major themes	Create four or five major themes in the study in words of participants	Create a node for each heading and put text that applies into the node
Title the manuscript	Create a title in words of the participants—to make report realistic, to catch attention of readers	Create a node based on short phrases found in the text; create alternative titles in this node as they appear in analyzing the texts
Include quotes in the manuscript	Identify good quotes that provide sound evidence for the themes, description, interpretation, and so forth	Create a general node and place all good quotes in that node; create a node for quotes under each theme or category of information
Phrase study in words of participants	Locate commonly used words or phrases and develop them into themes	Use word search procedure, string or pattern search, and place contents into a node; spread text around the word (or phrase) to capture the context of the word (or phrase)
Create a comparison table	Compare categories of information	Use matrix feature of program
Show levels of abstraction in the analysis	Present a visual of the categories in the analysis	Present the "tree" diagram
Discuss metaphors	Find text in which metaphors are presented and group into categories	Set up one node for metaphors with children of different types of metaphors; place text in nodes by types of metaphors

Source: From J. Creswell, *Qualitative Inquiry and Research Design: Choosing Among Five Traditions*, p. 162, copyright © 1998 by Sage Publications, Inc. Reprinted by permission of Sage Publications, Inc.

within their school; sometimes aspects of several categories would be evoked simultaneously. In such cases, relevant passages were coded for all categories referenced.

The initial categories of this study were family, peers, schoolwide/communitywide generalizations, ethnic self-identity, values, personal changes, intergroup relationships, ethnic group status, perceptions of ethnic groups, mixed ethnicities, differential treatment, and future plans. Initial categories evolved and new categories emerged as the transcripts were read and coded. In this process of changing and recoding data during analysis, the researcher continually built upon and extended theoretical notions about the findings. An example of this occurred in coding for references to personal values. It became evident that comments frequently clustered in various subcategories: education, family, religion, social, ethnic, and maxims. Two weeks after the initial reading and coding was completed, the researcher read each transcript a second time, verifying the consistency of the initial coding and updating codes to reflect expanded or consolidated categories. Coding in more specific subcategories permitted a finer degree of analysis within the database.

In addition to the categorical coding, demographic coding allowed for comparisons across various subgroups of students interviewed. Demographic variables included grade, gender, school, ethnic mix, birthplace, years of residence in urban or rural communities, and household (both parents, one parent, or other). For example, all of the coded statements about ethnic self-awareness were divided into subcategories by school, age, gender, ethnic mix, and years of Hawaii residence. Similarities and differences among subcategories were the basis for identifying patterns.

As this example illustrates, the use of computer software will not do the data analysis for you, but it will help retrieve categories from a large amount of narrative (text) data. You will still need to make many decisions about how to code your data. You will also want to revisit your data and verify that the computer "got it right"! (This is akin to estimating the outcome of a math problem for which a calculator has been used. Does the outcome make sense?)

Data Interpretation Techniques

You may wonder, why bother with interpretation, especially since interpretation involves taking risks and making educated guesses that might be off base? According to Wolcott (1994), qualitative (action) researchers must accept "the risks and challenges of the interpretive mode," because in doing so we can "demonstrate to others (and reassure ourselves) that, in spite of their undistinguished origins, our works and the implications to be drawn from them are socially significant" (p. 258). In other words, Wolcott argues for the importance of interpretation because as teacher researchers, our interpretations matter to the lives of our students. In addition, the process of interpretation is important because it can challenge teacher researchers' taken-for-granted assumptions and beliefs about the educational processes they have investigated.

The list of techniques for data interpretation that follow are adapted from Wolcott (1994, pp. 39–46) and Stringer (1996, pp. 87–96) but have been reframed to apply specifically to teacher researchers.

Extend the Analysis

One technique that is low on the data interpretation risk scale is to simply extend the analysis of your data by raising questions about the study, noting implications that might be drawn without actually drawing them. As Wolcott (1994) suggested, "This is a strategy for *pointing* the way rather than *leading* the way" (p. 40, italics added). For example, "While it appears as though the teen theater improvisation model positively impacts audience participation, a number of questions are raised by this strategy." In this example from Cathy Mitchell's Teen Theater group's use of improvisation (see Chapter 2), the analysis of data can be extended by raising questions about the intervention that were not asked as part of the original investigation but which may signal the beginning of the next action research cycle.

Similarly, in the Highland Park High School vignette, the research raised questions such as: Is the total elimination of letter and number grades the best way to deemphasize grades? Is there a way to deemphasize grades that requires less paperwork on the teacher's part? What is an appropriate role for students to play in determining their own grades? How can grades be deemphasized while teachers still maintain specific criteria/outcomes for students?

CONNECT FINDINGS WITH PERSONAL EXPERIENCE

Action research is personal business, so it makes sense to personalize our interpretations. For example, you may present your findings with the prelude: "Based on my experiences in conducting this study, this is what I make of it all." Remember, you know your study better than anyone else; after all, it's been conducted in your classroom or school and focused on your students. You have been there for every twist and turn along the way, trying to make sense of discrepant events just when you thought you "had it right." Share your interpretations based on your intimate knowledge and understanding of schools and classrooms and teaching and learning. For example, Deborah South (Chapter 1) had experienced the frustration of working with unmotivated children and the apparent futility of a study skills intervention. When faced with the "So what?" question, she based her interpretation not only on the analysis of data (test scores, surveys, interviews, and observations) but also on the memories and emotions of adolescent off-task behavior—a powerful interpretive lens.

SEEK THE ADVICE OF "CRITICAL" FRIENDS

If you have difficulty focusing an interpretive lens on your work, rely on your trusted colleagues to offer insights that you may have missed because of your closeness to the work. Offer your accounts to colleagues with the request that they share with you their possible interpretations. For example, the group of teachers at Highland Park High School found that their interpretations were enriched by the multiple viewpoints that came as a result of their collaboration. Remember, these colleagues may be people you have never met face-to-face but with whom you have talked in action research chat rooms on the Internet. Similarly, you may ask your informants (students, parents, teachers, and administrators) for their insights.

But beware! The more opinions you seek the more you will receive, and often these suggestions come with the expectation that you will accept the advice! Over time you will develop reciprocity with a cadre of trusted, like-minded colleagues who will selflessly fulfill the role of critical friends. Take the time to build these relationships and reap the rewards they offer. For example, when Deborah South concluded from her data analysis and interpretation that her study skills class was the "cause" of her students' lack of motivation, her critical friends in her action research class protested that interpretation and provided her with ideas for alternate explanations. What Deborah gained from the feedback of her critical friends was a commitment to change the "intervention" that was being touted as "the solution" to the "unmotivated students" problem in the school.

CONTEXTUALIZE FINDINGS IN THE LITERATURE

Uncovering external sources as part of the review of related literature is a powerful way for teacher researchers to provide support for the study's findings. Wolcott (1994) suggested that qualitative (action) researchers "draw connections with external authority. Most often this is accomplished through informed references to some recognized body of theory in one's special field, or to the recognized classics, in the tradition of the literature review" (p. 34). Making these connections also provides teacher researchers with a way to share with colleagues the existing knowledge base in a specific area of focus and to acknowledge the unique contribution the teacher researcher has made to our understanding of the topic studied.

TURN TO THEORY

Let me first offer a modest definition of theory as "an analytical and interpretive framework that helps the researcher make sense of 'what is going on' in the social setting being studied" (Mills, 1993, p. 103). Theory serves a number of important roles for action researchers. First, theory provides a way for teacher researchers to link their work to broader issues of the day. As Wolcott (1994) suggested, "One interpretive tack is to examine a case in terms of competing theories and then proclaim a winner or, more often, attempt some eclectic resolution" (p. 43). Second, "theory allows the researcher to search for increasing levels of abstraction, to move beyond a purely descriptive account" (Mills, 1993, p. 115). That level of abstraction "allow(s) us to communicate the essence of descriptive work to our colleagues at research meetings" (Mills, 1993, p. 115). Last, theory can provide a rationale or sense of meaning to the work we do. As educators we have all been influenced by learning theories that provide a safe haven for our own work. Share the theories that appear to help make sense of your data.

For example, Clem Annice's story of the use of technology to enhance mathematics learning for the students at Billabong Elementary School (Chapter 5) is influenced by theories about how students best learn math. Some of these theories are evident in the references to how students were using technology for "drill-and-kill" activities and how access to calculators was limited because calculator functions had been removed from the computers. The vignette suggests that other theories explain how students best learn math by challenging the "rote learning" theory that appeared well established at Billabong Elementary.

KNOW WHEN TO SAY "WHEN"!

Finally, if you don't feel comfortable with offering an interpretation, don't do it. Be satisfied with suggesting what needs to be done next and use that as a starting point for the next action research cycle. Restate the problem as you now see it and explain how you think you will fine-tune your efforts as you strive to increase your understanding of the phenomenon you have investigated. Wolcott (1994) cautioned, "Don't detract from what you have accomplished by tacking on a wimpy interpretation" (p. 41). (See Research in Action Checklist 6–2 for a list of data interpretation techniques.)

Sharing Your Interpretations Wisely

As educators we have all, at some time, been exposed to what are variously called "fads," "the pendulum swing," the "bandwagon," and so on. Thus, many of us may hesitate to embrace anything new or different that comes our way in schools, calming ourselves with the mantra "This, too, shall pass!" If we, as professional educators, attempt to use our action research findings only as a soapbox from which we

Data Interpretation Techniques

____ Extend the analysis by raising questions.
____ Connect the findings with personal experience.
____ Seek the advice of critical friends.
____ Contextualize findings in the literature.
____ Turn to theory.

simply have sought findings to confirm our beliefs and values, then we risk being alienated by our colleagues. Avoid being evangelical about your interpretations, connect them closely to your data and analysis, and share your newfound understandings with colleagues in an appropriate manner.

Summary

This chapter has explained the concepts of and provided techniques for data analysis and data interpretation. Data analysis is undertaken when researchers want to summarize and represent data that have been collected in a dependable, accurate, reliable, correct, and "right" manner. Researchers interpret data to make sense of the research findings, to answer the question "So what?"

Data analysis techniques included identifying themes; coding surveys, interviews, and questionnaires; asking key questions; doing an organizational review; developing a concept map; analyzing antecedents and consequences; and displaying findings.

Data interpretation techniques included extending the analysis by raising questions, connecting findings with personal experience, seeking the advice of critical friends, contextualizing findings in the literature, and turning to theory.

For Further Thought

1. How will you analyze each data source that you have indicated in your data collection plan? Remember: Don't collect data when you don't know what you are going to do with it.
2. How would you distinguish between data analysis and data interpretation?

7 Action Planning for Educational Change

This chapter discusses different steps in action planning that help ensure that teacher researchers are able to implement positive educational change based on the insights they gain through action research. **Action planning** basically attempts to answer the question, "Based on what I have learned from my research, what should I do now?"

A Steps to Action Chart is presented to guide teacher researchers through the action planning process. The chart identifies the findings of the study, the recommended action that targets a given finding, who is responsible for specific actions, who needs to be consulted or informed about the findings of the study and the concomitant actions, how to monitor the effects of your actions through the collection of data, a timeline for when the actions and monitoring will occur, and any resources that will be needed to carry out the action. A blank Steps to Action Chart is also included for your personal use.

Finally, this chapter will discuss action planning within the context of challenges that face the teacher researcher and the conditions under which action research and the educational change that follows it can occur.

After reading this chapter you should be able to:
1. Complete an action plan by working through a Steps to Action Chart.
2. Become aware of challenges that confront the action researcher in the action planning process.
3. Become aware of conditions that facilitate educational change in school environments.

Reflecting on Admission Criteria

Jack Reston

This vignette is the story of an elementary school principal who modeled the process of action research for his teachers, many of whom were involved in their own action research projects at the same time. Jack's story is particularly powerful because it illustrates the willingness of a school principal to investigate the effect of a policy he had developed. Further, Jack tackled difficult problems facing many teachers and principals: how to keep children in school and the importance of being in school. The result of the study was an action plan that required the change of a district-wide absenteeism policy.

I was selected to serve on a committee of administrators to review current policies concerning students' absenteeism. The task of the committee was to write a new student absenteeism policy, which led to the adoption of a new absenteeism policy and procedure. I recognized throughout this process a need to look into student absenteeism with more depth and understanding, and for this reason I selected the topic of student absenteeism for my action research project.

I initiated my research project with a review of our school's attendance rate profile for the last 5 years. The profile showed little or no change in the attendance rate. This was a concern because I cross-referenced the attendance rate with the funds allocated for various attendance incentives designed to motivate students and could easily see that the dollars spent on incentives were not affecting the attendance rate. I sat at my desk and thought about all my current and past efforts. It was clear that I was not truly passionate about student absenteeism. I had never taken time to clearly understand its causes or researched the best solutions to prevent it. I was passionate about my belief that a child's success in life depends on a solid educational foundation. I was passionate about my belief that students cannot afford to miss class at any time. I was passionate about my belief that absenteeism is a symptom or gauge of a student experiencing failure in school.

I began by asking three questions:

1. What student characteristics are associated with student absenteeism?
2. What are some longitudinal effects of student absenteeism?
3. What are some effective strategies to prevent student absenteeism?

I reviewed current studies, literature, local and national profiles, written surveys, and interviews. I found that absenteeism was highly associated with dropping out of school, academic failure, and delinquency. I learned what students and parents in our school believed about the relationship between school and absenteeism. I concluded that I really did not understand the belief systems of families at risk for poor attendance in school. I conducted a massive survey of students and parents within a four-day period of time. Surveys gathered data concerning such things as respectfulness of students, safety in school, conflict management, discipline, school rules, self-esteem, and academics. In addition, the survey gathered data on mobility rates, volunteerism, and levels of education in parents. The identity of the families surveyed was kept unknown. Instead, the surveys were coded as "at risk" or "not at risk" data.

I collected data from the surveys in three stages. First, each family in the school was mailed a survey. The surveys arrived at the homes of students on a Saturday. Completed surveys were returned to the school prior to 9:00 AM on the following Monday. Second, each student in the entire school was surveyed in their classroom at 9:00 AM on Monday. Third, selected students and parents were interviewed between Monday and Tuesday to collect data similarly gathered on the surveys.

Student teachers from a nearby university and local educators with experience in action research interviewed selected students and parents. The interviews were conducted over the telephone or face-to-face. I compiled all of the data and began searching for a better understanding of at-risk students and parents at my school. I found these people believed the following:

- Other students did not respect them.
- They did not use conflict management skills.
- Adults in the school did not handle discipline effectively.
- School rules are not fair.
- There are behavior problems associated with this group.
- At-risk students perform poorly in academic areas.
- At-risk students in this school are not motivated by rewards such as drawings for prizes and certificates.

This information led to major changes in our approach to improving attendance in school. First, we stopped spending large sums of money for rewards and drawings. Although these are nice things for students, they are ineffective in dealing with the problem of poor attendance. Second, we recognized punitive measures were having little effect on attendance. This led us to the belief that students succeeding in school were more likely to attend school regularly.

We began a concentrated effort to improve the success of students at school both academically and emotionally. This included the use of student/parent/teacher/principal contracts, daily planners for students, individual conferences between the student and the principal every 14 days to review grades and behaviors, better assessments to locate students having academic problems, improved instructional techniques and alignment of curriculum, and more concentrated efforts to improve the self-esteem of students.

In conclusion, I found the following to be true in our effort to improve student absenteeism:

1. Students need to be successful in school.
2. Students need to be connected to the school.
3. Students need friendships with students and adults at school.
4. Students need to develop the skills to deal with life's daily anxieties.
5. The school needs to develop meaningful relationships with the family.

Based on these findings, I worked with teachers and parents to develop quick responses that unite the student, parent, educator, and community in a preventive effort to minimize absenteeism.

To SUPPORT KURT LEWIN'S PROPHETIC STATEMENT, "No action without research; no research without action" (cited in Adelman, 1993, p. 8), this chapter discusses how teacher researchers can ensure that action is a natural outcome of their action research efforts. Without action, we have done nothing more than replicate what we set out to avoid—doing research on someone for our own benefit, whatever that may be. But the reward for us all in this process is taking action to improve the educational experiences of our children—action is at the very heart of the action research endeavor.

In Jack Reston's vignette we see a principal and members of the school community (children, parents, teachers, student teachers) who persevered in trying to solve an important problem that faces many schools—how to keep children in school. Reston's action plan identified a number of actions targeted to the findings of the study: developing students' skills to deal with the anxieties of life and school, developing strategies to ensure student success in school, developing meaningful relationships with families, improving instructional techniques and curriculum alignment, using strategies to develop meaningful relationships/partnerships with families, and so on. In the action planning process, Reston had reflected on the findings of the study and what he now understood about the problem of absenteeism. As a result of this reflection, he was better able to plan the next steps in the action research process.

Action planning is a natural next step in the action research process. Using the guidelines in this chapter, you will be able to ensure that the necessary steps are taken to bring your efforts to fruition.

Developing Action Plans

At this phase of the action research process, the teacher researcher is basically trying to answer the following question: "Based on what I have learned from this investigation, what should I do now?" At this point, teacher researchers should reflect on the taken-for-granted assumptions that guided them to the investigation in the first instance and determine what course of action to take next. This reflection allows time for both teachers and administrators to determine what they have learned from their investigations and the related professional literature and to decide on the necessary steps to action.

To facilitate this process, consider using a Steps to Action Chart similar to those shown in Tables 7–1 and 7–2. (Table 7–1 shows a generic Steps to Action Chart; Table 7–2 shows the Steps to Action Chart created by Jack Reston for his study of student absenteeism.) By working through the steps included on the chart, teacher researchers will have a list of:

- What they learned (findings).
- The recommended actions that target a given finding.
- Who is responsible for specific actions (responsibility).
- Who needs to be consulted or informed about the findings of the study and the associated actions.
- Who will monitor or collect the effects of actions.
- Dates when the actions and monitoring will occur.
- Any resources that will be needed to carry out the action.

Elements of this chart will look familiar to you. Monitoring and data collection efforts will once again involve you in the action research process. In each case, you will focus on a new problem, such as "What are the effects of this action on student performance?", and develop specific data collection/monitoring techniques to answer the question. Although not included on the chart, the monitoring/data collection techniques (see Chapter 3) would lead to data analysis and interpretation (see Chapter 6) with findings and further steps to action. Hence, the cycle repeats itself again and again. It may be that you are entirely satisfied with an intervention and that the proposed action is to continue with its implementation. This routinization of instruction still suggests that as a reflective teacher you will continue to collect data—to monitor the effects of your instruction on your students' performance and attitude. At that point, as a self-renewing school faculty or as an individual teacher with a reflective professional disposition, you will continue your systematic

TABLE 7–1 Steps to Action Chart

Summary of Findings Research Questions	Recommended Action Targeted to Findings	Who Is Responsible for the Action?	Who Needs to Be Consulted or Informed?	Who Will Monitor/ Collect Data?	Timeline	Resources
1.0 Research question #1					When will action/ monitoring occur?	What will you need in order to carry out your action?
1.1 Finding #1 1.2 Finding #2		• Teacher • Team	• Teacher • Team			
2.0 Research question #2		• Department head • Principal • Parents • Students	• Department head • Principal • Parents • Students			
2.1 Finding #1 2.2 Finding #2 2.3 etc.						

inquiry into some other aspect of your practice. (See Research in Action Checklist 7–1 for a list of steps to action.)

LEVELS OF ACTION PLANNING

Action planning can occur at a number of different levels within the school: *individual, team*, and *schoolwide*, depending on the scope of the action research effort. Action planning also may take place at a number of these different levels during a single investigation. For example, the problem under investigation may have had a schoolwide focus, such as to determine the effects of an innovative reading curriculum (with an emphasis on constructing meaning) on student performance (as measured by statewide assessment scores and monthly criterion-referenced tests). Participation in the schoolwide effort also necessitated that teachers meet in grade-level teams to plan appropriate reading interventions and to analyze regularly collected data. Finally, individual teachers had to adapt the intervention as appropriate for their own students' needs. In this case, action planning was undertaken at all levels within the school.

Individual

Typically, **individual action planning** will be characterized by teacher researchers who have worked through an action research cycle, either as part of a course, licensure, or grant requirement or by teacher researchers who are undertaking action research as a regular component of their practice. Individual teachers can still work through the Steps to Action Chart (see Table 7–1) and in so doing remind themselves of the steps that need to be taken to implement action and monitor the effects of the action.

In all likelihood, individual teacher researchers will have focused their action research projects and interventions on an issue related to curriculum, instruction, assessment, classroom management, or community involvement. In these areas, the resulting action plan will focus on activities such as:

- Curriculum development. Findings of a study related to curriculum development (and implementation) would provide the teacher researcher with specific actions for the next cycle of curriculum development (for example, the inclusion of new and/or revised lessons), additional learning artifacts (resources and materials), and so on. Following the Steps to Action Chart, the individual teacher researcher would be responsible not only for all actions but also for consulting with grade-level colleagues, department heads, district-level curriculum specialists, parents, and the school principal.
- Instructional strategies. Findings of a study related to the implementation of new instructional strategies (e.g., cooperative learning, high-level questioning strategies, increase in "wait time," teaching reading across the curriculum, and so on) would provide the teacher researcher with specific actions for the next cycle of developing and implementing any new instructional strategies. Following the Steps to Action Chart, the individual teacher researcher would be responsible for all actions, including consulting with grade-level colleagues, department heads, district-level teaching specialists (for example, a Teacher

TABLE 7–2 Jack Reston's Steps to Action Chart

Summary of Findings Research Questions	Recommended Action Targeted to Findings	Who Is Responsible for the Action? T – Teacher S – Student P – Principal PA – Parent/s	Who Needs to Be Consulted or Informed?	Who Will Monitor/ Collect Data?	Timeline	Resources
1.0 What student characteristics are attributed to student absenteeism? 1.1 Lack of respect 1.2 Poor conflict management skills 1.3 Lack of self-discipline 1.4 Behavior problems 1.5 Poor academic performance	1.1 Model respect for others. 1.2–1.4 Develop skills to deal with life's daily anxieties. 1.5 Improve strategies to develop success in school.	1.1 T, S, P 1.2–1.4 T, S, P, PA 1.5 T, P	1.2–1.4 PA	T, P: 1. Observations 2. Intentions 3. Surveys 4. Test data	Ongoing throughout school year.	None
2.0 What are some longitudinal effects of student absenteeism? 2.1 Dropouts 2.2 Academic failure 2.3 Delinquency	2.1–2.3 Students need to be connected to school. Develop strategies to build a sense of "belonging" at school.	2.1–2.3 T, P, S		T, P: 1. Observations 2. Intentions 3. Surveys 4. Test data	Ongoing throughout school year.	None

3.0 What are some effective strategies to prevent student absenteeism?						
3.1 Student/Parent/Teacher/Principal contracts	3.1 Implement contracts.	3.1 S, PA, T, P	3.1 S, PA	T, P: 1. Observations 2. Intentions 3. Surveys 4. Test data	Ongoing throughout school year.	
3.2 Daily planners	3.2 Purchase & use planners.	3.2 P				3.2 $$ for planners
3.3 Diagnostic tools	3.3 Work with district office to administer diagnostic tests.	3.3 P	3.3 District office			
3.4 Self-esteem strategies	3.4 Implement self-esteem curriculum.	3.4 T				
3.5 Improved teaching & curriculum	3.5 Encourage ongoing professional development.	3.5 T, P				3.5 $$ for P.D.

Blank Steps to Action Chart

Summary of Findings Research Questions	Recommended Action Targeted to Findings	Who Is Responsible for the Action?	Who Needs to Be Consulted or Informed?	Who Will Monitor/ Collect Data?	Timeline	Resources

Steps to Action

_____ Findings of the research.
_____ Recommended action.
_____ Responsibilities.
_____ Sharing findings with colleagues.
_____ Ongoing monitoring (data collection).
_____ Timeline for action.
_____ Resources.

on Special Assignment [TOSA]), parents, and the school principal. The teacher may identify specific additional professional development activities that need to be undertaken (and budgeted for) prior to the next action research cycle.

- Assessment strategies. Findings of a study related to the use of innovative assessment strategies (for example, the Highland Park High School "Emphasizing Learning by Deemphasizing Grades" example in Chapter 6) would provide the teacher researcher with specific actions for the next cycle of implementing an innovative assessment strategy. Following the Steps to Action Chart, the individual teacher researcher would be responsible for all actions, including consulting with grade-level colleagues, department heads, district-level curriculum and instruction specialists, parents, and the school principal.

- Classroom management strategies/plans. A common area of focus for beginning teachers (preservice and inservice) is classroom management. Findings of a study related to implementation of a new classroom management plan would provide the teacher researcher with specific actions for the next cycle of teaching. Following the Steps to Action Chart, the individual teacher researcher would be responsible not only for all actions but also for consulting with grade-level colleagues, department heads, district-level curriculum and instruction specialists, parents, and the school principal.

- Community involvement. Findings of a study related to community involvement (for example, Jack Reston's vignette at the start of this chapter) would provide the teacher researcher with specific actions for the next cycle of how to improve community involvement in solving local school problems. Following the Steps to Action Chart, the individual teacher researcher would be responsible for all actions, including consulting with grade-level colleagues, department heads, district-level curriculum specialists, parents, the school principal, and probably the district superintendent.

Although the primary audience for the findings from any of these studies is the individual teacher, it is important for teacher researchers to tap into the kind of support networks one will find at universities. As Elliott (1991) suggested:

A small band of isolated teacher researchers can tap into a reflective counter culture in the form of an action-research network which transcends school boundaries and is linked to a teacher education institution. Membership of such a network can provide the kind of cultural resources which strengthen the capacity of aspiring teacher researchers to resist the time pressures operating on them from inside schools. (pp. 66–67)

As discussed later, in Chapter 8, this networking transcends not only school boundaries, but also global boundaries via participation in online action research listservs and chat rooms. This kind of cyberspace network can strengthen the resolve of teachers who must work in isolation to continue with the process through the action planning stage and into the next revolution of the cycle.

Team

In an era of devolution of authority to schools to make decisions about appropriate curriculum and instruction and school-based decision making through "site councils," it is common to see teams of teachers, administrators, and sometimes parents working collaboratively on action research projects. Often these groups grow out of networks developed in an action research course among teachers with similar areas of interest and expertise. At other times they grow out of grant requirements for grade-level or discipline-based teams to work collaboratively on a school improvement focus. Regardless of the catalyst for the network, these **teams** all share a common focus at this stage in the action research process—to mobilize their collective energies to move forward with action. This process can be facilitated by working through the Steps to Action Chart and collaboratively determining who has responsibility for what, when, and where. Resolution of any issues that emerge at this stage is critical to the continued success and longevity of the action research team. At this stage the primary audience for the action plan is the team members. However, action research teams must seek appropriate ways to transcend the traditional boundaries that have historically seen small teams of teachers burn out without feedback and support from the environments in which they work.

Schoolwide

Schoolwide action research, as the name implies, is about all of the members of the school community working together with a single goal in mind. For example, a schoolwide emphasis on improving reading, writing, or math is a common area of focus in elementary schools. Similarly, and sadly, it is not uncommon to see a high school focus on the effects of a drug and alcohol curriculum on student attitude, understanding, and levels of use. However, the distinguishing feature in these examples is that they have been agreed on by the whole school faculty as the focus for a schoolwide improvement effort that will be driven by the findings of an action research effort. Cooperation, collaboration, and communication are no less important in the action planning phase than they were during the other steps of the process.

The challenge at the schoolwide level is how to actively engage all the participants in goal setting that is integral to the action planning process. There will always be finger pointing and denial, and it will take a skilled facilitator to move a faculty through the Steps to Action Chart if progress is to be made. Do not underestimate the necessity of meaningfully engaging all of the school community in this action planning process, or you will risk perpetual isolation in the world of playground supervision— been there, done that, bought the umbrella!

ACTION SHOULD BE ONGOING

This discussion about action planning is not meant to suggest that action occurs only at the end of the action research process. The very dynamic nature of teaching necessitates that teachers make many changes to instruction during the course of a day based on the formative feedback (data) collected as an integral part of the teaching process. For example, preservice teachers are often requested to include on lesson plans "Evaluation" statements to the effect of "How will you know if your students have achieved your instructional objectives?" In other words, what data will you collect that informs your post-planning at the end of the day? Often these data are collected intuitively and informally in noninvasive ways. It is such a normative aspect of teaching that we take it for granted. As teachers we have been programmed to collect, analyze, and interpret data quickly and efficiently so we can suggest "findings" and take necessary "actions" (remediation, reteaching, related material, extension activities) that enable learning to proceed in a connected fashion.

THE IMPORTANCE OF REFLECTION

Action planning is also a time for reflection—reflection on where you have been, what you have learned, and where you are going. Action planning and reflection give you an opportunity to identify your individual or collective continuing professional development needs. This reflection is facilitated by the review of the related literature you collected early in the action research process in concert with your own findings. The following questions may also be helpful prompts for reflection:

- What were the intended and unintended effects of your actions?
- What educational issues arise from what you've learned about your practice?

Clearly, these are not questions that elicit quick and easy responses. They urge you to look back at your practice from the enlightened viewpoint of someone who has systematically inquired into the effects of teaching on student outcomes. In undertaking such reflection, you will position yourself to act responsively to the findings of your study. The remaining sections of this chapter will help you to further identify challenges you may face when attempting to implement change and will guide you in meeting those challenges and effecting positive educational change in your school.

Some Challenges Facing Teacher Researchers

As you reflect on the critical steps to action, consider the challenges that all teacher researchers face both when doing action research and when attempting to effect educational change based on the results of their inquiry. If indeed we are going to avoid living out Sarason's (1990) prophecy of "the more things change, the more they will remain the same" (p. 5), then we must be prepared to address these obstacles. These hurdles include a lack of resources, resistance to change, reluctance to interfere with others' professional practices, reluctance to admit difficult truths, the challenge of finding a forum to share what you have learned, and the difficulty of making time for action research endeavors.

LACK OF RESOURCES

The scarcity of resources is perhaps the greatest obstacle to action planning you will face. Many excellent action research and change efforts have been blocked by the lack of resources and materials to use in the classroom. But by being innovative and remaining energized by what you have learned about your practice, you will find ways to make change happen. This may mean using creativity to solve materials management issues. Don't wait for an administrator, central office person, or philanthropist to offer what you need to be successful. Go after the grants, however small, to fund the resources you identify as critical to the success of your intervention. (See Chapter 8 for further discussion of grant sources available for teacher researchers.) Use the data you have collected, analyzed, and interpreted as a way to build a case for resources that may be presented to Parent-Teacher Associations, district-wide committees, school boards, granting agencies, and so on to make a case for what you need.

Action researchers also need professional as well as material resources. If action research is to become a part of your professional disposition and be continued over time, it must benefit both your own continued professional development and student outcomes. Identification of promising practices will suggest the kinds of professional development you need to seek, either individually or collectively. If your local university or school district can't provide the professional development you seek, use the Internet to find out who does. Again, use your findings to make a compelling, persuasive case for the kind of professional development you need—not what someone else thinks you need.

RESISTANCE TO CHANGE

Any type of change, however small, may be viewed as threatening by some. After all, the status quo is familiar and comfortable. But the era of schools that refuse to innovate is past. The ever-changing social and political environment in which we live necessitates that teachers become sophisticated instructional leaders and decision makers who have the skills to empower students and other individuals in their learning communities. Participation in and support of the action research process is critical if there is to be a shift in the culture of schools to the reflective practitioner culture of the self-renewing school. Living the commitment to a dynamic school culture as opposed to living the traditional "advocate of constraint" persona will go a long way toward revitalizing an individual school's culture and bringing about positive change.

For example, Jack Reston's investigation of the effect of the school/district policy on absenteeism showed that attendance rates had remained the same despite costly student incentives that were an integral part of the policy. Once he realized that the current intervention was having no impact, Jack knew he had to take responsibility for trying to change the system to make Eastview Elementary School an environment where all children (especially those at risk for absenteeism) would want to come to school. That meant changing even fundamental things, such as the way administrators interacted with students and the amount of time he spent with them individually. In doing so, he overcame several factors, including the institutional resistance to change.

RELUCTANCE TO INTERFERE WITH OTHERS' PROFESSIONAL PRACTICES

Unfortunately, there seems to be a prevailing cultural value in schools of "Don't mess around in someone else's professional practice"—especially if you are not invited. The dilemma here for the teacher researcher arises from a conflict between the desire to persuade colleagues to experiment with or embrace new practices that have been shown via action research to have positive effects and a "respect for the professional expertise of colleagues and their right to exercise authority within the confines of their own classroom" (Elliott, 1991, p. 59).

Often teacher researchers faced with this dilemma back away from their investigations and change efforts to "keep the peace" with colleagues. However, if we are to learn from our own and others' professional practice, we must be willing to set aside the traditional protection of each other's classrooms and to embrace as a community of learners the proposed action plan that emerges from our research.

How you approach this professional collaboration with other teachers in your school is as important as trying it at all. It is critical to the success of your action research and change efforts, particularly at the schoolwide level, not to have alienated yourself from others by appearing to be a member of some "enlightened elite" who now knows all of the answers to the problems that affect students' inability to do well on statewide assessments! You will have gone a long way to revitalizing the professional disposition of teaching if you have been able to nurture your own and your colleagues' understanding of the problems you have investigated and built a teamwide commitment to implementing action based on your findings. Collaboration can help break down these stubborn professional barriers.

RELUCTANCE TO ADMIT DIFFICULT TRUTHS

If we view action research and action planning as one way to empower teachers, we should also be aware of the increased accountability these efforts place on teacher researchers. We can't have it both ways: If we want the authority to make the changes we have recommended based on our action research findings, then we must be prepared to look into the mirror and face what we see. After all, if each of us has the power to make the most important decisions in our schools—that is, the ones that have the greatest impact on students—then we must also not abdicate responsibility when things don't go our way. If what we learn is that, despite our best efforts and intentions, our interventions have not succeeded, then we must be prepared to look objectively at the data and make new recommendations for change in our quest to provide the best education possible for our students.

For example, Deborah South (Chapter 1) had hoped to find in her action research project that the group of "unmotivated" students in her study skills class would respond positively to her instruction and guidance. Instead she noticed an alarming and demoralizing trend: Students' grades were dropping. Deborah had to wrestle with this "difficult truth" and carefully consider her own responsibility for the students' performance before coming to a conclusion about the best way to effect change to benefit these "unmotivated" students.

FINDING A FORUM TO SHARE WHAT YOU HAVE LEARNED

The potential for an action plan to serve as the catalyst for reflective conversation between professionals is limitless. Elliott (1991) argued that such data sharing "promotes a reflective conversation and is at the heart of any transformation of the professional culture" (p. 60). However, an open conversation about what the data from the study suggest (analysis and interpretation) and how these findings have been transformed into a proposed action plan will not always be an easy one.

What is needed is a forum (local, national, or global!) for teachers to share their accounts and a recognition by the profession that change-oriented action research is an important part of the professional competencies of being a teacher. For example, preservice teacher preparation programs are incorporating action research into the requirements of some preservice programs. Individual schools are providing teachers with opportunities to showcase their action research skills as part of an annual teacher evaluation cycle; state and federal grants incorporate action research as part of the instructional improvement cycle; school-based decision-making teams are embracing an action research model to guide their school improvement efforts; and state teacher-licensing agencies are incorporating action research into continuing license renewal requirements.

Although teacher researchers typically have not published their findings, the sharing of teacher researchers' stories has also been facilitated by Web-based action research sites. Teachers can now use a global forum to share their stories, the actions they have taken based on their research, and what they have learned in subsequent action research cycles. (These online journals include *Educational Action Research, Networks, Action Research International*, and *Action Research Electronic Reader*.) The sharing of action plans and what teacher researchers learn in the process is critical to the emerging teacher-as-researcher culture. (See Chapter 8 for practical guidelines for "getting the word out.")

MAKING TIME FOR ACTION RESEARCH ENDEAVORS

We have already discussed the challenge of making time for action research in your busy daily schedule. Just when you thought the action research cycle was over and you are ready to return to "just teaching," you are thrust back into the process with further reflection about the actions suggested by the findings of your study and the who, what, and when of the next cycle.

"You mean I need to take more action and monitor its effects? But I don't have the time to do one more thing!" This exasperated call for putting the brakes on the process is not uncommon or unreasonable. By the time you have arrived at action planning, you may be all but spent and happy to claim that the status quo is working just fine. If you fall into this category of teacher, I would suggest that you follow your instincts. Allow yourself time to reflect and plan at a bearable pace. You are no good to the students in your care if you are burned out. (As the parent of a child in eighth grade, the last thing I want is my child's teacher all worn out from a year of doing action research!) The goal is to evolve to the point where action and research become a part of your professional life, but not at the expense of the energy that you need to be vital, creative, and exciting in your daily teaching. After all, if the action research process cannot be normative and undertaken without adversely affecting your primary focus of teaching children, then it *should not be done*.

On the other hand, if you have arrived at the action planning phase with renewed energy and enthusiasm for your work, if you are committed to implementing a locally contextualized innovation that you believe will contribute to the well-being of the students in your care, and if you have maintained a clear sense of direction, mission, and purpose, then move forward in the process and share your stories by whatever medium you can! It will be your stories of success and being a lifelong learner that will change the culture of teaching. These are intimate changes that cannot be forced on any of us from outside—they must come from the passion within.

Regardless of international, national, state, and local trends and initiatives, the individual teacher researcher's ability to resolve the issue of time constraints will ultimately determine whether action research is routinized into the classroom. However, if we as professionals cannot find time to do the work associated with it, then action research will be discarded on the dust heap of other promising educational initiatives.

Facilitating Educational Change

The goal of action research is to enhance the lives of students and teachers through positive educational change. We have just discussed several common challenges that teachers face when attempting to effect educational change based on action research findings. In addition to being prepared to address those challenges, you can help create an environment that is conducive to change. The following are eight conditions that facilitate educational change (adapted from Fullan, 1993; Miller & Lieberman, 1988; Sarason, 1990).

Teachers and Administrators Need to Restructure Power and Authority Relationships

The first condition for fostering action research and encouraging educational change is that teachers and administrators need to restructure power and authority relationships. Power relationships in schools have the potential to empower or underpower action planning efforts. **Power** is not being used in a pejorative sense here—teacher researchers have the potential to harness the collective power of their colleagues, including administrators, to bring about meaningful change through a democratic, liberating, and life-enhancing process. For this to happen, participants in the action research process must be prepared to ask the hard questions related to implementing action based on the findings of the study: What is the recommended action? Who is responsible for doing what? Who needs to be consulted or informed? How will the effects of the implementation be monitored? When will tasks be completed? What resources are needed?

Asking these questions invariably leads to discussions about who has the final decision-making power in the school. In an era of school-based decision making, it is likely that a team of teachers, parents, students, and administrators will have the authority to answer action planning questions and to make decisions. However, whether your school has a professional or a bureaucratic model of school-based decision making in place will determine the amount of influence you will have individually or as a team. According to Conley (1991), the bureaucratic model emphasizes the formal authority of administrators to delegate responsibilities to subordinates, to formulate rules to govern subordinate behavior, and to implement centralized control, planning, and decision making. In contrast, the professional model emphasizes the professional discretion and expertise of teachers in diagnosing and addressing student needs, with an aim to provide teachers the rights they expect as professionals.

Power should be seen as an investment, not as a means of controlling people. According to Miller and Lieberman (1988), "If we look at power this way, teachers and principals can hold leadership roles, and, working together, they can help the schools build a professional culture" (p. 653). This view emphasizes a reflective practitioner culture that empowers rather than underpowers teachers.

Deborah South was empowered, for example, to make changes to the study skills program for unmotivated students based on what she learned from her action research study. Jack Reston was empowered to change the absenteeism policy for his school and to recommend changes to the district's absenteeism policy based on his new understandings of what worked and didn't work for keeping children in school. Viewed in this way, power was an investment in the quality of the educational experiences of many children.

BOTH TOP-DOWN AND BOTTOM-UP STRATEGIES OF CHANGE CAN WORK

In effecting educational change, both top-down and bottom-up strategies of change can work (Hord, Rutherford, Huling-Austin, & Hall, 1987). **Top-down strategies** can be thought of as changes that are mandated by school/district/state administrators without giving teachers an equal voice in the decision-making process (bureaucratic model). Alternatively, **bottom-up strategies** can be thought of as change that is driven by teachers when given the authority to make decisions (professional model). The debate over whether top-down or bottom-up efforts at change produce the greatest effects has flourished for many years. Fullan (1993) concluded, "What is required is a different two-way relationship of pressure, support and continuous negotiation" (p. 38), such as a continuous discourse between administrators and teachers involved in a collaborative action research project.

For example, the teachers at Highland Park High School worked collaboratively with the school's assistant principal and involved him in the team's action research activities. In this respect, there was obvious support from the school's administration for the action research effort. Alternatively, the teachers at Billabong Elementary School (Chapter 5) were quite resentful that the principal had mandated a math text for the school without consulting teachers in the process.

TEACHERS MUST BE PROVIDED WITH SUPPORT

Additionally, teachers involved in change efforts brought about by action research must be provided with support. Support for teachers in their endeavors ideally would come from all quarters: students, other teachers, the school administration, students' families, government officials, and so on. For example, Jack Reston's investigation into absenteeism could not have occurred had it not been for the support of the parents, teachers, and student teachers (who helped with interviews). Deborah South relied heavily on the emotional support of her critical friends in the action research class when she shared the analysis and interpretation of her study of unmotivated students.

EVERY PERSON IS A CHANGE AGENT

Both individual and collective efforts are critical to successful change, and every person has the potential to be a change agent. The action research vignettes in this book illustrate the potential for change to happen at the individual, team, and schoolwide levels. But perhaps the key point of all these examples is that it took the desire of an individual teacher or principal to initiate the action research process and to effect positive educational change based on the findings. As Fullan (1993) reminds us, "Each and every teacher has the responsibility to help create an organization capable of individual and collective inquiry and continuous renewal, or [change] will not happen" (p. 39).

CHANGE TENDS NOT TO BE NEAT, LINEAR, OR RATIONAL

Equally important, those involved in action research must recognize that change tends not to be neat, linear, or rational. Consider as an example the work of Cathy Mitchell and the Duct Tape Theater (Chapter 2). Although Cathy was able to confirm that her objective of making teen theater a more meaningful experience was sound, she also recognized that the approach of interactive improvisation did not have the desired effects. The audience did not respond to the "Violence Improv" scene as she expected and, as a result, her action research project did not provide her with the tidy solutions she hoped for. Although recommitted to her goal, Cathy is still faced with figuring out new ways to make teen theater a more meaningful experience. For Cathy, the processes of action research and change will be recursive and cyclical.

TEACHER RESEARCHERS MUST PAY ATTENTION TO THE CULTURE OF THE SCHOOL

A sixth condition is that teacher researchers must pay attention to the culture of the school. Change efforts should always be viewed in the context of the culture of the school and classroom in which the action research effort is being conducted. For example, until Jack Reston investigated the effectiveness of his school's absenteeism policies, it was assumed that the current reward system of drawings and certificates was effective. Instead, he found that the reward system made no difference for at-risk students. As a result, he tried to isolate what intervention would make a difference to these children. He used surveys and interviews to attempt to thoroughly understand the culture, values, and belief systems of the families of children at risk for absenteeism. Based on his findings, he was able to recommend meaningful changes to the school's policy on absenteeism that specifically responded to the needs of this group, especially their need to feel connected to the school.

The Outcome of Any Change Effort Must Benefit Students

A somewhat obvious condition for doing action research and effecting educational change is that the outcome of any change effort must benefit students if it is to be continued. Action research can provide a method for recording, measuring, and analyzing the results of an educational practice or intervention. For example, the data collected by James Rockford in his study of the effectiveness of keyboarding software on the class word processing rate provided conclusive evidence that the keyboarding software being tested was very effective and that time spent on computers at schools was critical. These persuasive data gave James confidence in the benefits of this educational intervention and supported his recommendation that teachers take students to the computer lab every day, monitor keyboarding habits, and see that each student received a minimum of 10 minutes of practice per day.

Being Hopeful Is a Critical Resource

Finally, being hopeful is a critical resource if teachers are to perform action research and stay the course of change. Recall the words of Cathy Mitchell, whose teen theater action research project was described in Chapter 2:

> The most important part of this project is that I felt renewed energy for my work. Last year at this time I was busily seeking a replacement for myself and announcing to everyone that I wasn't going to direct teens anymore. I didn't even consider that there was a problem that could be addressed and remedied. It feels really good to expect something to happen in my working life as a result of the research and reflection that I myself have done.

As a result of her action research inquiry, Cathy has created a powerful resource for herself—the hope that she will discover new ways to make her work meaningful for teens. Even though she once felt like quitting, she writes that this new hope is powerful enough to sustain her through future change efforts.

For educational change to be successful, all those involved must be optimistic about the results of the transformation. (Of course, they also need to be realistic: Being hopeful is not the same as being naïve.) Reform efforts can sometimes generate negative emotions and a sense of hopelessness because the individuals involved may be on the defensive from external attack or part of small groups of reformers suffering burnout (Fullan, 1997). But if we are going to make progress with reform efforts, we have to weather the negative emotions to succeed.

At the action planning stage of the action research process, you may again have to confront negative emotions from other stakeholders in the process. This is a critical turning point in the action research process: You can easily adopt the position that this is a lost cause, or you can rely on the most critical resource any of us have—*hope*. Individually, we all must take a stand on whether our investigations have yielded findings that warrant taking action. If we have done a good job, we should have collected findings that are trustworthy and true. Reflect on the hope you felt when you first began your project, then use that hope to sustain you through the action planning process. "Being hopeful and taking action in the face of important lost causes may be less emotionally draining than being in a permanent state of despair" (Fullan, 1997, pp. 231–32).

Recognize that we can do little to really change how a colleague thinks, acts, and feels—we must all answer to ourselves and the search for self-efficacy that comes with being a professional educator. If any of us reach a point in our professional lives when we feel that we can no longer make a difference or no longer struggle in the face of adversity (limited time or resources, for example), then it is probably time to try another professional calling. In education, whether it's a lack of chalk, paper, or RAM for the computer, none of us have ever had a blank check to finance the time and resources we think we need to be the best we can be. But what sets us apart from other professionals is the belief that we can make a difference in children's lives, with or without the resources.

Schools are complex social settings, and those of us who have taught at a number of different schools know how they can differ from community to community. You are in the best position to know what lessons you can apply from this broad discussion of educational change to your own situation. But we can all learn from each other's experience by sharing our stories. Whenever possible, share your action research stories with others. In doing so, you will help revitalize the professional disposition of teachers.

What Do Teachers Gain Through All of This Work?

If you are now living this process, perhaps in a quiet, unassuming way, what follows will validate your work as a professional—contribute to your sense of self-efficacy—for it is within that we all find the rewards that teaching has to offer. Returning to our earlier discussion about critical/postmodern perspectives of action research, you will recall an emphasis on what we believe as a professional community and what we as individual teacher researchers have gained through all of this work that has systematically guided us to action.

Having invested a great deal of time and energy into investigating the taken-for-granted relationships and practices in your professional life, you have now arrived at the point where the "rubber meets the road." Will you really initiate action and continue the process? If you answer in the affirmative, you have gone a long way toward embracing some of the tenets of a socially responsive approach to research: You have engaged in a democratic process that has encouraged the participation of your colleagues. The process has been equitable, with the participants all having one voice. The experience has been liberating and has freed you from accepting with blind faith something that may have been forced on you. Finally, the experience has been life enhancing for you as a professional and for the students who will benefit from your teaching.

For me, the ultimate payoff for teacher researchers who have stuck with the process, have learned and internalized the action research skills, and are now committed to action and self-renewal is the belief and knowledge that those who are the real beneficiaries of your work are the students in your care. There can be no argument against this powerful and altruistic goal.

Summary

Action planning is an effort to answer the question, "Based on what I have learned from my research, what should I do now?" This chapter has presented a Steps to Action Chart that addresses issues related to what you as a teacher researcher have learned (findings), what recommended action targets a given finding, who is responsible for specific actions (responsibility), who needs to be consulted or informed about the findings of the study and the concomitant actions, how you will monitor the effect of your actions by collecting data, on what dates the actions and monitoring will occur, and what resources will be needed to carry out the action.

This chapter also discussed how to overcome the challenges faced by action researchers who seek to implement positive educational change: lack of resources, resistance to change, reluctance to interfere with others' professional practices, reluctance to admit difficult truths, difficulty of finding a forum to share what you have learned, and lack of time for action research endeavors.

This chapter also noted eight factors for facilitating change in a school environment: (1) teachers and administrators need to restructure power relationships; (2) both top-down and bottom-up strategies for change can work; (3) teachers involved in change efforts brought about by action research must be provided with support; (4) every person is a change agent; (5) those involved must recognize that change tends not to be neat, linear, and rational; (6) teacher researchers must pay attention to the culture of the school; (7) the outcome of any change effort must be beneficial to be continued; and (8) being hopeful is a powerful resource.

For Further Thought

1. Develop an action plan based on your action research findings and present it using the Steps to Action Chart format.
2. How would you apply what you have learned about the challenges of implementing educational change to overcome potential obstacles that you may encounter in taking action?

CHAPTER

8 | Writing Up
Action Research

There is little point to writing up qualitative research if we cannot get anyone to read what we have to report, and no point to research without reporting. (Wolcott, 2001, p. 7)

Perhaps one of the most difficult tasks confronting teacher researchers is finding the time and inclination to commit to paper what they have learned about their area of focus. For university researchers who live in a "publish or perish" world, the motivation to write up and publish their research is far more extrinsic. However, teacher researchers are more concerned about the pressures and complexities of daily classroom life—after all, their number one priority is the planning, implementation, and evaluation of engaging learning experiences for the children in their classrooms.

Yet, teacher researchers can help fellow teachers as well as themselves by writing about action research in a prescribed way—in an organized report. Think of this last step as helping to close the gap that has historically existed between research and practice (something alluded to in Chapter 1 with the work of Mary Kennedy). It is important to be familiar with a form that is most commonly accepted for publication in journals and certainly for satisfying traditional university course requirements.

Two primary motivations for writing up your action research include the following:

1. The act of writing helps each of us better understand the story we are trying to tell.
2. A written record provides us with a permanent, accessible record for our professional and personal use.

Many of my students find themselves writing, not by choice but by mandate (you may well be in the same situation!). In fact, some of you may see the very act of writing up your studies as unpleasant . . . just one more term paper to complete, another hoop to jump through. On the other hand, you may not mind writing but still may be frustrated by some of the nuts and bolts issues associated with writing and finding an audience for your work. Read on! I can't guarantee that the outcome of your writing journey will be publication in a prestigious journal or book, but I can guarantee you that if you invest the time and energy into writing your research story, you will at least benefit your students as well as give yourself the opportunity to have it read by like-minded folks. And what could be more altruistic than helping other teachers help their students? What's that saying about if a tree falls in the forest and nobody hears it, did it make a sound? The same is true for writing up our research efforts. If you don't share your stories, how will anyone know you ever did anything that contributed to the teachers' body of knowledge?

After reading this chapter you should be able to:
1. Write about your action research.
2. Target a professional publication for your work.
3. Submit your work for publication.
4. Identify the keys to successful writing of action research.

Before our discussion about formally writing about your action research, we need to discuss the value of writing up your action research experience and findings.

Why Should I Formally Write About My Action Research?

Perhaps one of the most difficult concepts I have to "sell" to teacher researchers is the importance of "writing up" their research efforts; they struggle to see the value of it. These teachers are focused on understanding the impact of what they do in classrooms and on how and what their students learn. In short, these professional teachers are committed to improving their own practice but do not necessarily see the purpose of sharing what they have learned with a wider audience. Often teacher researchers have declared to me:

> I developed my action plan based on what I learned. . . . I am making a difference in my own classroom for my own kids. What does it matter if somebody else reads about what I did and learned?

> Writing up what I have done and trying to publish the story is not rewarded or recognized as important by my school and district. Why bother if nobody cares?

Again, this is a difficult argument to win when one argues on the basis of giving back to the profession and contributing to the knowledge base, and blah, blah, blah! Yet, as members of a profession, we have to get beyond the point that writing up research is something that is done by academics in ivory towers.

The value in writing up your research is that the process of writing requires the writer to clarify meaning—choose words carefully, thoughtfully describe that which is experienced or seen, reflect on experiences, and refine phrasing when putting words on a page. You may learn something important about your students and their learning—something you may have missed had you not considered your words on the page—as you formally write about your research. Furthermore, the act of putting information on paper for your peers necessitates honesty, accuracy, clarity, and thought, thereby encouraging you to create a better product than if you had simply made a mental note of your action research as you left school at the end of the day. So, keep this reason in mind as you engage in this writing phase of your research:

> *Clarification*—Writing your research requires clarity and accuracy of expression. Writing about your research activities encourages thought and reflection, and perhaps creates new questions that are resolved, which shape and complete your research.

Other reasons to write up your research include:

- *Validation*—Publishing your research and the feedback you will receive from your reviewers and readers will validate who you are as a professional educator and what you do.
- *Empowerment*—Reflecting on your practices through writing will empower you to continue to challenge the status quo and be an advocate for your children.
- *Generative*—Writing is a generative activity that culminates in a product, something tangible that you can share with colleagues, supervisors, and parents.
- *Accomplishment*—Writing up your research will provide you with a sense of accomplishment. It is both humbling and exciting when colleagues read your work and compliment you on your accomplishments!

Format and Style

Format refers to the general pattern of organization and arrangement of the research report. The number and types of headings and subheadings to be included in the report are determined by the format used. Style refers to the rules of grammar, spelling, capitalization, punctuation, and word processing followed in preparing the report. Formats may vary in terms of specific headings included, and research reports generally follow a format that parallels the steps involved in conducting a study. For example, although one format may call for a discussion section and another format may require a summary or conclusions and a recommendations section (or both), all formats require a section in which the results of the study are discussed and interpreted. All research reports also include a condensed description of the study, whether it be a summary of a dissertation or an abstract of a journal article.

Most colleges, universities, and professional journals either have developed their own, required style manual or have selected one that must be followed. Check with your instructor about the style used in your institution. Do this before beginning writing, because rearranging a format after the fact is tedious and time consuming.

Type of Reference	Reference Format
The following are examples of many of the types of references you may need to include in your research paper. These examples follow the APA style guidelines set forth in the fifth edition of the *Publication Manual of the American Psychological Association*.	
Book	Bandura, A. J. (1977). *Social learning theory.* Englewood Cliffs, NJ: Prentice Hall.
Book, Edited	Gibbs, J. T., & Huang, L. N. (Eds.). (1991). *Children of color: Psychological interventions with minority youth.* San Francisco: Jossey-Bass.
Book, Chapter	O'Neil, J. M., & Egan, J. (1992). Men's and women's gender role journeys: Metaphor for healing, transition, and transformation. In B. R. Wainrib (Ed.), *Gender issues across the life cycle* (pp. 107–123). New York: Springer.
Book Review	Schatz, B. R. (2000). Learning by text or context? [Review of the book *The social life of information*]. *Science, 290,* 1304.
Journal Article	Klimoski, R., & Palmer, S. (1993). The ADA and the hiring process in organizations. *Consulting Psychology Journal: Practice and Research, 45*(2), 10–36.
Electronic Sources, Retrieval Information	Eid, M., & Langeheine, R. (1999). The measurement of consistency and occasion specificity with latent class models: A new model and its application to the measurement of affect. *Psychological Methods, 4,* 100–116. Retrieved November 19, 2000, from the PsycARTICLES database.
Abstract	Nakazato, K., Shimonaka, Y., & Homma, A. (1992). Cognitive functions of centenarians: The Tokyo Metropolitan Centenarian Study. *Japanese Journal of Developmental Psychology, 3,* 9–16. Abstract obtained from *PsycSCAN: Neuropsychology,* 1993, *2,* Abstract No. 604.
ERIC Reference	Mead, J. V. (1992). *Looking at old photographs: Investigating the teacher tales that novice teachers bring with them* (Report No. NCRTL-RR-92-4). East Lansing, MI: National Center for Research on Teacher Learning. (ERIC Document Reproduction Service No. ED346082)
Dissertation (unpublished)	Wilfley, D. E. (1989). *Interpersonal analyses of bulimia: Normal-weight and obese.* Unpublished doctoral dissertation, University of Missouri, Columbia.

FIGURE 8–1 APA Reference Formats

Source: All examples from *Publication Manual of the American Psychological Association* (5th ed., pp. 215–281) by the American Psychological Association, 2001, Washington, DC: Author. Copyright © 2001 by the American Psychological Association. Reprinted with permission. Neither the original nor this reproduction may be republished or distributed in any form or by any means or stored in a database or retrieval system, without the prior written permission of the publisher.

One such manual, which is increasingly being required as a guide for theses and dissertations, is the *Publication Manual of the American Psychological Association*, also called the APA style manual (currently in its fifth edition). If you are not bound by any particular format and style system, the APA style manual is recommended as it is the most widely accepted academic format and style system used by colleges, universities, and journals. In addition to acquiring and studying a copy of the selected manual, it is also very helpful to study several reports that have been written following the same manual. For example, look at existing action research write ups to get an idea of format and what is expected. To the degree possible (e.g., with respect to tables, figures, references, and student examples of tasks) this text you are reading reflects APA guidelines, as does the following discussion. Figure 8–1 illustrates some of the basic APA reference formats. Are you sold on the idea of writing? If so, let's forge ahead with examining an example of an action research article.

Sample Annotated Action Research Article

The following research article is reprinted here so that you may examine the general structure and components of written action research. I hope that you will refer to this example frequently as you write your first action research report. Just as you've been trained to observe your students, be observant as you read the following article and consciously note the various components of this written report: the headings, some of the phrases that are characteristic of particular sections of the write-up, and the meaning of each section. As you will soon see (or perhaps you came to this realization earlier), the organization of an action research write-up is not rocket science. In fact, the sections that follow predictably mirror the core chapters of this book and the Steps in the Action Plan: the Area of Focus Statement, Research Questions, Review of Literature, Data Collection, Data Analysis, and the Action Plan. (Look at the Table of Contents of this book—look familiar?)

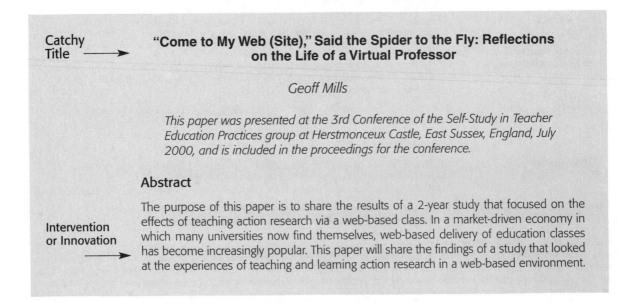

Catchy Title →

"Come to My Web (Site)," Said the Spider to the Fly: Reflections on the Life of a Virtual Professor

Geoff Mills

This paper was presented at the 3rd Conference of the Self-Study in Teacher Education Practices group at Herstmonceux Castle, East Sussex, England, July 2000, and is included in the proceedings for the conference.

Abstract

Intervention or Innovation →

The purpose of this paper is to share the results of a 2-year study that focused on the effects of teaching action research via a web-based class. In a market-driven economy in which many universities now find themselves, web-based delivery of education classes has become increasingly popular. This paper will share the findings of a study that looked at the experiences of teaching and learning action research in a web-based environment.

Introduction

In recent years, Oregon universities have moved to decrease the amount of "satellite" time associated with distance learning classes and to increase the amount of support made available to students "on-line." As a result of the Learning Anywhere, Anytime Project (LAAP) grant by the Oregon University System, the Education Department at Southern Oregon University is pioneering the development and implementation of completely web-based graduate classes in education. This paper is based on my experiences of teaching a web-based version of action research for two terms in 2 consecutive years.

Context →

The Action Research course is a 10-week introductory, graduate level class focused on the development, implementation, and evaluation of action research. One of the goals of the web-based class is to maximize the interaction between the instructor and the students, and among the students. In order to encourage this interaction, students "post" their responses to weekly tasks as well as respond to other students in the class. Additionally, the class utilizes a listserv and a discussion board (chat room). In order to complete the course, students are required to write a review of related literature, respond to weekly postings and tasks, and complete an action research project. Students register for the class and request a copy of the required text by calling a toll-free number or registering on-line. The course is based around the text *Action Research: A Guide for the Teacher Researcher* (Mills, 2000) and is supplemented with PowerPoint presentations that can be downloaded from the course web site. A complete overview of the class can be accessed at the following URL using the password "research" to enter the class: http://www.collegecourse.com/sou/ed/ed519/.

Action research involves teacher researchers in a four-step process that includes the following: identifying an area of focus, data collection, data analysis and interpretation, and action planning. In doing action research, teacher researchers have developed solutions to their own problems and as such are the authoritative voices as to what works in their particular settings. They exhibit a professional disposition that is encapsulated in their willingness to challenge the taken-for-granted assumptions that influence their daily instructional practices. By modeling the action research process for my graduate education students, I believe that I am able to nurture the development of a teacher researcher professional disposition and, in some ways, to demystify the process. My students are able to witness the development of an emerging action research project that involves them in the data collection process. They are also able to see a teacher who is committed to improving his own

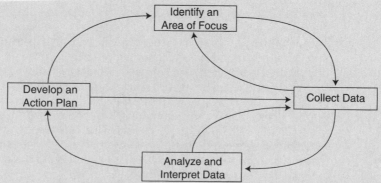

FIGURE 1   The Dialectic Action Research Spiral (Mills, 2000, p. 20)

teaching through the use of an action research model. For many of my students, this is a revelation in itself—that someone who teaches at a university would actually want to improve his practice! Therefore, this paper is structured using the action research conceptual framework I use to teach action research (see Figure 1).

Area of Focus Statement

Area of
Focus
Statement

———→

The purpose of this study was to describe the effects of web-based instruction in a distance learning action research class on student outcomes and attitudes. This area of focus statement satisfies my central tenets of action research in that it involves teaching and learning, is something that is within my locus of control, is something I feel passionate about, and is something I would like to change or improve (Mills, 2000, p. 27).

Research Questions

Research
Questions

———→

1. What is the effect of web-based instruction on students' communication with each other? With the instructor?

2. How do students' learning styles effect their success in a web-based class?

3. How do online resources meet students' needs to access course materials?

Review of Related Literature

Literature
Review

———→

As an expatriate Australian, I am positively predisposed to distance learning. As a young teacher in a small rural "outback" town in Australia, my only option for continuing my education was via correspondence education. In the United States, correspondence education is not widely accepted as an acceptable form of education by those of us working in universities. But why is this the case when other developed countries (like Australia!) have wide acceptance of distance learning via correspondence? I believe that this issue gets to the heart of the propositions many of us hold about effective pedagogy, whether it is in a live or web-based learning environment, and provides the framework for the related literature to be considered here.

There is a dearth of literature that addresses what is for me one of the most critical aspects of classroom learning environments—the nature and quality of the interaction between teachers and students, and between students with other students. This pedagogical concern can be viewed in broader terms to include "the identification of learning goals, philosophical changes in teaching and learning, reconceptualization of the teacher's role, evaluation of student and instructor, and the stimulation of interactivity" (Schrum, 1998, p. 56). In order to foster interaction in a virtual classroom, Berge (1999) points out that teachers must utilize interactions of a synchronous (communication occurs in real time) or asynchronous (technologically mediated in time) nature. I taught my action research class based on an asynchronous model—students who registered for the class could take it anywhere, anytime—although they were encouraged to follow a 10-week outline of tasks and activities. Similarly, the class was characterized by asynchronous communication—there was never the expectation that the class would meet in "real time" or with any face-to-face interaction. But as I will discuss later in this paper, this kind of communication provided me with a significant challenge in the way I developed rapport with my students. Levin (1997) characterizes this challenge in the following way:

> I can neither see the puzzlement in an online learner's eyes or the "aha" twinkle when a student gets the point. One of the attractions of asynchronous computer

mediated communication, also poses another challenge: anytime, anywhere, but alone. If you believe as I do that learning should be viewed as the social construction of meaning and knowledge, then this isolation poses a stiff challenge to learning. Online learning is conducted largely within text (p. 6).

As you will see, I find this inability to see the twinkle of my students' eyes a drawback in my ability to develop a rapport and understanding of the complex worldviews they bring to the learning environment. However, there is little evidence in the literature to suggest that students of web-based instruction (WBI) classes perform differently compared with traditional classes.

Teachers and students who participate in WBI classes appear to hold somewhat contrasting views of the distance learning experience that are challenging to reconcile. For example, faculty are consistently concerned about the quality of the teaching/learning experience and the degree of interactivity that occurs. Alternatively, students are generally positive about the experience and report that the convenience of this medium meets the needs of the nontraditional (distance learning) student who balances work, family, and study (Daugherty & Funke, 1998). The same study reports that faculty perceptions of WBI can be categorized as follows: lack of technical support, lack of software/adequate equipment, lack of faculty/administrative support, the amount of preparation time required to create and grade assignments, and student lack of knowledge and resistance to the technology. Alternatively, students tend to acknowledge the utility of the Internet and the "discovery" learning that occurred through the use of Internet resources and, according to Daugherty and Funke (1998), "appeared genuinely impressed by the variety and quality of the learning materials offered via the Web" (p. 30). In an earlier study, Harasim (1987) reported an even greater list of perceived advantages of on-line learning, from an increased interaction in quantity and intensity to motivational aspects related to text-based communication (p. 124). Students value being able to communicate in a text-based environment to a far greater degree than they would in a traditional live class—a finding that is supported in my own study and to which I will speak later in this paper.

Data Collection

Qualitative data collection techniques were used as the primary research methods for this study. However, the traditional ethnographic technique of "participant observer" was limited to written communication and postings at the course listserv and discussion board (chat room). The only time I met with students "face-to-face" was in the rare instance when a student drove to the university to talk to me, or when I interviewed the students at the end of the course. There was never an opportunity to observe the students in their own learning environments at home (where all of the students "attended" the course).

Data
Collection

Data Sources

- *Surveys*—Students filled out surveys throughout the class in order to provide insights into their experiences during the term in which the class was taught and follow-up surveys during which time they reflected on their experience in the class and its application to their regular teaching environment.

- *Interviews*—Following the surveys, students were invited to meet with me to further discuss their experiences throughout the class. As Agar (1980) suggests, information from interviews can serve as the "methodological core" against which observational data can be used to "feed" ongoing informal interviews. The interviews can best be categorized as informal ethnographic interviews that allowed me to inquire into the experiences of the students in the on-line class and to follow-up on comments individual students had made in response to survey items.

- *Matrix*—All of the listserv postings were printed and analyzed in terms of the number of postings and the types of communication that were occurring. This constant "lurking" on the Web was a valuable data source.

- *Artifacts*—Students submitted final action research projects in "display" form, which varied from multi-media presentations posted to the course's web page to audio and video presentations with accompanying poster boards.

Data Analysis and Interpretation

The following themes emerged from the analysis of the surveys, interviews, observations, and students' projects.

The Frequency and Type of Communication

Themes

The frequency and types of communication varied considerably throughout the length of the course. Frequently, students reported being "overwhelmed" with the volume of e-mail that was an integral part of the weekly class participation. Although not every e-mail required a response from the instructor, like the students in the class, I found the daily task of responding to e-mail quite daunting.

The Benefits and Drawbacks of Listserv Communication

Students considered the benefits of listserv communication as follows:

- Comfort level of being able to give feedback in an on-line setting. Many students expressed high levels of satisfaction with being able to give and receive feedback without feeling pressured to "talk" in class.

- Frequency of responses individual students received appeared related to their area of focus and the frequency of responses they made to other students in the class, that is, if the content area was something a number of students had in common, they tended to gravitate toward each other. The matrix of frequency and kinds of responses indicated that quiet students received less feedback on their projects.

Students considered the drawbacks of listserv communication as follows:

- The overwhelming volume of e-mail messages. It did not appear to matter whether there were 10 or 20 students registered in the class—both groups described the volume of e-mail as "overwhelming."

- Delay in receiving feedback. Some students expressed frustration with not receiving "immediate" feedback from the instructor and/or colleagues in the class.

- Lack of nonverbal cues. A number of students requested that we "post" digital photographs so that we could "put a face with a name." There appeared to be interest in getting to know each other but a virtual classroom environment was not the ideal setting for establishing rapport.

Related to the use of the listserv and e-mail was the use of a discussion board (chat room) during the second offering of the class. My intent in implementing the discussion board was to cut down on the frequency and total number of e-mail postings. However, the use of the chat room appeared to cause more problems than it solved due to technical problems of access to the discussion board. Students were given the option of using one communication network or the other. Ultimately, this did not work and caused a division in the class that challenged the continuity of the communication among all students.

Learning Styles and Traits for Success in a Web-Based Class

Themes

The completion rate for students in the first offering of the class was 50% and increased to 63% in the second offering. I believe that this completion rate raises questions about matching students' learning styles with the medium of instruction. For example, my traditional "live" offerings of this action research class average about an 85% completion rate. The majority of students (70%) indicated that if traveling distance to the university was not a factor, they would have preferred a "live" class.

On-Line Resources

Students indicated a high level of satisfaction with the availability and quality of on-line resources available on the Internet. However, there were some students who expressed concern about the "black hole" of time that accompanied searching for materials on the Web. Similarly, students who were new users ("newbies") expressed concern about the amount of time it took for them to acquire the skills to search the Internet in an effective and efficient manner.

Action Plan

Action Plan

Based on the themes that have emerged from this study, I plan to make the following changes in the future offerings of my web-based, distance learning action research:

- Restructure the class tasks so that the interaction between students, and between the students and the instructor, are manageable. Any future use and implementation of the chat room strategy would have to come with an assurance that **all** students would be able to access the discussion board. This is critical for effective communication—perhaps the one aspect of a web-based learning environment that is critical to success.

- Learning styles—Although there appears to be a dearth of literature that discusses the importance of students' learning styles as they relate to web-based learning, I believe that it is critical that students are somehow screened in order to determine the likelihood that they will succeed in a virtual classroom environment. For example, in future offerings of the class I will interview all students prior to giving permission to register for the class to determine their comfort level with (a) the use of computers and the Internet, and (b) their comfort level with being an independent, "self-starter" learner who can work on tasks in a relatively self-directed fashion. I will try to identify an instrument that can assist with this task and for which there is predictive validity.

- On-line resources—I will continue to explore the use of on-line resources to facilitate independent teacher research, such as supporting students' efforts to retrieve copies of journal articles, which is an otherwise expensive activity.

- Rapport building—In order to build rapport with my students, and between students, I will include an interactive, face-to-face communication facilitated by distance learning technologies. Rapport may also be facilitated by the use of cameras mounted on the top of computers. Finally, I will incorporate the use of a dial-up teleconference during which time students can present their term projects. For example, students could "post" their projects to the listserv, which could then be downloaded prior to a designated class session. Using a toll-free university phone tree, students could participate in a teleconference and be able to scroll through each other's projects during a presentation. All of these strategies will function to facilitate the development of rapport and decrease feelings of isolation.

Final Thoughts

As I mentioned earlier, I am positively predisposed to distance learning modalities. I believe that it addresses issues of equity and access to education for all. This is particularly true at my university, which provides services to many teachers working in rural communities.

However, with spiraling tuition costs, many of these teachers also question whether or not they are getting "value for money" when they choose to learn in isolation. Do equity and access equal good pedagogy? How is it that on-line courses maintain the integrity of a graduate education? What characteristics distinguish an on-line course from a correspondence course? This study has raised more questions for me than it has answered. I am challenged by the opportunities that current distance learning modalities offer and strive to balance issues of equity and access against quality. Ultimately, perhaps, the responsibility for choosing to learn via an on-line environment rests with the learner. Similarly, the responsibility for overcoming some of the inherent problems associated with teaching in an on-line environment must rest with the teacher. Through the implementation of an action research approach, I have reflected on the limitations of teaching in a web-based environment and am committed to address them in future class offerings.

References —→

References

Agar, M. (1980). *The professional stranger: An informal introduction to ethnography*. Orlando, FL: Academic.

Berge, Z. (1999). Interaction in post-secondary web-based learning. *Educational Technology, 39*(1), 5–11.

Daugherty, M., & B. L. Funke. (1998). University faculty and student perceptions of web-based instruction. *Journal of Distance Education, 13*(1), 21–39.

Harasim, L. (1987). Teaching and learning on-line: Issues in computer-mediated graduate courses. *CJCE, 16*(2), 117–135.

Levin, D. (1997). *Institutional concerns: Supporting the use of Internet discussion groups*. ED 416481.

Mills, G. E. (2000). *Action research: A guide for the teacher researcher*. Upper Saddle River, NJ: Merrill.

Schrum, L. (1998). On-line education: A study of emerging pedagogy. *New Directions for Adult and Continuing Education, 78*, 53–61.

Now that you've seen a sample of something you might produce, let's discuss some nuts and bolts ideas on writing up action research.

Rituals and Writing

One of my favorite books on writing is Howard Becker's *Writing for Social Scientists: How to Start and Finish Your Thesis, Book, or Article* (1986). As Becker points out, many writers hold certain irrational rituals as necessary precursors to the act of writing:

> From one point of view, my fellow participants (in the writing workshop) were describing neurotic symptoms. Viewed sociologically, however, those symptoms were magical rituals. According to Malinowski (1948, pp. 25–36), people perform such rituals to influence the result of some process over which they think they have no rational means of control. (p. 3)

A survey of friends and colleagues suggested the following magical rituals were powerful predictors of successful writing sessions. How do they compare with your own?

- Writing can only occur between the hours of 7:00 AM and 12:00 PM.
- At least six sharpened pencils and a yellow legal pad must be in place next to the computer.
- Writing can only be done longhand using a blue pen and white legal pad.
- The house must be clean before writing starts.
- Everything must be in order (materials, lighting, soft music, etc.) before writing can commence.

ESTABLISHING A WRITING ROUTINE

There is no easy way around the pragmatic issue of time—writing takes time and we never have enough time to do all that we have to do, professionally and personally. The only advice I can offer here is to somehow make writing part of your professional life and responsibility. Capture the minutes and hours where they fall—before school, after school, preparation periods, cancelled faculty meetings, failed parent conferences, and professional development days. Argue for the time as part of your faculty meetings and professional development days . . . and be prepared to ante up when asked to share the outcome of your efforts.

I know of no other way besides attacking personal family time to get my writing done. In the short term, our loved ones will put up with "I need to stay home and get this writing (or grading, lesson planning, or test development tasks that teachers take home) done. You go ahead and enjoy the movie (dinner, picnic, hike, river rafting, skiing)." We could all fill in the blank based on our professional life as a teacher.

However you make it happen, I am assuming that there will come a time when you sit down in front of a keyboard, or with a blank pad of paper, and start the task of writing up your action research. I can picture you now—pencil in hand, keyboard at the ready—poised to pen the story of your action research! Go to that place for a while. Get ready to write!

In the spirit of sharing tips for successful writing, see Figure 8–2 for some tips on what *not to do*. You might identify with some of these.

On a more practical note, here are some guidelines for writing and editing:

- Write at the same time every day, a time when you know you won't be disturbed.
- Write up your story as though you're sending an e-mail to a friend. Pretend that your friend needs it explained in simple terms.

- Think about all the things at school that I need to do before tomorrow.

- Scan my desk to see if someone has left me a note about a meeting, sports practice, birthday party that I need to go to **NOW.**

- Check my voicemail.

- Check my e-mail.

- Check my checkbook to see if it is balanced.

- Call my wife/child/colleague/friend/enemy to see what they are doing.

- Walk down the hallway to see if I can find someone to talk to.

- Dream about winning the lottery.

- Make an appointment to see my dentist.

FIGURE 8–2   Geoff's Tips for Being Able to Avoid Writing

- Tell a story as you write. Most teachers are good storytellers. Whether it is telling third graders about Columbus' voyages, how chicks hatch in an incubator, or an embarrassing incident that occurred "way back when" when you were in school, teachers are compelling storytellers who can capture the imagination of their students. This is true regardless of the content matter. These skills can be transferred to the way in which we share our action research stories. And I do not use the term *storyteller* in a pejorative sense here—storytellers can still employ rigor in their work.

- If you're having trouble getting started, "write it the way you talk." The editing can come later. Tell your story with an audience of colleague teacher researchers in mind and the words will flow naturally. If you get hung up on writing for a larger "academic" audience, the words will not come easily and sentences may be stilted and formal. There is also no reason to use big words.

- Organize your thoughts around an outline and tell your story in a way that stays true to the facts of your study. Make it coherent and make sure your story flows.

- In the early stages don't worry too much about how well the text reads or whether it is full of grammatical errors. Write without consideration for grammar, syntax, or punctuation—just write. Concentrate on getting the story out. Look for progress, not perfection.

- Write whatever comes to mind. Then go back and hunt for what you are really trying to say—it's there.

- Have you ever thought to yourself, "I wish I had done that differently"? Writing is like that, and then you get to do it differently—editing your own work is a delight. Write boldly and then say it again—better.

- Writing, then editing, then rewriting, and then re-editing clarifies thoughts into a coherent package. Even a gem needs to be mined roughly, cut ruthlessly, then buffed.

- Nobody knows my work better than I do. Writing is an exercise in learning about your own work. I'm always surprised how much better I know it when I've discussed it with my computer a few times.
- Edit after you have all your thoughts on paper. I may be a poor writer, but I am a fast writer! I churn out words faster than you can imagine. The problem is they take a lot of editing, wordsmithing, revising, rethinking, and replacing along the way. What you see here is not my first draft—or my last. It also has benefited from the collective wisdom and skills of a development editor, copy editors, people with Ph.D. degrees in English and Literature, and friends who are pretty good writers. In short, as readers of research we should not hold ourselves to unrealistic expectations of grandeur. Any of us can write well given the time, effort, and assistance needed to produce "good" writing. Set realistic expectations for yourself somewhere between "The first draft is the last draft!" and "This will never be perfect—I'll just stick with it for another few years!"
- If you accept that your first draft is not your last draft, living with mediocre text becomes easier to accept. Put another way:

  > The only way I can get anything written at all is to write really, really sh__ first drafts. . . . All good writers write them. This is how they end up with good second drafts and terrific third drafts. (Lamott, 1994, cited in Wolcott, 2001, p. 55)

I am sure that you can add to these lists with your own rituals and tips. My advice to you is consistent with the advice I once gave to my third-grade students when teaching them to play the recorder: "Make as much noise as you want to for the next 2 minutes. Get it out of your system. When the time is up we will focus on playing the music on the page. Go ahead and blow!" A suggestion: Write down your avoidance list and stick it next to wherever it is that you write. Check it occasionally, but get the behaviors out of your system. Consider it therapeutic and try and catch yourself being "good," that is, staying on task with your writing. Think of a little reward system (if you are somewhat extrinsically motivated like me, that is). Here are a few things I "treat" myself to when I have dedicated myself to some writing time (not in order of preference): a run, time to play with my son and wife, something sweet (you know, some sugar to help with the fatigue!), an adult beverage, food, sleep, or all of the above.

Now that you have identified your avoidance techniques and treats, let's get down to the business of writing: structure, how to submit the write-up to a journal, using a consistent style, and assessing content. Later we'll discuss article length, choosing a title, getting feedback, and final editing.

An Outline for an Action Research Report

Review the following list. Does it look familiar?

- Area-of-focus statement ("The purpose of this study was to . . . ")
- Related literature
- Defining the variables
- Research questions
- Description of intervention or innovation

- Data collection
- Data considerations (issues of validity, reliability, and ethics)
- Data analysis and interpretation
- Action plan (e.g., "Steps to Action Chart")

This is the basic outline I have used with teacher researchers for many years and it has proved to be a useful approach. You may need to adapt the structure of your article to fit your audience. This outline is not set in stone—a statement that will no doubt be supported by your own professor (if you are taking a class), school (if you are writing up your action research as part of an evaluation model), or journal editor (if you are submitting your story to an action research journal). Nevertheless, this outline is a useful way to start organizing your thoughts about your story. Later in this chapter, you will see a rubric of essential elements to include in your report and points to consider for each of the items in this list.

Other Structures in Action Research Reports

As an alternative to using this outline, you can look at the "Notes for Contributors" in action research and teacher research journals that you might want to target for publishing your story. These sections provide guidelines for authors to consider before submitting work to the journal's editor or editorial board. For example, *Networks*, the online action research journal discussed in Chapter 7, offers the following "Criteria for Acceptance of Articles":

The journal does not demand that submitted articles be in any particular format or genre and encourages contributors to experiment with new forms appropriate to their topic and purpose. At the same time, articles should, where relevant, meet the following criteria:

- address an issue of significance to other teachers and teacher researchers;
- provide information about methods of collection and analysis of evidence that will be useful to other teacher researchers;
- provide adequate information about the institutional/educational context, bearing in mind an international readership;
- present a clear and coherent account, with appropriate warrant for the conclusions reached;
- comment on the implications and issues arising from the research in a way that can potentially contribute to an ongoing debate;
- appropriately take account of and acknowledge the work of other writers; and
- be written in an interesting, reader-friendly style.
  (http://www.oise.utoronto.ca/ctd/networks/contributorNotes.html)

Similarly, *Educational Action Research* calls for contributions from practitioner researchers (in fields varying from education to nursing, medicine, and other "social settings") with the following guidelines:

Two kinds of papers are particularly welcome: (1) accounts of action research and development studies; and (2) contributions to the debate on the theory and practice of action research and associated methodologies. Readability and honest engagement with problematic issues will be among the criteria against which contributions will be judged. The journal can be construed as carrying out, through its contributors and reviewers, action research on the characteristics on effective reporting, and the Editors will, therefore, welcome exploratory forms of presentation (Notes for Contributors).

As a teacher researcher reading these guidelines, you are probably struck by one overriding feeling—anxiety! What is meant by "honest engagement with problematic issues" anyway? And how will it be judged? What are the criteria? To take this anxiety one step further, let's look at who the people are who publish in journals. My hunch is that 99% of articles published (and probably submitted) to **refereed journals** (a fancy way of saying that more than one "qualified" person reads the submission) are by teachers teaching and researching in higher education. However, this does not mean that it must continue to be that way, and I have been delighted with the teacher researcher articles published in *Networks*, a journal that seems to live up to its billing as being a journal by teachers and for teachers. (For a comparison of action research journals that you may want to target for publication see Figure 8–3.)

So, what do these "Notes to Contributors" and my outline have in common? Is there a rubric that will help me decide whether I am meeting the publication's benchmark? Unfortunately, there is no easy answer to this conundrum. I have a drawer full of rejection letters for what I thought were "reader friendly" journal articles that addressed an "issue of significance"! I also know "published" academics who, despite their reputation and experience, still manage to get rejected on occasion. Of course, this is the magic of the **blind review** process, a practice by which

Journal Name	Publisher	Address	E-mail or Web Site	Phone Fax	Description
Networks: An Online Journal for Teacher Research	University of Toronto	NA	http://www.oise.utoronto.ca/ctd/networks/	NA	An online journal that provides a forum for teachers working in classrooms (elementary–university) to share their experiences and learn from each other. Also publishes book reviews and discussions on current issues in teacher research.
Reflective Practice	Carfax	Carfax Publishing Taylor & Francis Ltd 325 Chestnut St. 8th Floor, Philadelphia, PA 19106 USA	http://www.tandf.co.uk enquiry@tandf.co.uk	(800) 821-8312 (US & Canada) Fax: (625) 821-2940 (US & Canada)	A refereed journal "about and for the enhancement of practice through reflection." Articles are focused on the connections between reflection, knowledge generation, practice, and policy.
Educational Action Research	Triangle Journals	Triangle Journals Ltd P.O. Box 65, Wallingford, Oxfordshire OX10 04G United Kingdom	journals@triangle.co.uk http://www.triangle.co.uk	NA	A refereed journal that publishes accounts of action research in education and across the professions. Also provides a forum for dialogue about current action research issues.
Action Research International	Southern Cross University	NA	http://www.scu.edu.au/schools/gcm/ar/ari/arihome.htm	NA	A refereed journal of action research that seeks to publish papers about the integrated theory practice of action research. Papers may be a work in progress, a completed study, a theoretical paper, or a book review.

FIGURE 8–3 Action Research Journals

articles submitted for publication are presented to reviewers without name and institutional affiliation to avoid bias. The editorial board wants to ensure that the article is accepted on its merit, not the author's reputation. Therefore, let me offer the following modest advice for attending to contributors' notes.

General Guidelines for Submissions to Journals

- *Attend to the context of your study.* Craft a narrative that guides your audience to the site at which your study occurred. For example, let's compare a good and bad context narrative from the sample paper " 'Come to My Web (Site),' Said the Spider to the Fly."

  > Good example: "As a result of the LAAP grant by the Oregon University System, the Education Department is pioneering the development and implementation of completely web-based graduate classes in education. This paper is based on my experiences of teaching a web-based version of action research for two terms in consecutive years."

  > Poor example: "This study is based on my experiences of teaching a web-based class on action research."

  The good example provides the reader with information about the setting (a university), the audience (graduate education students), the length of the study (two terms in consecutive years), and that the course development and implementation was funded by a grant (Learning Anywhere, Anytime Project grant). This brief statement provides the reader with helpful information about the study that is otherwise overlooked (in the poor example).
- *Use a clear, reader-friendly writing style.* Don't try and model your writing after the kinds of articles you have read in prestigious research journals. Be realistic in your goal and write using the same voice that you use to tell the story of your research to your colleagues. (See the guidelines for writing listed earlier in this chapter.)
- *Peruse the journals you are considering* for your submissions and notice the structure and writing style of the researchers whose work has been accepted and published.
- *Include a brief description of what you did.* Attend to any issues related to data collection, analysis, interpretation, and data collection considerations (e.g., validity, reliability, ethics).
- *Write in an honest, open manner.* Don't try to hide behind jargon and don't make statements that you can't substantiate. Let your data speak for themselves. In other words, what is the gist of what your data show? Say it. Remember what Kennedy (1997) said (see Chapter 1) about teachers not reading research because it is not accessible. Now is your chance to explain it as if you were discussing it over coffee with a colleague or with your Uncle Fred who may not know anything about your research. Make it understandable.
- *Keep readers' attention.* If you are like me, you read something that is "published" and make a judgment like "Not bad," "Engaging," "Pretty bad," or "I'll give it another few pages before I put it in the round file." For whatever reason, we intuitively know what will keep our attention. For example, I read fiction books, not textbooks, for pleasure. Indeed, these are different genres and we should

not be surprised by the fact that we are engaged in reading bestseller novels and not academic writings. (I joke with my non-teacher friends that I know a good cure for insomnia—and its title starts with Action Research!) But does enjoyable, engaging reading (and, hence, writing) have to be mutually exclusive from academic writing? Consider writing up your teacher researcher studies in a way that makes them engaging for you and your audience.

- *Follow a style* (e.g., American Psychological Association [APA] style) used in action research journals.

Perhaps the underlying lesson here is that if we have a story to tell, and a compelling way in which to tell it, then there is a good chance that an editorial board will agree with you!

Choosing a "Journal" Style

Teacher researchers often ask me what "convention" they should follow when writing a term paper or preparing an action research study for publication. There is no simple answer to this. I usually suggest one of the following approaches:

- Choose an article from the journal you are targeting for your write-up and follow the conventions used by the author. Rationale: If the journal published the article using the conventions contained therein, then the editor will probably accept your mirroring of it!
- Follow the conventions outlined in the *Publication Manual of the American Psychological Association* (5th edition), also known as the APA style manual. For those of us trying to publish in education journals, it is the most widely accepted style to follow.

At the risk of trying to oversimplify a 412-page style manual, the list below suggests conventions that you should attend to in your writing. And remember, if in doubt, go to the *Manual* itself. I offer this as a simple reminder of the conventions that most often plague my teacher researcher colleagues.

APA *Publication Manual* Conventions

Punctuation

- *Period*: Use a period to end a complete sentence.
- *Comma*: Use a comma between elements in a series of three or more items.
- *Semicolon*: Use a semicolon to separate two independent clauses that are not joined by a conjunction.
- *Colon*: Use a colon between a complete introductory clause and a final explanatory phrase or clause.
- *Dash*: Use an em-dash (—) to indicate only a sudden interruption in the continuity of a sentence.
- *Quotation marks:* Use double quotation marks to introduce a word or phrase used in an ironic comment, to set off the title of an article or chapter, or for a direct quotation of less than 25 words.
- *Parentheses*: Use parentheses to set off structurally independent elements, for citations, and to introduce abbreviations.

Preferred Spelling

- *Merriam-Webster's Collegiate Dictionary* is the standard spelling reference for APA journals and books. (Consult www.apastyle.org for current information.) For example, appendix, appendices; criterion, criteria; phenomenon, phenomena; curriculum, curricula, *or* curriculums.
- *Check part of speech*: write up (verb), write-up (noun).
- *Hyphenation*: Refer to the dictionary to determine if you should use a hyphen. For example, is follow-up or followup the correct form to use?

Abbreviations

- APA prefers that authors use abbreviations sparingly.

Reference Style

- *Periodical*: Mills, G. E. (1999). Teacher research and the professional disposition of teaching. *New England Mathematics Journal, 31*(2), 5–17.
- *Book*: Mills, G. E. (2000). *Action research: A guide for the teacher researcher.* Upper Saddle River, NJ: Merrill Prentice Hall.
- *Online reference*: Hansen, L. (2000). The inherent desire to learn: Intrinsically motivating first grade students. *Networks, 4*(2). January 15, 2002, from http://www.oise.utoronto.ca/nctd/networks.
- Six or more authors in a reference, use "et al."

This listing of APA editorial style cannot really summarize a 138-page chapter on editorial style! Once you identify the journal you are going to target for publishing your work, find out the preferred editorial style for your manuscript. Consult the complete APA style manual for specific details. However, most of the teacher researchers with whom I work struggle with simple issues related to punctuation, spelling, and references. To this end I offer the guide above—for everything else, go to the source.

SELF-ASSESSING YOUR WRITE-UP

The following rubric (Figure 8–4) may be one way of self-assessing whether your write-up is ready to be sent to a journal for consideration. If you rank yourself with 3s on all of these categories, you are probably ready to submit your article for publication. What follows is an example of how the rubric was applied to the article " 'Come to My Web (Site),' Said the Spider to the Fly."

Assessing an Article Using Rubric Criteria

In the following outline I have self-assessed my article reprinted in this chapter using the criteria in the rubric.

a. *Organization and Use of Conventions—3.* The article complies with an acceptable format and uses correct grammar, spelling, and punctuation.
b. *Area of Focus—3.* The article includes a clear area of focus statement: "The purpose of this study was to describe the effects of web-based instruction in a distance learning action research class on student outcomes and attitudes."
c. *Data Collection—3.* The article includes a clear statement outlining the data sources used for the study: surveys, interviews, matrix, and artifacts.

Category	1	2	3
A. Organization of Conventions	• Write-up does not follow any format • Many errors in grammar, spelling, and punctuation	• Write-up partially follows a format • Grammar, spelling, and punctuation are generally accurate	• Write-up follows a format • Grammar, spelling, and punctuation are free of errors
B. Area of Focus	• There is no clear area of focus for the study • Research questions are vague (e.g., "Is on-line learning good?")	• The area of focus is too broad or too narrow • Research questions are poorly written (e.g., "What is the effect of on-line learning?")	• There is a clear area of focus statement ("The purpose of this study was to . . . ") • Research questions are clear and appropriate (e.g., "What are the effects of web-based instruction on student outcomes?")
C. Data Collection	• Few data sources are evident • Data sources do not match the research questions	• Multiple data sources are evident • Data sources roughly match the research questions	• Multiple data sources are evident and there is an attempt to triangulate the data • A variety of data sources is used • Data sources match the research questions
D. Review of the Literature (Refer to Chapter 2 "Writing a Review of the Literature" for suggestions about writing this section)	• There is no attempt to connect the study to existing research	• Five recent sources (within the past 3 years) are cited • One or more sources that do not relate to the study are cited • One or more sources are incorrectly cited	• Five or more recent sources are cited • Irrelevant sources are not cited • Citations are made correctly, per APA style or another style required for the audience
E. Context	• No context for the study is provided	• Context is provided but is vague	• Context is well-written and provides the audience with a clear understanding of where the study was conducted
F. Writing Style	• Narrative is hard to read	• Narrative uses headings that guide the reader • Writer uses jargon	• Narrative is clear, coherent, and reader friendly • Evidence is provided to support statements (e.g., see reprinted research paper in this chapter)
G. Action Plan	• There is no action	• Components of the action plan are missing or incorrectly stated • There is not a clear connection between data analysis and the action plan	• There is a clear connection between the findings of the study and proposed changes in practice (e.g., an action plan may start with the following: "Based on the themes that have emerged from this study, I plan to make the following changes. . . . ")

FIGURE 8–4 Action Research Write-Up Rubric

This section might have been improved by including a data collection matrix (see Chapter 3).

d. *Review of Literature—3*. The article includes a succinct literature review that is directly related to the area of focus. Specifically, the review focused on the challenges of synchronous and asynchronous components of online courses. This section might have been strengthened by the use of sub-headings to guide the reader, or by the inclusion of a literature matrix (see Chapter 2).

e. *Context—3*. The article provides the reader with a context for the study and how it is related to the Learning Anywhere Anytime Project grant.

f. *Writing Style—3*. I wrote it so it must be good, right?! The narrative is reader friendly.

g. *Action Plan—3*. The article includes an action plan that clearly outlines the next steps in the search for excellence in online teaching and learning. There is a clear connection between the data and the suggested future changes.

After you've completed the second draft of your write-up, consider each of these points to assess whether you are ready to share your work with others.

INTEGRATING TEACHING, RESEARCH, AND WRITING

Classroom teachers face a stressful challenge every day—they must inspire children in their classes for 8 hours each school day. And, of course, the day doesn't end there—there is always planning, grading, perpetual cleaning of the classroom, organizing, creating, professional development, and parent-student-teacher conferences. No wonder that teacher researchers express concern about finding time to write.

So, if writing is not a way of life for teacher researchers, what advice can I offer that may help encourage and nurture writing? Let's assume for one moment that you have a story that you *want* to tell; then the issues become finding the time to tell the story to an interested audience and finding enjoyment in committing the story to words. So, as a teacher researcher, how can I find the time to write a story that I want to share with like-minded teacher researchers?

I believe that the secret lies in the ability to integrate teaching, research, and writing. For the teacher researchers with whom I have worked, the secret to writing has been a commitment to integrate the writing as part of their daily routine. It usually does not mean committing a large block of time to writing, but every little bit helps, especially when it is done on a daily basis. What follows is a list of creative strategies that teacher researchers have used to make time for writing.

- *Journal Writing Time*—Many teachers provide their students with dedicated class time to journal each day. Teacher researchers will often use this time to write their research. Furthermore, teacher researchers who practice this often tell me that if they model writing for their children during "journal time," children are more likely to spend the time writing! Keep your journal or legal pad within easy reach in or on top of your desk. Your observations should be fresh, so ideally you should jot down conversations or classroom observations while you're in school.
- *"Down Time" in School*—In rare cases, teacher researchers are able to carve out writing time by committing a planning period, a supervisory study hall,

a period that might be freed up by student teachers or art and physical education specialists, or library time to writing. And although I would not recommend that teachers leave their students during these times, all of the time, it can be an effective way to find some writing time during the contract day.

- *Professional Development Days*—Many school districts have collective bargaining agreements that allow for a day per term for teacher professional development. Teacher researchers can negotiate with their building administrators to use some of this time for writing. This argument can be enhanced when teacher researchers incorporate action research as a component of their annual evaluation process.
- *Vacation*—A commitment of 1 day during each vacation period on the school calendar can make huge inroads into the writing task. I know many teachers who take a day out of each vacation period to simply clean their classroom. Writing could become the new "cleaning" or "catching up" priority.
- *Time Dedicated to Grant Writing*—Grants from professional organizations, such as the International Reading Association and the National Council of Teachers of Mathematics, may be used to fund release time for the purpose of writing and publishing teacher research. The Teacher as Researcher Grants (http://www.reading.org/association/awards/research_teacher_as_researcher.html) of the International Reading Association support classroom teachers in their inquiries about literacy and instruction. Grants will be awarded up to (US) $5,000, although priority will be given to smaller grants (e.g., $1,000 to $2,000) in order to provide support for as many teacher researchers as possible. Completed applications must be received by January 15 each year. Similarly, the National Council of Teachers of Mathematics (NCTM) through the Mathematics Education Trust (MET) awards the Edward G. Begle Grant. This grant will provide up to $8,000 to support collaborative classroom-based research in pre-college mathematics education. Proposals should reflect creativity and emphasize innovative ways of teaching and/or assessing the students' learning of mathematics. Cooperative involvement of a college or university mathematics educator (a teacher of mathematics learning, teaching, or curriculum) and one or more grades K–12 classroom teachers is required (http://www.nctm.org/about/met/begle.htm).

How Long Should the Write-Up Be?

This is always a burning question for teacher researchers who are required to write up their action research projects in order to earn academic credit. My answer, "It depends," is usually not very helpful. It depends on the scope of the study, the kind of research that was conducted, the audience, the time allowed for writing, what the professor has stated in the syllabus, or what the "Notes to Contributors" for the targeted journal suggests.

For Submission to a Journal

Let's assume that you are targeting a journal for your write-up. The average length for a journal article typically is 2,500 to 3,500 words. I suspect that this is about twice the length of an average "term paper" (approximately 6 to 10 double-spaced,

$8\frac{1}{2}'' \times 11''$ pages). Again, don't worry about length. I know how overwhelmed I felt when I received the contract for the first edition of this book that stated it would be approximately 90,000 words! I couldn't conceive of the idea that I had 90,000 words to say on the topic, but like any teacher, I found that talking (and writing) about the focus of my writing, in this case action research, was easier than I had thought. If you break the task down into pieces of manageable length (as per an outline or table of contents), the task becomes less overwhelming.

For Distribution to Local Colleagues

The length of your write-up will also depend on your audience. For example, for colleagues in your school you may want to keep it to an "executive summary" of a page or two. Similarly, if you are sharing your study with a school board, principal, or PTA, then a brief summary probably is appropriate. However, if you are developing a paper that will be presented at a professional development seminar or conference, you might think about something along the lines of 1,000 to 2,000 words in length. Ultimately, you are the best person to decide whether you have included enough context and detail in the write-up so that you can affirmatively answer the question: What happened in this study? If in doubt, err on the side of detail rather than be criticized for providing readers with an incomplete picture.

SEEKING FEEDBACK

I would recommend that you seek feedback from trusted friends and colleagues, with one caveat: Be careful what you ask for because you will get it! Interpretation: If you ask someone for feedback, they will probably give it to you; however, you may not like what they have to say and not know what to do with it! The feedback I receive from my family and friends is, "Why do you want to spend your leisure time writing and not playing with us?" I have a few trusted colleagues who work with me and also teach action research. I know that when I ask them for feedback that they will be brutally honest with me. Similarly, I will often ask my students for feedback on my writing (in an anonymous, nonthreatening way)—after all, they are the audience with whom the success or failure of the text rests.

The point here is simple: Different audiences will give you different kinds of feedback that, if taken seriously, will ultimately result in a better outcome. This process is no more evident than in the development of a commercial textbook such as this one. The publishers use folks who are experts in grammar and content experts who check the content validity of the material in an effort to get it right. But for teacher researchers, seeking feedback should be a far more pragmatic activity. You will know your study better than anybody else; therefore, you provide your own content validity to your write-up. The feedback you will seek is more along the lines of:

- Does the write-up provide a complete picture of the research?
- Is the write-up reader friendly?
- Is the write-up engaging?
- Will someone (besides loved ones!) want to read it?

I offer one last suggestion here: Do not expect your friends and colleagues (and professors, for that matter) to do your editing for you. Before you send them a draft, make sure that you have attended to the basic editorial needs of grammar and punctuation. Otherwise you run the risk of focusing their attention on the structure of the narrative rather than the story itself.

What's in a Title?

When it comes to giving your write-up a title, I would suggest that you be somewhat creative. I think that we all probably underestimate the power of the title for attracting our readers. After all, if we can't get folks past the title, there is probably little chance that they will get into the story that follows. The following examples are illustrative of the importance of titles and the roles they play:

It's Memorable!

I have a friend who reads applications for competitive grants. His advice to me about successful grant writing has been this: Make sure you have a catchy title or acronym—something that the reader will remember. Now, I don't want to suggest that grant readers are so shallow as to be solely attracted to a title; however, folks are attracted to engaging titles and are more likely to pick up a text or journal article if their curiosity is piqued by the title. Of course, you are probably thinking, "Oh sure, what does this guy know? He came up with a really engaging title for his book!" I remember discussing the title with my friend and mentor Harry Wolcott. He suggested that I write down all of the descriptors that would convey the content of the book and try to organize them in a way that is engaging. With a textbook, or journal article for that matter, you need a title that will also be found by a keyword search, such as on ERIC. I remember asking friends for advice and receiving suggestions like: "Lights, Camera: Action Research!" I also think that I have written some pretty good conference papers that utilized catchy titles, such as the article reprinted in this chapter, " 'Come to My Web (Site),' Said the Spider to the Fly: Reflections on the Life of a Virtual Professor," "Talking Heads and Techno-Pages: Reflections on the Development of a Graduate Distance Learning Program," and "Herding Cats and Nailing Jello: Reflections on Being a Dean of Education." You may also notice that I have a habit of using a colon in my titles. I tend to use a catchy opening and follow the colon with a subtitle that clarifies what the paper is about. I like to have fun with titles and hope that my readers will find them fun as well—enough fun so that they will at least pick up the report in the first place.

It Provides a Focus

The other more practical purpose that a title can serve is to provide a focus for your writing. For example, the title for my article was both memorable and a focus for my writing. Specifically, the subtitle "Reflections on the Life of a Virtual Professor" kept me on track during the writing. That is, I was constantly reminded that I was writing about what it was like to be a "virtual professor." However, it may also be that the title changes during the write-up—a fact that reflects the writer's better understanding of the meaning of the study.

Polishing the Text

Let's assume that you have made it to the point where you are ready to submit your write-up for publication or presentation and you want to take one last shot at making the text as tight as possible. Wolcott (2001) provides a useful analogy to help with this process:

> Some of the best advice I've ever found for writers happened to be included with the directions for assembling a new wheelbarrow: Make sure all parts are properly in place before tightening. (p. 109)

I've never assembled a wheelbarrow, but if my experience with assembling a barbecue grill is anything to go by, I can relate to the analogy. The directions for the barbecue were quite explicit: "Ensure assembly is complete before igniting."

To apply the assembly metaphor to our polishing task, be sure to take the time to carefully read the narrative (instructions!) and attend to all details. Working with the narrative and getting it ready for publication is not the time to be in a hurry. You have endured many days, weeks, and months of doing action research. You are close to meeting your personal and professional goal and want to get the text off your desk (or hard drive). Now is not the time to be foolhardy and to try and light the barbecue before all the pieces are correctly positioned and tightened! Take time to do a word-by-word edit and delete unnecessary words and "excessive anythings" (Wolcott, 2001, p. 116).

In this chapter I have provided some simple suggestions for getting the word out. There is no substitute for perseverance and perspiration when it comes to writing. Your commitment to getting your word out and the positive impact it will have on your students and colleagues is the ultimate reward.

Summary

This chapter has examined the potential motivation for teacher researchers to write about their action research efforts and identified the professional publications (traditional and online journals) that are receptive to publishing action research accounts. The chapter included a sample annotated action research article and a self-assessment rubric for scoring teacher researcher accounts against the common themes that have emerged from teacher researcher journals' "Notes for Contributors." For example, teacher researchers should consider the following themes when submitting a write-up of their work to a journal: the context of their study; the use of clear, reader-friendly writing; a brief description of what they did; an honest, open manner of writing; the use of a "journal" style; and a writing style that keeps their readers' attention.

The chapter also includes an outline to follow when writing up an action research report that includes the following headings:

- Area-of-focus statement
- Related literature
- Defining the variables
- Research questions
- Description of intervention or innovation

- Data collection
- Data considerations
- Data analysis and interpretation
- Action plan

The chapter also provides a summary of a "journal" style of writing based on the guidelines provided by the widely accepted style formats presented in the *Publication Manual of the American Psychological Association* (5th edition).

Finally, the chapter provides suggestions for how teacher researchers can integrate teaching, research, and writing into their professional lives. For example, teacher researchers are encouraged to use journal writing time, school "down time," professional development days, vacation days, and grant-sponsored time as possible ways of carving writing time from an already hectic professional life.

For Further Thought

1. Develop a list of your personal writing rituals and how they help (or hinder!) your writing.
2. Develop an outline for your action research write-up that includes the headings provided in this chapter with an accompanying brief descriptive statement that captures what you will include in each section.
3. Review the "Notes for Contributors" for the following journals and decide which journal you will submit your action research report to: *Networks: An Online Journal for Teacher Research, Reflective Practice, Educational Action Research*, or *Action Research International*.
4. Develop a writing schedule for the development of your write-up and stick to it!

Sharing, Critiquing, and Celebrating Action Research Online

Whereas Chapter 7 showed teacher researchers how to ensure that action is planned with consideration of the findings of the study and the potential obstacles to implementing change, this chapter addresses different ways of sharing action research, criteria for judging action research efforts, the importance of celebrating our professional learnings, and the use of online action research resources.

This chapter addresses the benefits of sharing action research with others and discusses an alternativ'e to the traditional publication of research in professional, refereed journals: the electronic publication of texts. Electronic publication of action research texts offers another means for sharing action research with other classroom teachers and colleagues.

Teacher researchers are encouraged to celebrate their actions and to commit to action research as just the beginning of their lifelong learning. Also, teacher researchers are invited to explore a variety of Web-based resources available to them, including action research Web sites, listservs, and online and print action research journals.

Finally, the following criteria for judging action research reports are discussed: intractability of reform, audience, format, prejudices, professional disposition, reflective stance, action taken, the relationship between action and data, the ongoing monitoring of practice, suggested changes, and the responses of colleagues to the action research effort.

After reading this chapter you should be able to:
1. Identify strategies to use for sharing your action research inquiry.
2. Discuss how to celebrate your professional learning and contributions to the field.
3. Locate online action research resources such as Web sites, listservs, and journals.
4. Participate in online action research conversations by subscribing to a listserv.
5. Identify criteria for judging the quality of action research.

Reflecting on Reflective Teaching
MARY CURTIS-GRAMLEY

This is the story of a university professor who worked as the staff development coordinator for an urban elementary school. It provides us with the perspective of someone who worked in a long-term, consultant/facilitator role for 15 elementary teachers concerned with implementing an action research/reflective practitioner approach in their classrooms. It also illustrates the importance of collaboration in action research at every step of the process—from planning the inquiry to sharing, critiquing, and celebrating the results!

During the 1996–97 school year, teachers and specialists in an elementary school of approximately 310 students in kindergarten through fifth grade moved somewhat reluctantly into the world of action research. This first attempt to implement schoolwide action research projects provided many discoveries about ourselves as learners, researchers, and inquirers. Additionally, the experiences highlighted the value of collaboration in planning and conducting action research projects and in presenting the outcomes of the projects. Several vignettes from our experiences illustrate the value of collaboration in action research.

As a member of the school leadership team responsible for staff development, I helped guide the process of designing and carrying out the projects. One of the major challenges in conducting action research projects for this particular group of teachers was the first step: defining the question or problem to be studied. The delicate part of the facilitator's role for this part of action research is to guide teachers toward questions that accurately represent their real concerns and to help them articulate questions in ways that clarify the important elements. If action research is to be useful and engaging, then questions must focus on significant issues related to the success of students within the classroom.

While defining a concern and developing a question, one teacher began with some very general thoughts about gender imbalance in her classroom. She had sensed the impact of class composition, that is, 14 girls and 7 boys, on the interactions among the young students and on the climate within the classroom. The issues, however, were not well-formulated and were difficult to translate into specific questions. "Something is going on here," she noted. "But I am not sure what, and I don't know how to turn what I am sensing into a question." Furthermore, it was difficult to determine if there really was a problem and whether it was adversely affecting student success. Although undefined at the outset, this issue seemed to intrigue and puzzle the teacher, so we began to explore some of the specific behaviors the children were demonstrating. As we discussed the teacher's observations, it became clear that a major area of concern was the communication patterns of students and the teacher during large-group discussions and during times when students chose from a variety of independent and cooperative group activities. A question regarding communication patterns emerged from our discussions, and this teacher, who earlier had said she had no idea exactly what question to pursue, launched into her project with enthusiasm and commitment. Collaboration at this beginning stage of the project helped define a question that both motivated and framed the study.

The value of time spent on framing the question was further confirmed by a team of primary teachers who ultimately chose to examine the outcomes of children's participation in activities of their choice. A first-grade and a second-grade teacher in adjoining classrooms had collaborated in designing independent learning activities (ILA) for the students when they arrived in the morning. While the students appeared to thoroughly enjoy these types of activities, it was not clear whether the experiences were contributing to authentic learning. Additionally, the teachers were concerned about the types of activities certain children consistently chose.

Like the teacher whose classroom presented undefined issues related to gender, these teachers had a series of ambiguous concerns that were difficult to reduce to a single, researchable question.

In trying to help them clarify the question that would guide their project, I engaged in a series of observations during independent learning activity time. These observations and the discussions with the teachers regarding student choices and student participation helped clarify the major concern: "Were activities chosen during independent learning time truly valuable and, if so, what was their value?" Although this was a broad concern, we chose to analyze the issues pertaining to independent learning activities in relation to a curriculum framework adopted by the school. The curriculum framework served as a reference point and provided the structure within which the question would ultimately be framed: "What are the elements of independent learning activities that promote intellectual engagement and depth of knowledge?"

In this case, as in the previous one, the time spent discussing the issues with the teachers both helped them to develop a question and to analyze the issues more deeply. This type of dialogue can involve a group of teachers considering similar problems or individual teachers. Discussion at this initial stage of the process is extremely useful, especially for teachers who have had little or no experience with action research.

Although discussions at the end of the projects differed significantly from those at the beginning, all members of the school teaching staff benefited from sharing research discoveries at an all-staff celebration that took place at the end of the year. At the celebration, each teacher or team of teachers presented their projects and described the major discoveries. The teacher who focused on gender issues was both open and candid about her discoveries, acknowledging that at first it had been difficult to accept that she was ignoring the persistent requests for attention from one female student. Additionally, the fact that she was calling on two students to a much larger degree than any others in the class was an alarming yet important discovery. This teacher's willingness to share a part of her teaching that she wished to improve encouraged other teachers to look more honestly at their findings and become constructively critical of their own teaching.

At the year-end celebration, the teachers who had examined student participation in independent learning activities made a very interesting presentation in which they described the work of several children over a 3-month period. The children's work was then compared with the curriculum framework that had provided some definition for the projects. Teachers were able to see relationships of learning experiences to curriculum design, which was exceedingly helpful as the teachers worked to implement the framework. This project actually initiated analyses of independent learning experiences in several other classrooms.

Although all of the teachers finished the year with a favorable attitude toward action research, all did not begin with this mindset. Research to some of the teachers meant an irrelevant, sometimes contrived activity that usually generated findings of little value and certainly was not worth the effort or the distraction from the "real work of teaching." The interactions and discussions at the beginning of the project and the presentations and conversations at the end were like bookends to support and enclose very productive and positive experiences. Without exception, all of the teachers were looking forward to continuing their professional development by conducting action research projects.

I T IS UNLIKELY THAT by the time you have arrived at this point in the book you will have actually been through the full action research cycle and are ready to immerse yourself in the next cycle. It is likely, however, that you are currently engaged in the process, perhaps collecting data, undertaking early analysis, monitoring the appropriateness of your data collection, and so on. As the title suggests, this chapter is about examining and celebrating the insights gained through action research and the use of online resources. And although it may be premature, given the stage you are at in the process, to discuss its critical evaluation and "public debut," it is appropriate to consider some of those issues now.

Sharing Action Research

One way that teacher researchers can gain additional insight and satisfaction from their action research is to share their work with other members of the teaching profession. The act of sharing and celebrating the findings of action research is a critical component of the professional disposition of teaching that will ultimately revitalize the culture of teaching and move us from a *craft culture* to a *reflective practitioner* focused profession.

As discussed earlier, the historical gap between research and practice has also been fueled by the resistance of teacher researchers to share or publish their research with a wider community of learners. It is with this obstacle in mind that electronic sharing and publication are offered as alternatives for presenting teacher research reports as well as for engaging colleagues, and yourself, in the reinterpretation of your findings.

One technique for sharing action research that is frequently used is the use of interactive multimedia software as a way to share and engage colleagues in the text. I have seen teacher researchers use PowerPoint, HyperStudio, and Director to great effect by incorporating sound, pictures, and video into presentations. For example, a PowerPoint presentation might include a dozen or so slides as follows: Slide 1: Area of Focus; Slide 2: Research Questions; Slide 3: Data Collection Matrix; Slides 4–8: Summary of the data; Slides 9–11: Data Analysis and Interpretation; Slide 12: Steps to Action Chart.

I have witnessed teacher researchers develop their multimedia presentations with active engagement of the audience in mind. Maybe we are not far from an interactive presentation that allows participants to choose their own happy endings (as per some CD-ROM games that my 13-year-old plays with). Ultimately, the experience provides a venue for teacher researchers and colleagues to grapple with the fundamental question of "What is going on here?" in relation to the teacher researcher's area of focus. It is also a good time to try out your presentation with like-minded, supportive colleagues. For example, you could send your PowerPoint (or some other multimedia) presentation to friends and colleagues as an e-mail attachment and ask for constructive feedback.

Now is not the time to be self-conscious. Be bold. Attempt more, gain more (and perhaps experience more pain and embarrassment). Take a risk and be comforted by the knowledge that you have the potential to motivate colleagues to create meaning from the experience.

Electronic Means for Sharing Action Research

In an era of increasing use of technology to enhance teaching and learning, as evidenced by the influx of computers in schools and the homes of our students, we are constantly exposed to electronic media—the Internet, Web sites, online shopping for airfare bargains and, of course, professional literature databases such as ERIC! However, a public forum such as the Internet also provides for freedom of speech in ways that are not always socially acceptable, such as Web sites that highlight violence, child pornography, and so on. This situation is even more complex given the nature of "spyware," "pop-ups," and viruses that invade the hard drives of our computers. In short, anyone with the computer hardware, software, and necessary computer literacy skills can create a Web site on the Internet.

My assumption, however, is that most of us do not have all of the hardware, software, skills, and time (!) to develop a Web site. Furthermore, if we ignore the existing action research Web sites being used for sharing action research, we are limiting our conversation to teacher researchers who go exploring the Internet in search of new action research Web sites.

Electronic sharing allows teacher researchers to share their work and engage in conversation with professionals from around the world who are investigating similar problems. It is an opportunity for teacher researchers to learn from each other and to contribute to the existing knowledge base—something that they have not done historically.

A Word on Quality Control on the Internet

The electronic sharing of action research reports has not been without its challenges. Issues of quality and what should be placed in the public domain of the Internet are common concerns for all teachers and parents. Nevertheless, the potential of the Internet to provide a global forum for professionals should not be underestimated. The issue of quality becomes a professional and personal responsibility for those who choose to "post" information and opinions on the Internet. Associated with the issue of quality is the issue of control; that is, quality control. Who should be responsible for controlling the quality of action research posted on the Internet? Perhaps this is stating the obvious (or restating it, because we briefly discussed this in Chapter 2), but do not assume that everything you read, see, and hear online has been subjected to any scrutiny by experts. What comes across your screen could be shared by just about anyone, anywhere, and without any consideration of accuracy. You will quickly gain a renewed interest in the concepts of validity and reliability when you read postings from all over the world. This does not mean that what you find online is garbage (I wonder if they call this "space junk" in cyberspace?!). Rather, be cautious about accepting anything that you find in this medium as "published" or "refereed" just because it appears on a computer monitor. Apply the same personal evaluative criteria that you would apply to anything you read and your common sense will ensure good choices. Be a critical consumer of the information you find online.

Using the Internet to Get Connected

My experiences of teaching in an Australian primary school (K–7) and teaching at universities in Australia and the United States (and watching my 13-year-old son in school) is that teaching shares many of the characteristics of kindergarten and preschool play—as teachers we tend to work in isolation, engaged in parallel play in our own little sandboxes. It has been argued that one of the critical contributing factors to teacher burnout is the isolated nature of the profession. Clearly, many teachers find little solace in the isolation of their workplace. One of the characteristics of action research is that it is "collaborative" or "participatory." And although we hope that teacher researchers are able to engage in this systematic inquiry as a learning community, there is the distinct possibility that you will find yourself working alone on some aspect of the action research process. Regardless of the degree to which you participate in this activity with others, the ability to interact with other practitioners via the Internet can provide a valuable support system, a way to become "connected" to others with similar goals and interests.

Access to Web-based action research resources can provide teacher researchers with the sense that the world is smaller and can be easily reached from their home, school, or office computer. I was reminded of the shrinking nature of the world during a trip to Australia to visit my 90-year-old father, who appeared smaller and weaker than I had remembered him. Not only has the world shrunk over time, but so have some of the artifacts that I use as reference points—such as my dad. Each time I see him (usually every year), he greets with me with the same whimsical smile and turn of phrase, "Where did you come from?!" It's not that he doesn't remember who I am or where I live, but his reference point is a different era than mine, a time of steamship travel to fight in a war halfway around the world—two experiences I will never have. So, it was a surprise to him when I talked about being able to write to him by e-mail (electronic mail as compared to "snail" mail) via his assisted living facility's computer, or even directly to him via a fax located in the facility's main office. These were not easy concepts for him to grasp—even if he wanted to.

For those of us who find ourselves in our own little sandbox isolated from like-minded colleagues who do not offer to play with us, the Internet provides an excellent opportunity to participate in an ongoing dialogue with other teacher researchers.

What Different Types of Online Resources Can I Use?

The online resources offered at different sites typically fall into three categories: action research Web sites, listservs, and online journals.

ACTION RESEARCH WEB SITES

Many action research Web sites offer similar features and "links" to other sites of interest. We will briefly review five of these: PARnet (Participatory Action Research Network) based at Cornell University (United States), CARN (Collaborative Action Research Network) based at the University of East Anglia (United Kingdom), CARPP (Centre for Action Research in Professional Practice) based at the University of Bath (United Kingdom), Highland Park High School Action Research Laboratory (United States), and Queen's University action research Web site based at Queen's University (Canada).

Participatory Action Research Network (PARnet)

The welcome page to PARnet (http://www.parnet.org) provides the following context to the site:

> Welcome to the premier knowledge gateway for practitioners and scholars of action research around the world. Founded in the Spring of 1993, PARnet is the oldest action research web site on the Internet. Its non-affiliated institutional status and mission to facilitate a comprehensive community managed knowledge base give PARnet a unique role in the ever expanding assortment of action research sources on the Internet. (Participatory Action Research Network, http://www.parnet.org)

> Once you have entered PARnet, you are provided with the following choices:

- PARchives
- Calendar
- Websites
- Dialog
- Where to Study

Each of these headings provides you with links to areas such as the archives of the Arlist-L listserv (with an invitation to subscribe and with links to other listservs, archives, and information), a link to online action research publications, and a catalog of opportunities to study action research anywhere in the world! There is plenty here to occupy your time, but it is worth checking out a number of sites before deciding whether to subscribe to any given listserv or journal or to enroll in an action research course.

The Collaborative Action Research Network (CARN)

The Collaborative Action Research Network (http://www.did.stu.mmu.ac.uk/carn/whatis.shtml) is coordinated by a group of six members, three based at Manchester Metropolitan University (MMU) and three based at St. Martins College (SMC). CARN was founded in 1976 and "aims to encourage and support action research projects (personal, local, national, and international), accessible accounts of action research projects, and contributions to theory and methodology of action research" (CARN homepage).

Like PARnet, CARN is a wonderful resource for teacher researchers who wish to learn from and contribute to discussions about their action research efforts. CARN offers memberships to individuals who wish to access CARN Study Days, publications, and an annual conference. CARN also provides many links to other action research Web sites and a discussion list for CARN members interested in discussing issues in action research.

Centre for Action Research in Professional Practice (CARPP)

The Centre for Action Research in Professional Practice (http://www.bath.ac.uk/carpp) is housed at the University of Bath (United Kingdom). The Centre aims to provide support for teacher researchers who are developing their reflective practice. The Web site also provides links to graduate action research courses and degree programs at the University of Bath, upcoming conferences, full-text papers (written by Centre staff), and other online publications, including unpublished masters and doctoral theses.

Highland Park High School Action Research Laboratory (ARL)

If you would like to read more about the Action Research Laboratory (ARL) at Highland Park High School (United States) than what you read in the "Emphasizing Learning by Deemphasizing Grades" vignette that opened Chapter 6, I would recommend that you visit the lab's Web site at http://www.dist113.org. The Highland Park High School ARL has grown out of the work of Joe Senese and his high school teaching colleagues to meet the following goals:

- To provide teachers sufficient time to be able to reflect on their classroom experiences and to consult with and share with other teaching professionals (collaboration);
- To provide teachers with the ways and means in which to entertain new ideas of instruction, curriculum development, and assessment (experimentation);
- To provide teachers with the support to put into practice what educational research says will best help all students learn (research-base); and
- To provide the ARL teachers, their department members, and the faculty at large a living laboratory that proves that best practices can and will make a "successful" high school better (teacher empowerment/school reform).

The ARL has been in existence since 1995, and the number of teachers participating in the project grows each year. The Web site now contains links to publications by the ARL teams similar to the vignette from Chapter 6. This is a valuable Web site for teacher researchers who want to see how an action research model can be used as a model of professional development for teachers.

Queen's University Action Research Web Site

Another useful resource you may want to explore is the Queen's University action research Web site (http://educ.queensu.ca/~ar/) hosted at Queen's University in Ontario, Canada, and developed by Tom Russell. This excellent site includes links to action research activities conducted at Queen's University as well as links to the following valuable resources: action research papers presented at the Annual Meeting of the American Educational Research Association, action research assignments completed by undergraduate and graduate students at Queen's University, and links to many of the Web sites discussed in this chapter.

LISTSERVS

A **listserv** is an online discussion forum usually "hosted" by a university computer network. Different groups offer different listservs that are invitations to participate in discussions with other action researchers from all over the world. The most heavily subscribed action research listserv is **Arlist-L**, which can be subscribed to by following the directions provided by the Arlist-L homepage:

> To join Arlist, you need to send an e-mail message to listproc@scu.edu.au with nothing in the subject line, and this message only: subscribe arlist name1 name2. Of course, put your names instead of 'name1 name2'. Remember, this e-mail must go with your own e-mail address. . . . When you subscribe you will receive instructions on how to use Arlist. (http://www.scu.edu.au/schools/gcm/ar/arr/arlist.html)

A word of caution for new listserv users: If you subscribe to a listserv, be prepared to receive a reasonable volume of e-mail messages (maybe 5 to 10) per day. If you don't check your e-mail every day, this quickly adds up to a great deal of mail. Yet, participation in such an activity appears to be worth the effort. In the time that I have been a subscriber, I have "lurked" (read the messages only, and not actively participated in discussions) on the listserv and been impressed with the thoughtfulness of the discourse as well as the willingness of participants to suggest particular references that may be helpful. Similarly, the advice given to teacher researchers on how best to tackle a problem, what data collection techniques are most appropriate, how to proceed with data analysis and interpretation, and so on have been of high quality. For all of these reasons it is worthwhile for teacher researchers to subscribe to this free resource.

ONLINE JOURNALS

Increasingly, full-text, refereed, online teacher researcher journals are becoming available. Five such journals are *Educational Action Research, Networks, Action Research International,* the *Action Research Electronic Reader,* and *AR Expeditions.*

Educational Action Research

This journal can be accessed through the CARN homepage or directly at http://www.tandf.co.uk/journals/titles/09650792.asp (see Figure 9–1). The welcome screen provides some helpful information about the journal as well as subscription directions:

> *Educational Action Research* is a fully refereed international journal concerned with exploring the unity between educational research and practice. Increasing

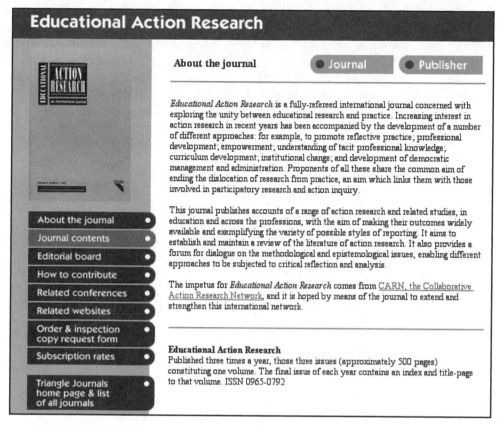

FIGURE 9–1 *Educational Action Research* **Screen Capture**
Source: Educational Action Research Home page at http://www.tandf.co.uk/journals/titles/09650792.asp.

interest in action research in recent years has been accompanied by the development of a number of different approaches: for example, to promote reflective practice; professional development; empowerment; understanding of tacit professional knowledge; curriculum development; institutional change; and development of democratic management and administration. Proponents of all these share the common aim of ending the dislocation of research from practice, an aim which links them with those involved in participatory research and action inquiry. (http://www.tandf.co.uk/journals/titles/09650792.asp)

By clicking on the "Online Contents" button, you can quickly access the journal's table of contents (by volume and number) and some articles for which full text is available. Authors are linked to an abstract of their paper and, if available, a link is provided to an online copy. In many cases the authors' e-mail addresses are also provided so that readers can communicate directly with them. This is particularly helpful to teacher researchers who wish to break down isolation and to seek feedback on their school-based action research efforts.

By providing the *Educational Action Research* table of contents online, the publisher has made a valuable contribution to bridging the gap between research and practice by addressing one of the potential obstacles hypothesized by Kennedy (1997), that is, the accessibility of research for teachers. By reviewing what is available online from a teacher-friendly journal, teacher researchers can access a journal article and even initiate a conversation with the author. This is a valuable way of seeking clarification about the content of published articles as well as an opportunity to gain advice from authors who are willing to help. For some of us reflecting back on the "good old days" when immersing oneself in the literature meant foraging through card catalogues and "the stacks," this virtual library and interaction with authors signals a giant step in the right direction.

Networks

An online journal for teacher research (http://education.ucsc.edu/faculty/gwells/networks/), *Networks* is the first online journal dedicated to teacher research that has full-length articles available (see Figure 9–2). This exciting journal has the potential to make a considerable contribution to the literature on action research by providing a forum for teachers to publish their action research accounts online.

The journal homepage also provides links to Notes for Contributors, Links, and Research News. As the homepage proclaims, this journal is an invitation to "share your classroom research with colleagues from around the world." Teacher researchers who wish to share their investigations, either completed or in progress, can submit a contribution to one of the following four sections of this online journal:

- Full-length articles (2,000–3,500 words) reporting a completed action research inquiry
- Shorter articles (300–750 words) describing a work in progress or raising issues related to such work
- Book reviews (750–1,000 words)
- A calendar of teacher researcher events providing teacher researchers with information about upcoming action research events

Contributions to be considered for publication in *Networks* can be submitted in any of the following forms:

- E-mail message to networks-j@oise.utoronto.ca
- A personal Web page address (URL) at which the text may be read
- Hard copy of manuscript, with or without accompanying disk (see *Networks* homepage)

(A complete discussion of *Networks* and other online and print journals appears in Chapter 8, "Writing Up Action Research.")

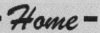

Welcome to NETWORKS: AN ON-LINE JOURNAL FOR TEACHER RESEARCH. This is the first on-line journal dedicated to teacher research.

With the help of readers and writers like you, this journal aims to provide a forum for teachers' voices, a place where teachers working in classrooms, from pre-school to university, can share their experiences and learn from each other. Join us as we embark on this exciting new venture! Share your classroom research with colleagues from around the world.

In each issue, you will find feature-length articles, as well as short reports of work-in-progress, book reviews, and discussions on current issues in teacher research. We welcome submissions on a wide variety of topics related to classroom research including: curriculum, methodology, ethics, collaboration, and community.

NOW:

Take a look at the Current Issue (September 2001) or visit our Previous Issues.

Drop in at the DISCUSSION FORUM; or visit RESEARCH NEWS to catch up on information concerning action research events. Best of all, become a CONTRIBUTOR: there's a section that tells you what's involved.

Join us as we create this exciting new venture! Share your classroom research with colleagues from around the world.

Thank you for visiting the NETWORKS web site.

| Home | Links |
| Discussion Forum | Research News |

FIGURE 9–2 *Networks* **Journal Screen Capture**
Source: *Networks* Home Page at http://education.ucsc.edu/faculty/gwells/networks/.

Action Research International

This journal can be accessed through the PARnet homepage or at http://www.scu.edu.au/schools/gcm/ar/ari/arihome.html (see Figure 9–3). According to the journal's homepage:

> *Action Research International* is a refereed on-line journal of action research. It has a distinguished international editorial panel, and is sponsored by the Southern Cross Institute of Action Research (SCIAR) within the Graduate College of Management at Southern Cross University, and by Southern Cross University Press. (http://www.scu.edu.au/schools/gcm/ar/ari/arihome.html)

The journal also provides links to other web sites and directions for how to subscribe to the journal and submit papers.

Action Research Electronic Reader

This journal can be accessed at http://www.scu.edu.au/schools/gcm/ar/arr/arow/default.html. Like the other journals, the *Action Research Electronic Reader* posts links to current and past refereed journal articles that can be downloaded to your computer. It also provides another venue for teacher researchers to publish their own stories.

AR Expeditions

AR Expeditions (http://arexpeditions.montana.edu/index.php) is one of the newer online action research journals available for teacher researchers. The *AR Expeditions* homepage provides the following introduction to the journal:

> *AR Expeditions* is an on-line professional journal promoting a creative and critical dialogue between members of the action research community including; educators in formal and informal settings, community members, university faculty, industrialists, politicians and administrators.
>
> *AR Expeditions* includes articles describing action research projects as well as strategies for conducting action research. The journal hosts an on-line continuous dialogue about issues in action research and discussions of articles with the authors and editors of the journal.
>
> *AR Expeditions* is designed to create a trusting, collegial, professional community in which action researchers acknowledge their individual expertise and accomplishments and are willing to share their risk taking, experimentation and new ideas in action research. (http://www.arexpeditions.montana.edu/index.php)

What makes *AR Expeditions* a little different than other online journals is the "dialogic" editorial review process outlined at the Web site as follows:

- The executive editor receives the article and sends an acknowledgment to the author. The article is posted for review in the editorial section of the AREXPEDITIONS web site, the article is assigned an editorial review discussion group on the web site,
- Two editors are assigned to review the article, they electronically submit their comments on the article to the editorial review discussion group, the reviewers notify the executive editor if the article is worth pursuing for publication,

Refereed on line journal of action research

Action research international is a refereed on-line journal of action research. It has a distinguished international <u>editorial panel</u>, and is sponsored by the <u>Institute of Workplace Research Learning and Development (WoRLD)</u> within the <u>Graduate College of Management</u> at Southern Cross University, and by Southern Cross University Press

The journal consists of an electronic discussion list to which papers can be submitted for comment, and a further list which carries the papers on acceptance. You may <u>submit papers</u>, or you may <u>join</u> the journal as a subscriber

 <u>Journal issues</u>

Other aspects of Action research international

<u>The operation of the journal</u>

<u>The editorial panel</u>

<u>Suggestions to intending authors</u>

<u>Subscribing to Action research international</u>

<u>Journal history</u>

FIGURE 9–3 *Action Research International* **Home Page**
Copyright © Bob Dick 2000. The URL of this page is http://www.scu.edu.au/schools/gcm/ar/ari/arihome.html. Maintained by Bob Dick.

- If the article is deemed worthy of inclusion in the journal, the author is invited to the editorial review discussion group to dialogue with the reviewers about the content of the article and their recommendations for revision, revisions are made and posted in the discussion group until the article is ready for publication,
- The article is published on the web site and the editorial review discussion group is open to the general readership for continued dialogue on the content of the article. (http://www.arexpeditions.montana.edu/docs/submissions.html)

(See Key Concepts Box 9–1 for a list of online addresses.)

Online Action Research: Challenges and Cautions

Although the use of the Internet may be convenient for some of us and perhaps even preferred over face-to-face contact (like using an automatic teller machine!), you should be aware of a few challenges and cautions.

KEY CONCEPTS BOX 9–1

Key Online Addresses	
PARnet	http://www.parnet.org
CARN	http://www.did.stu.mmu.ac.uk/carn/whatis.shtml
CARPP	http://www.bath.ac.uk/carpp/
Artist	http://elmo.scu.edu.au/schools/sawd/ari/artist.html or email: listproc@scu.edu.au
Action Research Electronic Reader	http://www.scu.edu.au/schools/gcm/ar/arr/arow/default.html
Educational Action Research	http://www.tandf.co.uk/journals/titles/09650792.asp
Networks	http://education.ucsc.edu/faculty/gwells/networks/
Action Research International	http://www.scu.edu.au/schools/gcm/ar/ari/arihome.html
Highland Park High School Action Research Lab	http://www.dist113.org
Queen's University Action Research Web Site	http://educ.queensu.ca/~ar/
AR Expeditions	http://arexpeditions.montana.edu/index.php

THE CHALLENGE OF TECHNOPHOBIA

The Internet can literally provide a "web" of connections and resources for you as a teaching professional. However, this wonderful resource cannot be accessed if you suffer from **technophobia**, or fear of things mechanical, electrical, or digital. This chapter is based on the assumption that you are willing and able to accept the challenge provided by the Internet and to profit from the interactions such a medium offers. Increasingly, graduates from teacher preparation programs (and high school for that matter) are required to demonstrate computer literacy skills. And although many of us remember an era sans automatic teller machines, computer chip cars, and regular flights to outer space, grappling our way into the 21st century technology base is, to paraphrase Apollo astronaut Neil Armstrong, "A giant step for humankind!"

Many of us face frustrations around the relatively simple act of turning on ("booting up") a computer. No doubt we all know adults (you might be one of them!) who are intimidated by computer technology and would have considerable difficulty completing such basic tasks even if they wanted to. Give yourself the time to make mistakes and be prepared to learn how to use the technology from the students in your class, because many of them have skills that far exceed our own. For example, my son has no difficulty turning on our home computer and inserting his CD-ROM game of choice. He is able to navigate through the games on the CD, and he demonstrates reading skills by being able to identify the correct buttons to click on. Using the mouse, he is also able to shut down the computer when he is finished playing. Similarly, he is able to load Netscape and visit his favorite Web sites (usually the NBA and iPod sites) and browse the Internet. Fortunately, he is too young to have accessed my credit card! Similarly, he has become adept scanning images into the computer and saving them in files to be used in a wide variety of school projects and assignments. He is also very comfortable with burning CDs of everything from the highlights of a family vacation (pictures) to his favorite songs. For the times, they are a changing!

If all of these computer-based opportunities sound inviting, but you do not have access to a computer at home or work—or if you do, and you just don't know where to begin—ask for help from your local university, department of education, public or school library, or even the students in your class. Somebody will be happy to get you connected.

THE CHALLENGE OF THE EVER-EVOLVING INTERNET

As mentioned earlier in the discussion on searching ERIC online (see Chapter 2), it is important to note the changing nature of Internet-based resources. In all likelihood some of the URL addresses included here will have changed by the time you use them. However, if you learn to use the various search engines (for example, Google, Yahoo!, Lycos, etc.), you will be able to locate anything that is discussed here even if its address has changed. In many cases, going to the address provided results in a link or forwarding address to the new location, much like the forwarding address provided by a post office when informed of a person's move to a new location. Simply update your "bookmark" so that you can return to the correct address quickly. Alternatively, you could visit the Merrill Education Web site that supports this text and use the updated links provided.

CAUTION: MONITOR YOUR TIME ONLINE

Online time can be engaging but expensive in terms of your time. This discussion of online resources is offered as an invitation to learn how to enhance your action research efforts, not as a way to devour your precious time. If you have access to the Internet and this virtual world is already commonplace for you, you have no doubt already learned to limit your time online. On the other hand, if this all sounds troublesome and confusing, then it would be prudent to take one small step at a time. Maybe, with the assistance of your school's resident computer "hacker," you can investigate a few of the sites I have recommended in this chapter and find a few of your own. (Every school has a "hacker," or "CG" a.k.a. "computer guru." Ask around—you'll be surprised at who it is! You should even check with the students in your class, some of whom probably have their own Web sites or keep their own blogs!) Whatever you do, don't let this journey into cyberspace eat up the time you have set aside for doing your action research. If you do, action research will quickly fall by the roadside to join other discarded educational innovations.

But Is It Really Research?—Criteria for Judging Action Research

As you should be aware of by now, action research is different from traditional educational research in many ways. By definition, it is research done *by* and *for* teachers and students, not research done *on* them. As such, the methods for *doing* action research and the methods for *sharing* action research are uniquely suited to its special purposes. Given these distinctions, what are the criteria for *evaluating* action research? Should these criteria be the same as those applied to educational research published in refereed journals?

Jack Whitehead (University of Bath, United Kingdom), an expert in the field, doesn't think so, on the basis that the findings of action research are usually formatted differently from the findings of traditional educational research. He maintains, "The spiritual, aesthetic and ethical standards of judgment in educational action research require multi-media forms of presentation which cannot, by their nature, be communicated through the pages of the linguistically constrained refereed journals" (Jack Whitehead, personal e-mail, 1998).

Ian Hughes, editor of the *Action Research Electronic Reader*, says that when making publication decisions, he "does not try for the standard which I imagine is appropriate to a peer-reviewed journal" and does not set "a standard which is impossibly high" because he is "not trying to compete with established academic journals" (Ian Hughes, personal e-mail, 1998). He believes that "the purpose and uses of my electronic reader are different." Because of this unique purpose, these are the informal criteria he uses when evaluating electronic action research texts for online publication:

- Would (in my imperfect judgment) the proposed paper be of potential use to this audience?
- Is the intended audience graduate students and practitioners of action research in fields including (but not limited to) health and community development?

- Does the article generally conform to accepted standards for publication in the social sciences, with references properly cited (in a format consistent within each article)?
- Does the paper contain original research or analysis (rather than being a re-hash of an existing publication)? Is there any hint of plagiarism?
- Is the article short, and written (if possible) in a simple and direct style? (Ian Hughes, personal e-mail, 1998)

Others offer additional advice about criteria for judging action research reports. Tickle (1993) recommended that teacher researchers assess the quality of their action research work and the work of others based on the following characteristics:

- **Prudence**—practical wisdom and the capacity to judge the most profitable courses of action.
- **Openness**—records, representation of action, reports of underlying theories, reviews of evidence of these, responsiveness to reviews, reinterpretations of accounts.
- **Communal self-reflection**—exposure of prejudices, both as practitioner and as researcher; engaging in collective examination of prejudices.
- **Courage**—in exposing curriculum proposals and practice, and in exposing research endeavors.
- **Growth**—a willingness to change and acknowledge change.
- **Contemplation**—living with the fermentation of understanding, especially of the theory-practice relationship, while seeking maturation.
- **Overview**—appreciating the interdependence of phenomena.
- **Configuration**—making meaningful form from complex information. (p. 235)

Creswell (2005) offers the following questions for teacher researchers to consider in evaluating action research:

- Does the project clearly address a problem or issue in practice that needs to be solved?
- Did the action researcher collect sufficient data to help address the problem?
- Did the action researcher collaborate with others during the study? Was there respect for all collaborators?
- Did the plan of action advanced by the researchers build logically from the data?
- Is there evidence that the plan of action contributed to the researcher's reflection as a professional?
- Has the research enhanced the lives of participants by empowering them, changing them, or providing them with new understandings?
- Did the action research actually lead to a change or did a solution to a problem make a difference?
- Was the action research reported to audiences who might use the information? (p. 565)

Another way to judge the quality of action research is to compare the written account of the process and findings to the characteristics of action research discussed in Chapter 1: Is it participatory and democratic? Does the knowledge gained from action research liberate students and teachers? Do teacher researchers have decision-making authority? Are teacher researchers committed to continued professional development and school improvement?

Tickle (1993) has argued that focusing too much energy on developing criteria for judging action research can have the unanticipated outcome of "freezing" would-be action researchers. These criteria, however, can help you judge the quality of your own work and decide how to improve the quality of your action research effort. Each of us who accepts the responsibility of being a self-governing professional must apply some or all of the criteria listed for judging the quality of the action research accounts that we read or experience in some other forum.

Based on a number of evaluative schema, including those listed above, I have devised the simple list of questions shown in Research in Action Checklist 9–1 to help you assess and evaluate your own action research efforts and the efforts of others.

Personal Reflection

All of this talk about cyberspace and virtual universities makes me think of my 90-year-old dad again and what his reaction to all of this would be. I suspect that it would invoke a wry smile, a subtle turn of the head, and a remark such as, "You know, son, you just can't beat sitting down with your mates (Australian for *friends*) at the pub and having a good old chin wag (Australian for *conversation*)." Maybe the message from an elder of the tribe and the message for accessing online action research resources are essentially the same—use the medium to talk to your teacher researcher friends in the "virtual" cyberspace community and enjoy the interactions

RESEARCH IN ACTION CHECKLIST 9–1

Criteria for Judging Action Research

____ **Intractability of reform**—Does your action research lead to an action?

____ **Audience**—What is the intended audience for your report?

____ **Format**—Have you presented the report using an acceptable format?

____ **Prejudices**—Have you shared any prejudices that may have affected your findings?

____ **Professional disposition**—How has the action research effort contributed to your professional disposition?

____ **Reflective stance**—In what ways has the action research effort contributed to your reflective stance on the way you view teaching and learning?

____ **Life-enhancing**—How have your efforts enhanced the lives of the students in your care?

____ **Action**—What action have you taken?

____ **Action-data connection**—How is the proposed action connected to your data analysis and interpretation?

____ **Impact**—How will you monitor the effects of your practice?

____ **Changes**—What would you do differently next time?

____ **Colleague response**—How did your colleagues respond to your findings and the actions recommended by your research?

and learning that occurs. (I haven't resolved the "pub" part of the story, but I am sure that cyberspace hackers are tackling such a pressing global problem at this very moment!)

Celebration—It's Time to Party!

For decades education and the profession of teaching have been the whipping post for all that ails society. As Deal (1987) argued:

> In the field of education, two decades of criticism, desegregation, innovation, and frustration have eroded faith and confidence in schools. . . . During these decades, schools were asked to solve the problems of the society, but to make their solutions inexpensive. Schools have been soundly criticized for not accomplishing feats that lie outside the ability of the society to perform. These have been turbulent times for educators, and there is no reason to believe that the turbulence will subside in the near future. (p. 9)

Like Deal, I am not overly optimistic that the turbulent times that teachers endured are all in the past. We continue to face tremendous obstacles: the national deficit, the spread of AIDS, terrorism and an increase in racial tension, and the poor performance of our children on international tests, just to name a few (c.f. the results of the TIMSS study, U.S. National Research Center, 1996). In a nutshell, if it's not one thing it's another, and those of us in the teaching profession are often blamed.

Although these assertions may not be warranted, over time these claims and others like them have eroded the self-esteem and sense of self-efficacy of teachers. And although being a teacher researcher is not the only solution, it *can* contribute to rebuilding our individual and collective self-esteem and sense of self-efficacy, because it provides an opportunity for us to celebrate, as a learning community, what we have learned as teacher researchers and how these learnings will positively affect the lives of children. In Deal's (1987) words, it is an opportunity to rebuild the "faith and confidence" that our constituents have in schools.

Teacher researchers can evoke faith and confidence in themselves and their schools by sharing their findings with the school community in ways that reinforce the importance of professional, systematic inquiry into one's practice and the resulting impact it has on children in schools. One way for this to happen is through a celebration of teacher researchers' learnings that may be supported by staff development funding, PTO/PTA contributions, or any other appropriate source of funding that can be located. Alternatively, teachers and other interested members of the school community can participate in a potluck dinner or perhaps coordinate the celebration with a state or national teachers' day of recognition that again provides a forum for teacher researchers to celebrate their action research achievements. As Stringer (1996) noted:

> Celebration is an important part of community-based work. It not only satisfies the very human, emotional elements of the experience, it works to enhance participants' feelings of solidarity, competence, and general well-being. It is a time when the emotional energy expended in particularly difficult activity can be recharged,

and when any residual antagonisms developed during the project can be defused and relationships among stakeholders enhanced. (p. 140)

A celebration can take many forms. Over the years, we have celebrated action research courses with poster sessions in which teacher researchers have informally shared their work using a performance of their choosing while incorporating food, drink, and music to accentuate the festive nature of the celebration.

There is no foolproof recipe for a successful party. We have all attended parties that have made us yearn to be somewhere else—even sitting in a dentist's chair has appeared more attractive! Rather than trying to suggest a recipe for a successful celebration, let's keep it simple: If you and your colleagues are excited about your learnings and express interest in "getting together" to celebrate your action research efforts, go for it. It is a great opportunity to recharge your batteries and to recommit to the process that will follow in the next action research cycle. If, on the other hand, this process has only reinforced your belief that your colleagues have nothing left to contribute to the profession, it may be more prudent to thank them for their contribution and make a dental appointment for a biannual cleaning (and hope that there is no need for a root canal)!

This Is Just the Beginning!

It should come as no surprise that I suggest toward the end of this book that now is really the beginning of your work. At this point, you have invested considerable time and energy reading about action research, learning how to do action research, locating action research within the broader framework of socially responsive research, developing your own action research efforts, clarifying an area of focus, establishing data collection techniques, undertaking data analysis and interpretation, and formulating an action plan through the use of a Steps to Action Chart. In short, you have done much work in a relatively short amount of time.

But now comes the real test of any educational innovation. Can it become a critical component of your regular, ongoing teaching practice? If you have found ways to overcome the potential obstacles to incorporating action research into the reflective practice stance you now have, you are well on your way to living the life of a reflective teacher researcher. Living this professional life, in the ways it has been described here, has the potential to change the culture of schools so that as a professional community we can once again evoke the faith and confidence of our communities in our schools and our profession of teaching.

We can all think of reasons why we shouldn't be incorporating action research into our craft culture—most notably because we are challenged by the impediments of time and resources. However, if you believe in what you are doing, you will find a way to make it happen. Call me an idealist if you will, but I am constantly impressed by the positive nature of teachers who, faced with adversity and challenges, are able to find ways to make a positive difference in children's lives. Make no mistake, that is what this action research journey has been about.

Armed with your knowledge, skills, values, and attitudes about action research, the work now begins as you routinize the practice and continue to monitor the effects of your innovations on students' learning, openly accepting the credo for professional practice and living the life of a lifelong learner. What you are learning about your practice will ultimately enhance the lives of the children in your care. If you are now motivated to continue with the action research process, one next logical step is to "Get the word out!"

Summary

This chapter explained ways for sharing, evaluating, and celebrating action research. Publication of action research stories in an electronic medium also provides a means for sharing action research with others. These techniques are viable alternatives to the traditional "papers" or journal articles that are rarely written, or shared, by teacher researchers.

The use of online action research resources can engage teacher researchers in discussion with like-minded teachers as part of a global learning community via the Internet. Web sites are valuable starting points for learning about what the Internet has to offer. Listservs and online journals are also valuable resources that can further teacher researchers' understandings of current literature and the nature of theoretical and practical debates being undertaken by the wider action research community. Finally, become aware of the challenges posed by the Internet and the need to be cautious in allocating your time and assessing the information you find online.

The criteria for judging the quality of action research include questions about the intractability of reform, audience, format, prejudices, professional disposition, reflective stance, action taken, the relationship between action and data, the ongoing monitoring of practice, suggested changes, and the responses of colleagues to the action research effort.

For Further Thought

1. What alternative techniques could you adapt to share the findings of your action research efforts?
2. How does your action research report satisfy the criteria for judging action research?
3. What online Web site resources did you identify as most helpful for your work? Why?
4. Subscribe to a listserv. What did you learn? What did you contribute to the discussion?
5. Visit the online journal sources listed in this chapter. What steps do you need to follow to get your story published?
6. What problems did you face in using the online resources? How did you resolve the issues?
7. What advice would you have for colleagues about using the Internet?

Appendix A

Action Research in Action: A Case Study of Curtis Elementary School and an Article Critique

This appendix includes a case study of Jonathan Stewart, a fifth-grade teacher at Curtis Elementary School. This account of Jonathan's study of the effects of an "altered curriculum" on student achievement in reading follows the framework for action research outlined in this text and includes a critique using criteria for judging action research from Chapter 9. The case is offered not as an ideal for action research but rather as yet another example (this time, a more detailed one) of what action research looks like in practice. This case also illustrates how action research can be embedded into the culture of a Professional Development School (PDS) through cooperative work between public school and university faculty.

After reading this appendix you should be able to:

1. Describe what good action research looks like in practice.
2. Apply the criteria for judging action research to the case study of Jonathan Stewart at Curtis Elementary School.
3. Discuss how you will represent your own action research projects.

The Setting: Curtis Elementary—A Professional Development School

Curtis Elementary School is a small K–5 urban elementary school with 256 children and 12 teachers. Located in the Pacific Northwest town of Cedarwood (population 18,000), Curtis Elementary was built in 1949. The limitations of the structure became evident when the school, like others in Cedarwood, received a grant to purchase computers for each classroom. The result—the school needed to be rewired to cope with the extra strain on the electrical system! The building is also considered to be "at risk" in the event of an earthquake and regularly undergoes structural inspections. A new wing was recently added to the school to house music and drama classes. The school also has an extensive playground that abounds with activity during the school day and a soccer/softball field that is used by community groups (such as the YMCA) for after-school sports.

For the most part, the teachers and principal have been working at the school for an average of 10 years and all report high levels of satisfaction with the teaching/learning environment. Curtis Elementary boasts a high level of parental involvement in school activities and a supportive Parent-Teacher Association as well as a supportive community. This support manifests itself in regular school-sponsored field trips, materials to enhance the curriculum (in particular computer software), and teacher appreciation luncheons.

The demographics of the school are as follows: 256 students, 12 classroom teachers, and 10 certified support personnel. The ethnic backgrounds of the students are Native American (2%), Hispanic American (4%), African American (5%), Asian American (5%), and White (84%). All of the teachers are White and most of them live in Cedarwood. Some of the teachers have children who attend the school. The general socioeconomic status of the community is revealed by the fact that 27% of the students are eligible for "free or reduced lunch," making the school eligible for federal Chapter One funding.

The principal has been at the school for 15 years and is highly respected by the teachers, children, and parents for his leadership, particularly through a period of embedding technology in the school to improve teacher productivity and enhance curriculum. The principal is described by his teachers as being "caring, thoughtful, and an educational leader," and he facilitates many of the decisions affecting curriculum and instruction through a consensus, school-based decision-making process. The principal has also worked closely with faculty from the local university in areas of program development and student teacher selection and placement in public schools in the region.

Curtis Elementary is a **Professional Development School (PDS)**, or "partner" school, with the local university. PDSs (analogous to teaching hospitals in the medical profession) are based on the following principles:

- **Reciprocity**—Mutual exchange and benefit between research and practice.
- **Experimentation**—Willingness to try new forms of practice and structure.
- **Systematic inquiry**—The requirement that new ideas be subject to careful study and validation.
- **Student diversity**—Commitment to the development of teaching strategies for a broad range of children with different backgrounds, abilities, and learning styles.

PDSs such as Curtis Elementary are "settings for teaching professionals to test different instructional arrangements, for novice teachers and researchers to work under the guidance of gifted practitioners, for the exchange of professional knowledge between university faculty and practitioners, and for the development of new structures designed around the demand of a new profession" (Holmes Group, 1986, p. 67). In PDSs, experienced teachers help teach and induct new members into the profession. In doing so, these experienced teachers also continue their quest to become better teachers themselves.

Curtis has used its PDS relationship with the university to drive school improvement efforts through action research. The partnership has created a synergistic relationship of public school teachers, preservice teachers, and university professors who can complement each other's skills. These are not research projects developed by professors to study teachers and children. They are collaborative, systematic, long-term efforts focused on improving teaching and learning. They are activities that can ultimately enhance the lives of children in classrooms. What follows is a description of the action research process as experienced by one teacher during a year at Curtis Elementary.

The Area of Focus: Constructing Meaning in Reading

The educators at Curtis Elementary have collectively agreed to make reading instruction a priority. As a team, they have decided that the general focus for action research efforts at Curtis Elementary will be on how children construct meaning in reading and how teachers can enhance student learning. After many collaborative discussions and reconnaissance activities, the members of the action research teams determined the school's area of focus would be: What is the effect of an "altered curriculum" on student performance? They defined an altered curriculum as an individual teacher's changes in what reading was taught and how it was taught based on professional development activities focused on constructing meaning in reading.

These decisions (and others like them) were based on reflective conversations like this one held at the weekly early morning faculty meetings at the beginning of the year:

Principal:	As you know, I've been working for the past few weeks trial-running interview questions and strategies with students in grades 3, 4, and 5. From these interviews, it's clear that children use a variety of techniques for constructing meaning in their reading.
Teacher 1:	One of the things I've been sitting here thinking about is the difference for our students between reading fiction and nonfiction.
Principal:	I think that you're right. I wonder what this means for the way that we teach children to construct meaning in their reading.
Teacher 2:	I read some research recently that indicated that children construct meaning by connecting what they are reading to other concepts they have learned.
Teacher 3:	That's real similar to what happens in mathematics when children construct meaning. They link their new knowledge to existing knowledge.
Principal:	Let me share with you one more story from a third grader. It appears as though she felt unable to trust her guesses about what was happening in the story, but she also gave me a vivid example of how she used visualization to construct meaning. I think that some of these examples point to how children use prior knowledge and context to construct meaning.
Teacher 4:	It makes me think about how we create opportunities for students to create meaning in all of the different strategies I use in my

classroom. But to be honest with you, while the information you have collected from the interviews with the students is so rich, I think that it's unrealistic to expect us to interview all of our students.

Principal: I think that you're right about that, which is why I think we should involve our preservice teachers in data collection. It will also satisfy a university course requirement for them. But I do think that these data are very rich and can help us understand how our students create meaning and what the effects of our reading strategies are on increasing their ability to construct meaning.

Web Sites

- ERIC Clearinghouse on Reading, English, and Communication
  http://www.indiana.edu/~eric_rec
- Reading for Meaning
  http://www.sasked.gov.sk.ca/docs/ela_mean.html
- Vocabulary Instruction and Reading Comprehension
  http://www.indiana.edu/~eric_rec/ieo/digests/d126.html
- Reading Comprehension Instructional Strategies—Elementary Level
  http://www.indiana.edu/~eric_rec/ieo/bibs/rdcompel.html
- How to Improve Reading Comprehension
  http://www.marin.cc.ca.us/~don/Study/7read.html

Readings

- Barrentine, Shelby, et al. (1995). Reading mini-lessons: An instructional practice for meaning centered reading programs. Grand Forks, ND: Center for Teaching and Learning, University of North Dakota.
- Cote, Nathalie, et al. (1995). Children's use of prior knowledge and experience in making sense of informational text. Paper presented at the annual meeting of the American Educational Research Association, San Francisco, CA. April 18–22, 1995.
- Cothern, Nancy B., et al. (1990). Using readers' imagery of literacy characters to study text meaning construction. *Reading Research and Instruction, 30* (1), 15–29.
- Dugan, JoAnn-Rubino, & Bean, Rita M. (1997). Side-by-side reading: Scaffolding meaning-making through literature discussions. Paper presented at the annual meeting of the American Educational Research Association, Chicago, IL. March 24–28, 1997.
- Hass, Christina, & Flower, Linda. (1988). Rhetorical reading strategies and the construction of meaning. *College Composition and Communication, 39* (2), 167–183.
- Keene, Ellin Oliver, & Zimmermann, Susan. (1997). *Mosaic of thought: Teaching comprehension in a reader's workshop.* Portsmouth, NH: Heinemann.
- Kucer, Stephen L. (1985). The making of meaning: Reading and writing, as parallel processes. *Written Communication, 2* (3), 317–336.
- Langer, Judith A. (1986). Reading, writing, and understanding: An analysis of the construction of meaning. *Written Communication, 3* (2), 219–267.
- Mosenthal, Peter B. (1987). Research views: Understanding meaning in reading. *Reading Teacher, 41* (2), 206–209.
- Oded, Brenda, & Stavans, Anat. (1994). The effect of "false" schema activation on the construction of meaning. *System, 22* (4), 497–507.
- Rowell, Jack A., et al. (1990). The construction of meaning from text: Possible effects of different reading strategies. *Educational Psychology: An International Journal of Experimental Educational Psychology, 10* (1), 39–55.
- Tierney, Robert J. (1990). Redefining reading comprehension. *Educational Leadership, 47* (6), 37–42.
- Wangberg, Elaine G. (1983). Instructional strategies for implementing a reading for meaning approach. *Reading Horizons, 23* (4), 259–262.

FIGURE A–1   Sources Provided by ERIC for Teachers at Curtis Elementary

Reviewing the Literature

A subcommittee of the teachers conducted a review of literature. They consulted sources already present in the school: professional journals, teachers with advanced preparation in reading, and faculty from the university. They also accessed literature via the Internet through the AskERIC Service for educators and the AskERIC Q&A service (askeric@askeric.org). A list of sources provided by ERIC for teachers at Curtis Elementary is shown in Figure A–1.

Creating an Action Plan

To guide them through their year-long action research projects, the teachers created action plans in conjunction with the principal. These action plans were used to guide and document the teachers' action research projects. Fifth-grade teacher Jonathan Stewart's action plan looked like this:

Creating Meaning in Reading
JONATHAN STEWART

Area of Focus Statement

I am concerned about the ability of students in my classroom to construct meaning as they read. I teach fifth grade and feel that in my teaching of reading I have resorted more to emphasizing volume (the number of books children read) than to creating meaning (whether or not children really understand what they are reading). I guess that by the time children come to my fifth grade class I have started to take for granted that they already know how to read and how to create meaning from what they read. As last year's statewide assessment scores indicated, I (and other teachers in this school) need to challenge the assumption that older children have already developed the skills to read and create meaning by the fifth grade. Therefore, the purpose of this study is to describe the effect of an "altered curriculum" on student achievement in reading.

Defining the Variables

As a whole faculty we defined an altered curriculum as an individual teacher's changes in how reading was taught based on professional development activities focused on constructing meaning in reading. Student performance was defined as the scores children earned on statewide assessment tests and teacher-made tests administered regularly during the year.

Research Question

What is the effect of an altered curriculum on student performance?

Intervention

The reading intervention that I implement in my class will be developed on the basis of the professional development activities we engage in as a faculty. I anticipate that these activities will include a renewed emphasis on comprehension skills and diagnostic techniques and a greater understanding of exactly how children create meaning from what they read. I am also hoping that the literature will reveal some promising practices that I might consider for use in my classroom.

Membership of the Action Research Group

All of the teachers in the school have adopted the same action research goal for the year. However, we are working individually with the specific interventions that we feel are most appropriate for the students in our individual classrooms.

Negotiations to Be Undertaken

The principal fully supports the action research process and will use individual teacher's documentation of the process and classroom observations of teaching as major components of the annual teacher evaluation cycle. I will need to negotiate my individual action research project with the principal, especially if I need to purchase any resources.

Timeline

- *Summer*—Search ERIC for literature. Do professional reading. Attend professional development activities offered by the university. Take graduate class in reading.
- *Fall*—Work with other teachers to determine appropriate professional development opportunities. Develop the specifics of my "creating meaning" reading intervention. Develop data collection strategies and collect some baseline data.
- *Winter–Spring*—Implement intervention and collect data. Meet regularly with colleagues to discuss the effects of the intervention.
- *Spring*—Analyze and interpret data and present findings to the faculty during an action research celebration. Plan the next cycle in the action research process.

Resources

- Paid non-contract time during summer to work on reviewing the literature.
- Support to attend summer institute on reading.
- Tuition reimbursement for cost of graduate credit.

Data Collection Ideas

- Interviews with students in my class.
- Observations during reading activities.
- Statewide assessment scores.
- Regular collection of student work.

Following the summer activities, Jonathan developed a formal data collection plan that included

multiple-choice activities, cloze activities, and oral storytelling activities, as outlined below.

Data Collection

During the school year I will use three different sources of data to help me "see" how my fifth graders are able to construct meaning when interacting with given passages of printed text. These data sources will include:

1. Multiple-choice, comprehension/recall activities using reading passages from grade levels 3 through 6.
2. Cloze procedures involving the students in the oral reading of a passage, at grade level, on Paul Bunyan, in which they will orally supply missing words from the text which complete the meaning of the passage.
3. Reading and retelling of a passage, at grade level, about the Bermuda Triangle (to name one example), in which the students will be allowed to read the passage as many times as they wish and to write/draw a retelling of the passage in their own words.

Data Analysis and Interpretation

Obviously, the only way I have of "knowing" that my students have reacted favorably to the curriculum and instruction changes used to implement my vocabulary focus on constructing meaning from the written work is to witness those students as they read, write, and interpret those same written words, both in context and individually. For the sake of brevity, I will simply share one situation that I have seen this year relating to each of the goals of increased vocabulary and meaning.

In the middle of a total group reading of *Thunder Cave* by Roland Smith, I was stopped by the class to recognize just how important it was that Jake, the young hero of the story, had been said to have handed a "folded" letter to a foreign official as part of a visa request process. This carried great meaning to me in that they had to realize (construct meaning) that, since the letter was to have come from his father in Africa and that he had just forged the letter on his own computer only blocks away, the insight to fold the letter rather than just bring it in flat was absolutely necessary for the story to hold credibility to both the official and the reading audience. (Note: When my class brought this passage up to the author, who visited our school in person, he had to admit he had never thought about it in quite that much detail, but he was glad that he had done it correctly by their critical standards of reading!)

During our annual Storytelling Unit this year, it was specifically brought to my mind by several of my 25 students, as they were "learning by heart" their tell-able tales, that some words used by the re-tellers of the chosen tales you just "had to memorize to use well" or the meaning of the story would change. As one student put it, "If they (the audience) can't understand that her venomous personality was snake-like, then I'll just have to add a line that lets them know that she really behaved like a snake and even looked like one at times." (Note: One student asked to be allowed to perform the same story she had done last year in fourth grade because she felt that this year she really understood what the story was about and could tell it in a more believable way.)

Student writings and rewritings show how they are constructing meaning either as a response to something they have already read or in thinking about how they want their readers to react to what they have put down on paper. For example, the following student dialogue evolved between a classmate and a peer proofreader and captures the essence of creating meaning:

"Charlie, how badly is this guy supposed to be hurt in this part of the story?"

"Not too bad. He's just got a cut on his forearm from the knife and it's bandaged up already."

"Then don't you think that gushed is a little strong for the way the blood was coming out of the bandage? Maybe it should be ooze or seep?"

When the children are having the discussions, asking the questions, and making the clarifying statements with each other, the teaching is invisible and at its highest level. Words weave wondrous webs!

Of the various factors of meaning construction I observed through the use of the data collection techniques, the most striking to me was the pivotal importance of each student "knowing or not knowing" the meaning of the vocabulary used in the story—not just the words "at grade level" that are the basic glue for the verbal presentation, but rather the "extended or specialized" terms that truly gave personality, character, and depth to the writing. Especially through the cloze procedure I was able to witness, with my own ears, the mental processing that some readers could, and others could not, employ to generate a meaningful and appropriate word choice to continue, complete, and in many cases, enrich a pre-initiated idea.

I was most aware of my students' reactions to and use of heightened vocabulary to increase their construction of meaning through three different activities:

1. Students recognize through a word replacement activity that it is very difficult to maintain the meaning of a well-written passage or sentence if you are trying to replace certain specifically selected words in that segment.
2. Students have "voiced" the feelings and mental pictures brought forth in their minds by different passages, both read and listened to, during various curricular reading assignments.
3. Student writing samples demonstrate how well they absorb and use different writing styles, voice, and word selection to create a more interesting, engaging, and detailed piece of writing.

The Findings

Based on my data analysis and interpretation, I will present the following findings of my study of the effects of an altered curriculum on student achievement to the other teachers and the principal:

- A high level of the skills and knowledge developed in professional development settings transferred to my classroom practice.
- Students understand the difficult nature of word replacement in activities where they try to replace words and maintain the meaning of a passage.
- As students have learned to create meaning during reading, they can discuss the feelings and mental pictures evoked by the passage.
- Students' ability to create meaning of what they read is also evident in their abilities to

TABLE A–1 Jonathan Stewart's Steps to Action Chart

Summary of Findings Research Questions	Recommended Action Targeted to Findings	Who Is Responsible for the Action? T—Teacher S—Student P—Principal PA—Parents	Who Needs to Be Consulted or Informed?	Who Will Monitor/ Collect Data	Timeline	Resources
1.0 What is the effect of an altered curriculum on student performance?					Ongoing throughout school year.	
1.1 High level of transfer of P.D. skills and knowledge to classroom practice.	1.1 Continue to monitor transfer of P.D. skills and to modify and evaluate vocabulary intensification efforts.	1.1 T	1.1 T, P	1.1–1.4 Multiple-choice activities. Cloze procedures.		1.1 $$ for P.D. and tuition reimbursement.
1.2 Students' understanding of word replacement strategies was high.	1.2–1.4 Continue to implement strategies that improve students' abilities to create meaning in their reading and writing.	1.2–1.4 T, S	1.2–1.4 T, P, S, Pa	Retelling passage/ story activities.		1.2–1.4 $$ for curriculum materials.
1.3 Students were able to create meaning during reading and to discuss feelings and mental pictures.				Student journal writing.		
1.4 Students were able to create meaning through their own writing.						

create interesting, engaging, and detailed writing of their own.

Action Planning

Though I have long been a person who loves to play with words and understands their massive power, I have never really tried to pass on that idea of literal word power. I plan to continue to emphasize looking for, reading, discussing, understanding, and employing the added power that well-used vocabulary can create in both oral and written expression.

My focus on vocabulary reinforcement will be extended through the following areas of reading and written expression with my students: group novels, published poetry, current events magazines, storytelling collections, student-created stories, narratives, opinion papers, descriptions, research papers, and oral presentations.

I plan to use the following in-class techniques to monitor, modify, and evaluate the impact and effectiveness of my vocabulary intensification efforts: observations of student learning, reflections with students (oral, written, individual, and group), and continued assessment using the data-gathering techniques mentioned earlier (multiple-choice activities, cloze activities, and oral storytelling activities). Students will also make regular journal entries recording their own observations of how different wording has affected their construction of meaning.

I have already implemented several teaching and curriculum changes as a result of this action research project. One helpful technique was my asking students to look up certain vocabulary words from novel selections, to know the meaning of the word as it was used in the selection, and then to try to replace the word with another word or phrase that maintained the flow and intent of the chosen sentence. Students are already finding out why the author chose a particular word for the intent of the sentence.

I am sure that as I start the next cycle of action research I will be "constructing meaning" of my own about how children construct meaning. The constant inquisitive nature of my fifth-grade learners will ensure that we are continually thinking together about our reading and how to improve ourselves. (See Table A–1.)

On-Line Resources

Throughout the year, I visited the following on-line sites to research the literature, check for promising practices and current trends within the professional organizations in the area of reading, and discuss my action research work-in-progress with other teachers across the nation:

- ERIC—I used the AskERIC Q&A service to conduct an electronic search of the literature related to my area of focus.
- Association for Supervision and Curriculum Development (http://odie.ascd.org).
- International Reading Association (http://www.ira.org)—The IRA offers grants to support teacher research (up to $5000) through their Teacher as Researcher Grants. I also discovered that the IRA homepage had links to their Research and Policy Division and links to upcoming research conferences and meetings.
- PARnet—I visited the PARnet website (http://www.parnet.org) to see if any other teachers were working on similar action research projects.
- Arlist—I subscribed to the action research listserv and monitored conversations.

Sharing the Findings

The faculty at Curtis Elementary met once a month for regular professional development activities related to the "creating meaning in reading" area of focus. Most of these activities were held after school and culminated with a dinner discussion at a restaurant or a faculty member's house. These forums for discourse are embedded in the culture of Curtis Elementary and are funded by the school's professional development fund.

Critiquing Action Research

Now, let's take a few moments to apply the criteria for judging action research (from Chapter 9) to Jonathan Stewart's action research project. Before proceeding with this activity, take a few minutes to write down your reactions to the study and whether you think that it is "good" action research.

AUDIENCE

Who was the intended audience for the action research report? Jonathan's report was intended primarily for himself and his principal, but it found a wider audience with other teachers at Curtis Elementary. With this audience in mind, it would appear as though Jonathan's report satisfies these criteria. The principal was satisfied with the detail included in Jonathan's report and felt that it provided him with another "window" into Jonathan's teaching practices and his ability to make curriculum and instruction changes on the basis of data.

FORMAT

Was the report presented using an acceptable format? All teachers' reports of their action research projects at Curtis Elementary were shared using the same format—a brief written report using these headings: area of focus, review of literature, action plan, data collection, data analysis and interpretation, steps to action, and online resources. This faculty had collaboratively determined that this was an acceptable format for sharing their action research inquiries with their colleagues and the principal.

PREJUDICES

Are there any prejudices that might affect the findings of the study? Jonathan does not explicitly state any prejudices he may have had regarding the area of focus. There is no indication of whether or not Jonathan had preconceived notions about the outcomes or conduct of the study.

PROFESSIONAL DISPOSITION

How has the action research effort contributed to the teacher's professional disposition? This is perhaps best summed up in Jonathan's words when he says, "I am sure that as I start the next cycle of action research I will be 'constructing meaning' of my own about how students construct meaning. The constant inquisitive nature of my fifth-grade learners will ensure that we are continually thinking together about our reading and how to improve ourselves." This statement appears to capture the spirit of a professional disposition of a teacher who is committed to being a lifelong learner and is willing to make changes if needed.

REFLECTIVE STANCE

In what ways has the action research effort contributed to Jonathan's reflective stance and how he views teaching and learning? Jonathan's professional disposition now appears to embrace a reflective stance and show a willingness to continue with the action research process to monitor the impact of his intervention during the next year.

LIFE ENHANCING

Have Jonathan's efforts enhanced the lives of the children in his care? It appears from Jonathan's narrative and examples of the children's voices that the ability to read and write, with an increased understanding of the meaning of the text, has been enhanced.

ACTION

What action did Jonathan take based on his findings? Jonathan implemented a reading curriculum that enhanced vocabulary development through reading and written expression activities involving group novels, published poetry, current events magazines, storytelling collections, student-created stories, narratives, opinion papers, descriptions, research papers, and oral presentations. Students also incorporated regular journal entries, recording their own observations of how different wording has affected their construction of meaning.

ACTION-DATA CONNECTION

How is Jonathan's proposed action connected to his data analysis and interpretation? Jonathan's narrative includes some references to data that informed his decision making, including observations of students as they read, write, and interpret written words in context; multiple-choice comprehension/recall activities; cloze procedures involving oral reading tasks; and writing, drawing, and retelling passages from stories. The data presented in Jonathan's case suggest a strong action-data connection. That is, Jonathan's proposed actions are connected to the data he collected, analyzed, and interpreted.

IMPACT

How will Jonathan continue to monitor the effects of his practice? Jonathan will continue to monitor his "altered curriculum" to enhance student construction of meaning in reading by using many of the same data collection techniques he incorporated into his first action research cycle.

CHANGES

What will Jonathan do differently during the next action research cycle? Jonathan will continue with his reading intervention as it was originally developed, but he is open to incorporating any new promising practices that emerge from his continued professional development opportunities. Jonathan will also add to his data collection strategies the use of journal writings in which students reflect on how they create meaning in reading.

COLLEAGUE RESPONSE

How did Jonathan's colleagues respond to the actions recommended by his research? Jonathan, like the other teachers at Curtis Elementary School, presented developments in his action research project throughout the school year. This ongoing discourse about what was being learned during the study is not captured in Jonathan's narrative, but is a regular part of life at Curtis Elementary. Jonathan's account could have included more information about how colleagues responded to his research and how it compared to the findings of other teachers who worked on the same area of focus.

Celebrating Action Research

At the end of the school year, the faculty at Curtis Elementary participated in an "Action Research Fair," during which the learning community celebrated their individual and collective insights about the impact of their "creating meaning in reading" interventions on student achievement. This event provided an opportunity for the teachers, preservice teachers, and university faculty to celebrate the action research process and to recommit to another year of professional development and goal setting.

Final Thoughts

We have now been through the full cycle of the action research process. We have read about the historical antecedents and theories that underpin action research. We have read about (and ideally, put into practice) each of the four steps in the process. We have read action research vignettes that breathe life into the process and demystify what action research might look like in practice. We are now ready to move on to the next action research cycle.

Action research is a process, but it is also a way of thinking and being. Becoming a teacher researcher means making a commitment to continually reflect on the way things are in our classrooms and schools and striving to learn what we can do to make them better. Your decision to do action research—your commitment to this way of thinking and being—contributes to the revitalization of the teaching profession. Your willingness to embark on this intimate, open-ended, creative journey called action research will be rewarded with the knowledge that our students are the benefactors of our search for excellence in education.

Summary

This appendix provided a case study of Jonathan Stewart, a fifth-grade teacher at Curtis Elementary School. This case study captured much of what Jonathan did during his study of the effects of an "altered curriculum" on student achievement in reading. The case study also included a critique of the study using criteria for judging action research from Chapter 9. This case also exemplified how action research can be embedded into the culture of a Professional Development School (PDS) through cooperative work between public school and university faculty.

For Further Thought

1. What did you learn from Jonathan Stewart's case study that can help with your own action research?
2. How would you apply the criteria for judging the quality of action research to Jonathan Stewart's case?
3. How can you develop a collaborative action research network that involves your school's principal and teachers with other educators (such as preservice teachers, university faculty, etc.)?

Appendix B

Descriptive Statistics and Action Research

Count What Counts! Using Descriptive Statistics

Data analysis and interpretation can also involve the use of descriptive statistics to help make sense of your findings. My advice here is simple: Count what counts! If it makes sense to tally and count events, categories, occurrences, test scores, and the like, use an appropriate descriptive statistic. However, I do not feel compelled to include elaborate statistical measures simply to add a perceived sense of rigor or credibility to your inquiry. Recall from Chapter 1 that action research is a very different kind of inquiry than traditional research and as such is less concerned with the claims that scientists use statistics to make. Treat descriptive statistics as one of an array of many useful tools that can help teacher researchers gain insight into their data and communicate them efficiently to others.

In this appendix we will briefly discuss measures of central tendency (mean, mode, median) and variability (standard deviation). For a more detailed explanation of the appropriate use of these statistics, I recommend Gay, Mills, and Airasian (2006). Many readily available computer programs, such as SPSS 12.0 Student Version, may be accessible for computing statistics at your school or university. Remember, there are many excellent math specialists in your school or district, so don't hesitate to call on those resources with questions.

WHY USE DESCRIPTIVE STATISTICS?

Descriptive statistics give us a shorthand way of giving lots of information about a range of numbers using only one or two numbers. For example, Chapter 3 discussed the use of attitude scales (Likert scales and semantic differentials) to measure students' attitudes, and other quantitative data collection techniques used by action researchers (for example, teacher-made tests, standardized tests, and school-generated report cards). One way to provide a great deal of information about our students' attitudes (as measured by these instruments) is to use descriptive statistics to describe the students' attitudes. For example, we might describe students' attitudes to a new mathematics curriculum (see Chapter 3) by reporting the average response to the following item on a questionnaire:

1. I believe that the problem-solving skills I learn in class help me make good problem-solving decisions outside of school.

SA .　　　A　　　U　　　D　　　SD

By assigning point values—SA = 5, A = 4, U = 3, D = 2, SD = 1—and calculating the average response, we would be able to describe, on average, what children believed about the transfer of problem-solving skills to decisions made outside of school. In other words, the use of a number, in this case an average, conveys a great deal of information about students' attitudes and helps us make sense of our questionnaire data. Without the use of numbers we would be limited to talking about an individual student's response to each question and not in more general terms about the attitudes of all of our students.

MEASURES OF CENTRAL TENDENCY

Simply put, a measure of central tendency is a single number that gives us information about the entire group of numbers we are examining. Three common measures of central tendency are the *mean* (the average), the *mode* (the most frequently occurring score/s), and the *median* (the middle score). In education, perhaps the most common descriptive statistic used by teachers is the mean. It allows us to talk in generalities and to compare how the students in our class have performed "on average" in comparison to other students or over a given time period. As a teacher you have no doubt calculated many averages, but remember: The **mean** (M) is calculated by adding together all of the scores (observations) and dividing by the number of scores.

Mean = The sum of all the scores divided by the number of scores.

For example, you administer a mathematics test with 100 questions to the 30 students in your class. After grading the tests, you award the following scores: 95, 95, 92, 92, 90, 90, 90, 88, 88, 85, 85, 85, 82, 82, 82, 82, 79, 79, 75, 75, 75, 75, 75, 72, 72, 72, 69, 69, 69, 65.

$$\text{Mean } (\bar{x}) = \frac{\Sigma x \text{ (the sum of scores)}}{n \text{ (the number of scores)}}$$
$$= \frac{2424}{30}$$
$$= 80.8$$

The mean is greatly affected by extreme scores, because it is "pulled" in the direction of the atypical values. For that reason, the median is sometimes a better descriptor of the full range of scores. For the most part, though, the mean (or the average) is the easiest, most familiar measure to use.

The **median** (Mdn) is the middle score in a distribution when the scores are ordered from the highest to the lowest. If there is an odd number of scores (say 31), then the middle score (the 16th one) is the median. But in the distribution of the math scores above, there is an even number of scores. To find the midpoint in the distribution when there is an even number of scores, we must add the two middle scores in the rank-ordered distribution and divide by two. In this case, we would add together the two scores that are at positions 15 and 16, and divide by two. In this case it would be scores 82 and 82. Therefore, 82 is the median score.

The **mode** is the most frequently occurring score in a distribution. In the case of these math scores, the mode would be 75, because that score was received by 5 students in the class. A distribution of scores can have more than one mode (making it bimodal or multimodal) or have no mode at all. The mode is the least useful measure of central tendency in most educational research: It tells us only about the score received most often and doesn't give us any information about the other scores.

MEASURE OF VARIABILITY: STANDARD DEVIATION

As a teacher, you may have been exposed to standard deviation (SD) but perhaps did not fully understand its meaning. For example, you may have received test scores for your students following administration of a standardized test with individual scores, a class average, and a standard deviation. For our purposes, it is not important to see and memorize the formula for the standard deviation or even to know its origins. It is more important to understand the concepts of variability and standard deviation, to know what they mean, and to recognize when they would be appropriate to use.

A measure of variability tells us "how spread out a group of scores are" (Gay et al., 2006, p. 308). The standard deviation is the most important measure of variability for our action research purposes. Whereas the mean is a measure of a position in a distribution of scores (in this case, 80.8 on a scale of 1 to 100), the standard deviation is a measure of distance from that mean (Witte, 1985, pp. 53–56). In essence, the standard deviation helps us to understand approximately how much a particular score deviates from the average score.

As a teacher researcher, I might also be puzzled about whether a relatively large or small standard deviation is "good" or "bad." Perhaps a better way to think of a standard deviation as it relates to our mathematics test scores is in terms of equity. For example, the mean is 80.8 and the standard deviation is 8.59. (I calculated the standard deviation using SPSS Student Version 12.0 for Windows. However, if you have a larger data set, this is not the kind of calculation you want to do by hand; although for a small data set you can calculate the standard deviation by hand.) If the data set is too large to calculate by hand and you don't have access to SPSS, you can use computer programs such as Excel or a calculator with a statistics function to calculate the standard deviation.

In our example where the mean is 80.8 and the SD is 8.59, the majority (68% to be precise) of the children scored (roughly) between 72 and 89 (±1 SD from the mean). In short, most of them probably succeeded on the test, if in fact scoring between this range of scores suggests some kind of mastery of the content. Now, let's compare the standard deviation of 8.59 to a standard deviation of say 16. If this were the case, we might conclude that the majority of children scored between 64 and 97. Again the question is one of mastery and whether or not a score

KEY CONCEPTS BOX B–1

		Descriptive Statistics	
DEFINITION OF MEASURE	**TYPE USED IN ACTION RESEARCH**
A **measure of central tendency** is a single number that gives us information about an entire group of numbers.	• Mean (the average) • Mode (the most frequently occurring score/s) • Median (the middle score)
A **measure of variability** tells us how spread out a group of scores are.	• Standard deviation (a measure of distance from the mean that helps us understand approximately how much a *particular* score deviates from the *average* score)

of 64 suggests mastery of the content. The larger standard deviation suggests that the children's scores on the math test are more spread out and, hence, leaves us to question the degree to which the children have achieved mastery on the test. For the classroom teacher seeking mastery of subject matter on a criterion-referenced test (teacher-made test), a higher mean and smaller standard deviation would be a desirable outcome.

All of this leads us to the question, "So how does this help me understand my students' mathematics test scores?" Armed with the knowledge that the average score for the 30 students in your class is 80.8 and the standard deviation of this distribution of scores is 8.59, you can make the following statements:

- On average the children in the class scored 80 on the test.
- Approximately two-thirds of the children in the class scored between 72 and 89 on the test.
- The relatively small standard deviation and mean of 80 suggest that approximately two-thirds of the children achieved mastery of the content that the test covered.

Used in conjunction, the mean and standard deviation can provide you and your colleagues with a great deal of information about the data you have collected if you have determined that it is data that can be counted. See Key Concepts Box B–1 for some of the uses of descriptive statistics.

An Illustration

In my study of change in the McKenzie School District (Mills, 1988), I administered a survey to classroom teachers. One of the items on the survey was focused on the teachers' perceptions of how the district's at-risk program had changed classroom practices. Specifically, teachers were asked to respond to the following statement: To what degree has the at-risk program changed your classroom practice? The survey included an item that required teachers to circle a number between 1 and 5

(1 = no change, 5 = large change). A total of 52 teachers responded to the survey item with the following frequency:

Impact of At-Risk Program on Classroom Practices

	No Change 1	2	3	4	Large Change 5
Number of Respondents	7(13%)	18(37%)	17(35%)	10(15%)	0(0%)

I used the following descriptive statistics to describe the distribution of teachers' responses:

4,4,4,4,4,4,4,4,4,4,3,3,3,3,3,3,3,3,3,3,3,3,3,3,3,3,3,3,3,2,2,2,2,2,2,2,2,2,2,2,2,2,2,2,2,2,2,2, 1,1,1,1,1,1,1

$$\text{Mean } (\bar{x}) = \frac{\Sigma x}{n}$$

$$= \frac{134}{52}$$

$$= 2.58$$

Mode = 2.0 (most frequently occurring score—it occurred 18 times)

Median = 3.0 (the middle score in this distribution of 52 responses)

Standard Deviation = 1.02

For fun, let's calculate a standard deviation by hand so we have a good understanding of what was involved in arriving at a SD of 1.02! Since we are doing this example "for fun," let's use the following data set of student test scores. Although sample sizes of 5 are hardly ever considered acceptable, I will use this number of participants for illustration purposes.

	X	X^2
Iggie	1	1
Hermie	2	4
Fifi	3	9
Teenie	4	16
Tiny	5	25
	$\Sigma X = 15$	$\Sigma X^2 = 55$
	$(\Sigma X)^2 = 225$	

To summarize, symbols commonly used in statistical formulas are as follows:

X = any score

Σ = the sum of; add them up

ΣX = the sum of all the scores

$\bar{X}$ = the mean, or arithmetic average, of the scores

N = total number of subjects

n = number of subjects in a particular group

ΣX^2 = the sum of the squares; square each score and add up all the squares

$(\Sigma X)^2$ = the square of the sum; add up the scores and square the sum, or total

If you approach each statistic in an orderly fashion, it makes your statistical life easier. A suggested procedure is as follows:

1. Make the columns required by the formula (e.g., X, X^2), as just shown, and find the sum of each column.
2. Label the sum of each column; in the previous example, the label for the sum of the X column is ΣX, and the label for the sum of the X^2 column is ΣX^2.
3. Write the formula.
4. Write the arithmetic equivalent of the formula [e.g., $(\Sigma X)^2 = (15)^2$].
5. Solve the arithmetic problem [e.g., $(15)^2 = 225$].

The Standard Deviation

Earlier I explained the fact that the standard deviation is the square root of the variance, which is based on the distance of each score from the mean. To calculate the standard deviation (SD), however, we do not have to calculate variance scores; we can use a raw score formula that gives us the same answer with less grief. Now, before you look at the formula, remember that no matter how bad it looks, it is going to turn into an easy arithmetic problem. Ready?

$$SD = \sqrt{\frac{SS}{N-1}}, \text{ where } SS = \Sigma X^2 - \frac{(\Sigma X)^2}{N}$$

or

$$SD = \sqrt{\frac{\Sigma X^2 - \frac{(\Sigma X)^2}{N}}{N-1}}$$

In other words, the SD is equal to the square root of the sum of squares (SS) divided by $N - 1$.

If the standard deviation of a *population* is being calculated, the formula is exactly the same, except we divide the sum of squares by N, instead of $N - 1$. The reason is that a sample standard deviation is considered to be a biased estimate of the population standard deviation. When we select a sample, especially a small sample, the probability is that participants will come from the middle of the distribution and that extreme scores will not be represented. Thus, the range of sample scores will be smaller than the population range, as will be the sample standard deviation. As the sample size increases, so do the chances of getting extreme scores; thus, the smaller the sample, the more important it is to correct for the downward bias. By dividing by $N - 1$ instead of N, we make the denominator (bottom part!) smaller, and thus $\frac{SS}{N-1}$ is larger, closer to the population SD than $\frac{SS}{N}$. For example, if $SS = 18$ and $N = 10$, then

$$\frac{SS}{N-1} = \frac{18}{9} = 2.00 \quad \text{and} \quad \frac{SS}{N} = \frac{18}{10} = 1.80$$

Now just relax and look at each piece of the formula; you already know what each piece means. Starting with the easy one, N refers to what? Right—the number of subjects. How about (ΣX)? Right—the sum of the scores. And $(\Sigma X)^2$? Right—the square of the sum of the scores. That leaves ΣX^2, which means the sum of what?

Fantastic. The sum of the squares. OK, let's use the same scores we used to calculate the mean. The first thing we need to do is to square each score and then add those squares up. While we are at it, we can also go ahead and add up all the scores.

	X	X^2	
Iggie	1	1	
Hermie	2	4	$\Sigma X = 15$
Fifi	3	9	$\Sigma X^2 = 55$
Teenie	4	16	$N = 5$
Tiny	5	25	$N - 1 = 4$
	$\Sigma X = 15$	$\Sigma X^2 = 55$	

Do we have everything we need? Yes. Does the formula ask for anything else? No. We are in business. Substituting each symbol with its numerical equivalent, we get

$$SS = \Sigma X^2 - \frac{(\Sigma X)^2}{N} = 55 - \frac{(15)^2}{5}$$

Now what do we have? A statistic? No! An arithmetic problem? Yes! A hard arithmetic problem? No! It is harder than $\frac{15}{5}$ but it is not hard. If we just do what the formula tells us to do, we will have no problem at all. The first thing it tells us to do is to square 15:

$$SS = \Sigma X^2 - \frac{(\Sigma X)^2}{N} = 55 - \frac{(15)^2}{5} = 55 - \frac{225}{5}$$

So far so good. The next thing the formula tells us to do is to divide 225 by 5, which equals 45. It is looking a lot better; now it is really an easy arithmetic problem. Next, we substract 45 from 55 and get a sum of squares (*SS*) equal to 10.00. Mere child's play.

Think you can figure out the next step? Terrific! Now that we have *SS*, we simply substitute it into the *SD* formula as follows:

$$SD = \sqrt{\frac{SS}{N-1}} = \sqrt{\frac{10}{4}} = \sqrt{2.5}$$

To find the square root of 2.5, simply enter 2.5 into your calculator and hit the square root button ($\sqrt{}$); the square root of 2.5 is 1.58. Substituting in our square root, we have

$$SD = \sqrt{2.5} = 1.58$$

The standard deviation is 1.58. Now you know how to do two useful descriptive statistics.

However, numbers alone do not tell a complete story. They inform the reader about how a sample responded to a particular item. For example, the analysis of the earlier illustration related to classroom teachers' perceptions of how the district's at-risk program had changed classroom practices is incomplete using only descriptive statistics. To complete my reporting on this item, I included the following comments that were representative of the remarks that accompanied the question, "To what extent do you think that the at-risk program changed your classroom practices?" The responses were grouped under the categories of "Positive Impact" and "No Impact."

Positive Impact

Reminded me and reinforced the concepts of learning styles and how to provide for them in my classroom.

Having insight to these kids has allowed me to be more sensitive and caring toward them and to act more compassionately.

I am more aware of needs of the "total child" as well as the student.

No Impact

No time to plan and implement all of those ideas!

I feel that the services needed for at-risk students are not available.

I was already using many of the skills.

Have been dealing with at-risk students since becoming a resource teacher so was already aware of the problem.

I believe that I have always been aware of the problem. It's only new at the district level.

The statistical analysis combined with the quotes from the teachers who responded provided me with a good understanding of the teachers' perceptions of the impact the at-risk program had on their classroom practices.

BE CAREFUL ABOUT YOUR CLAIMS

A final caveat: Be careful about how you "interpret" the descriptive statistics that you use to analyze your data and be careful about the claims you make based on the use of a descriptive statistical analysis. Be clear about the limited significance that can be attached to averages and standard deviations. Remember that these statistics are used for description, not for identifying statistically significant relationships that can be generalized to the larger population.

Clearly, this discussion about descriptive statistics is quite brief. My experiences with teacher researchers is that, like me, they are somewhat math phobic and reluctant to incorporate statistics into their studies. But as Pelto and Pelto (1978) remind us:

> In fact, not only humans but also other animals are constantly counting things in the process of adapting to their environments. Basic processes of learning, as described by experimental psychologists, most often imply some kind of counting or measurement that permits an animal (human or other) to distinguish between one condition and another as a relevant stimulus for appropriate action. (p. 123)

If counting things positively contributes to understanding your research or suggests a relationship that warrants further investigation, then consider the use of whatever statistic is most appropriate. And, if you are math phobic but still want to examine whether statistics can give you insight into your data, do not hesitate to call on the skills of your critical friends and colleagues.

Appendix C

Displaying Data Visually

Appendix C includes examples taken from action research projects where the teacher researcher has displayed data visually for ease of data analysis and data sharing with other teacher researchers who wish to "see for themselves." Visual displays of data help the researcher to summarize information that in any other format may be clumsy and difficult to reduce to a manageable format. For the most part, the data collected, using the data collection techniques outlined in Chapter 3, have been recorded as narrative in fieldnotes. However, as we will see in this appendix, there are other ways to think about data reduction so that the teacher researcher can work with the data in a way that leads to a trustworthy analysis. As Miles and Huberman (1994) assert:

> Valid analysis requires, and is driven by, displays that are focused enough to permit a viewing of a full data set in the same location, and are arranged systematically to answer the research questions at hand. (pp. 91–92)

The examples provided in this appendix are intended to be illustrative of the ways in which teacher researchers can display their data visually in order to assist with analysis of the data, as well as sharing the data with their audiences.

Example 1: Writers' Workshop and ESL Students' Written Work and Attitudes

The following visual displays have been taken from a teacher researcher's study of the impact of a writing intervention (Writers' Workshop) on the quality of seventh and eighth grade ESL students' written work and their attitudes toward writing. Students' writing was assessed using a scoring rubric that measured "voice" and "ownership" in their writing (adapted from the Oregon Department of Education Writing Scoring Guide).

The teacher researcher's use of bar graphs to summarize and represent the pre-, mid-, and post-assessments for all ESL students is a helpful way of sharing the kinds of numerical data that would have been recorded in a grade book. These graphs also allow the teacher researcher to work with the data in a manageable way and to be able to draw conclusions about individual student performance over the

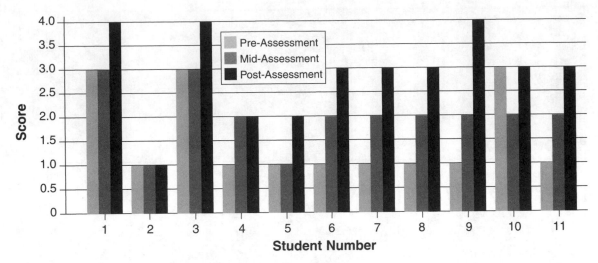

FIGURE C–1   Overall Student Performance Gains—VOICE

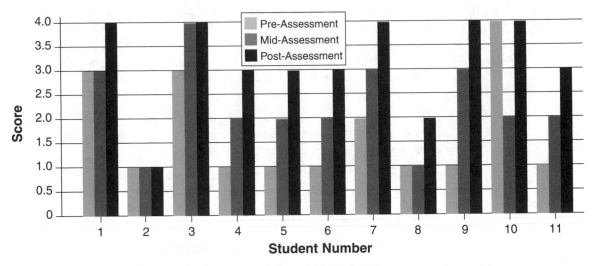

FIGURE C–2   Overall Student Performance Gains—OWNERSHIP

course of the writing intervention. Similarly, it provides the reader of the study with access to the same data—a powerful way of providing an "audit" for the outcomes of the study. (See Figures C–1 and C–2.)

Also this teacher researcher utilized a summary table of students' responses on a post-assessment questionnaire to the questions: Do you like to write? Why or why not? This summary of data, once again, allows the teacher researcher to provide illustrative examples of how the ESL students felt about writing in support of the themes "Likes to write" and "Does not like to write." (See Table C–1.)

TABLE C–1 Post-Assessment Questionnaire

STUDENT NUMBER	Question 1: Do you like to write? Why, or why not?	
	LIKES TO WRITE	DOES NOT LIKE TO WRITE
1	Yes, 'cause that's how I let out my expressions.	
2	Yes, because I just like it.	
3	I like to write a little bit, not much. The reason I like to write is because you can express your feelings.	
4		No, because I do not like to write a lot.
5	Yes, I do.	
6	Sometimes, I like writing when I'm bored.	
7	Yes, because it expresses.	
8		No, because we have to write a lot at school and I get tired to write all day and to think about all different topics to write about. After a while you run out of topics to write about.
9	Yes, because I can express myself.	
10	Yes, because it expresses my feelings.	
11	Yes, because I can tell about myself.	

In addition this teacher researcher used a similar format to summarize student responses to the questions: Do you think your writing has improved this term? How? What have you learned? (See Table C–2.) This visual display of data allows the teacher researcher to reduce the students' responses to a manageable level while at the same time capturing the essence of the students' comments. This activity also assists the teacher researcher's efforts to find themes that emerged from the students' comments. For example, all the students in this study believed that their writing had improved as a result of their participation in the Writers' Workshop

TABLE C–2 Post-Assessment Questionnaire

Question 3: Do you think your writing has improved this term? How? What have you learned?		
STUDENT NUMBER	**WRITING HAS IMPROVED**	**WRITING HAS NOT IMPROVED**
1	I've learned that it's better to make your own stories because you got more ideas.	
2	Yes, I learned to write better.	
3	I think my writing has improved a little bit, but not much.	
4	Yes, I have improved because every day I learn something new at school. I learned how to spell better.	
5	Yes, my writing is better because I wrote about what I wanted.	
6	Yes, by writing it longer.	
7	Yes, because I know how to spell more better.	
8	Yes, on spelling and commas, periods and more. I have learned where to put in my commas and periods.	
9	When I write about me or someone else I know, I learn a lot more things like writing everyday or express more myself.	

intervention—even though the overall student performance gains graphs indicated that at least two of the students did not improve—as measured by the rubric.

Example 2: Teaching Mathematics Using Manipulatives

This example is taken from a second-grade teacher researcher's project that focused on the impact of math manipulatives on students' learning and "on-task" behavior. This project also involved five other teachers' perceptions (six in all) of the impact of math manipulative use on student on-task behavior. Figure C–3 summarizes the six

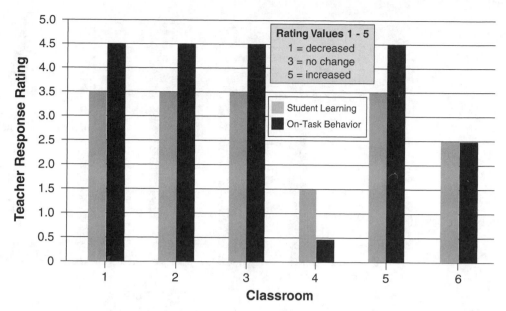

FIGURE C–3 Results of Teacher Questionnaire: Effects of Math Manipulative Use on Student Learning and On-Task Behavior

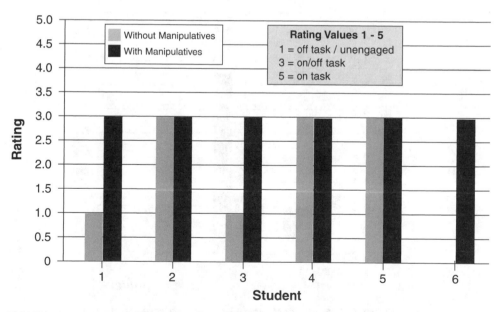

FIGURE C–4 Math Mystery Format—On-Task Behavior

teachers' perceptions of the impact of the use of math manipulatives on student learning and on-task behavior. It is interesting to note that the teacher of classroom 4 indicated that while there was no

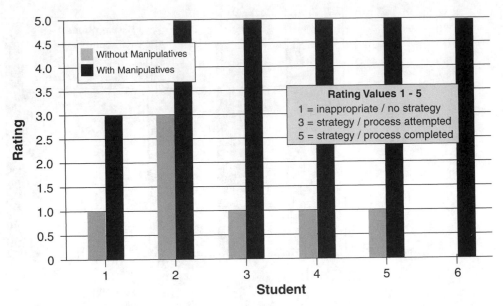

FIGURE C–5   Math Mystery Format—Strategy/Process

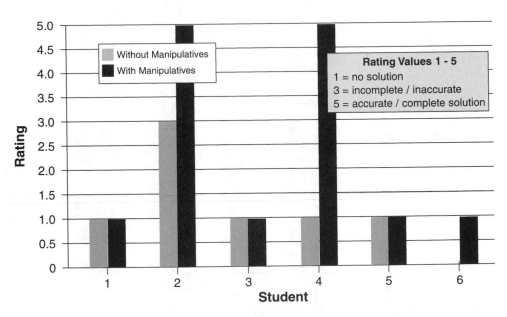

FIGURE C–6   Math Mystery Format—Completion/Accuracy

change in student learning there was a decrease in on-task behavior. This anomaly is evident in the visual representation of the data.

The following figures also use bar graphs to display the data that compares on-task behavior (Figure C–4), strategy/process

(Figure C–5), and completion/accuracy (Figure C–6) for six students in a second-grade math class over the course of a "Math Mystery" series of lessons that were taught with and without manipulatives. Again, the use of the visual display allows the teacher researcher to reduce all of the data for the six students to a manageable format for analysis. In this case, the teacher researcher concluded that while most students' abilities to develop problem-solving strategies and processes improved with the use of manipulatives, only two students' completion and accuracy improved with the use of manipulatives.

Example 3: The Impact of Book Sharing on Student Motivation to Read

This example is taken from a first-grade teacher's study of the impact of a "book sharing" intervention on students' motivation to read. This teacher researcher used a matrix to summarize the 15 students' responses to a series of questions that were given as a pre- and post-assessment and allowed the teacher to classify the responses as either a "positive change" or "no change" in attitude (see Table C–3). The teacher researcher was able to use this data display (along with bar graphs showing positive changes in student attitude toward reading) to support concluding statements such as "More students enjoyed reading during play time than before the intervention."

Example 4: Mapping Teacher's "Locus of Control" and "Movement"

Sometimes, teachers may want to track their "locus of control," that is, whether a particular individual child or group of children in a classroom demand a majority of the teacher's time and effort. This kind of data collection is greatly enhanced by the use of a visual display that records the frequency of student-teacher interactions during a lesson. In this particular example, the teacher researcher would ask a colleague to record the frequency of interactions between the teacher and the students and to keep a tally (see Figure C–7). Similarly, the privileged observer can keep track of the teacher's movement around the classroom (lines connected to numbers). From this visual display of data the teacher researcher may conclude, for this particular teaching episode, that most of the teacher's time and energy was focused on a few children seated in a group at the rear of the classroom. This kind of data would challenge the teacher to consider other questions such as "Why?" and "What was happening to cause this lopsided attention to a few children?" Again, this visual display provides the teacher researcher with a powerful way of capturing data that would not otherwise be easily recorded.

Example 5: Concept Map

In Chapter 6 (Data Analysis and Interpretation) you will find another visual representation that is a useful tool to aid data analysis and interpretation—a concept map. In this example I have used a map to outline the factors that affected absenteeism in Eastview's study. Again, this display provides the teacher researcher and reader with a conceptual view of all the factors that might affect absenteeism at the school (see Figure C–8).

TABLE C–3 Comparison of Student Responses from Pre- to Post-Assessment Survey

STUDENT	Do you like to read? PRE	POST	Do you like to be read to? PRE	POST	Do you read every day? PRE	POST	Do you like going to the library? PRE	POST	Do you like to read during free time at school? PRE	POST	Do you like to read instead of play? PRE	POST
1	Yes	Sometimes	Yes	Yes	Sometimes	Sometimes	Yes	Yes	Sometimes	Sometimes	Sometimes	Yes
2	Yes	Sometimes	Yes	Yes	No	No	Yes	Yes	Sometimes	Sometimes	No	No
3	Sometimes	Sometimes	Yes	Yes	No	Sometimes	Yes	Yes	Sometimes	Sometimes	No	Sometimes
4	Sometimes	Yes	Sometimes	Yes	Yes	Yes	Sometimes	Sometimes	No	Sometimes	Sometimes	Sometimes
5	Sometimes	Sometimes	Yes	Yes	Sometimes	Sometimes	No	Sometimes	Sometimes	Sometimes	No	Sometimes
6	Yes	Sometimes	Yes	Yes	Sometimes	Yes	Yes	Sometimes	Yes	Yes	No	No
7	Sometimes	Sometimes	Sometimes	Sometimes	No	Sometimes	Yes	Yes	Sometimes	Sometimes	No	Sometimes
8	Sometimes	No	Yes	Yes	No	No	Yes	Yes	No	No	No	No
9	Yes	Sometimes	Sometimes	No	No	Yes	No	Yes	Sometimes	Yes	No	Yes
10	Yes	Yes	Sometimes	No	Yes	Yes	Yes	Yes	Yes	Yes	Yes	Yes
11	Sometimes	Yes	Yes	Yes	Yes	No	Sometimes	Sometimes	Sometimes	Yes	Sometimes	Sometimes
12	Yes	Yes	Yes	Yes	No	Yes	Yes	Sometimes	Yes	Sometimes	Sometimes	Sometimes
13	Sometimes	Sometimes	Yes	Yes	No	Yes	No	Sometimes	No	No	No	No
14	Yes	Sometimes	Yes	Sometimes	Sometimes	Yes	Yes	Yes	Yes	Yes	Sometimes	No
15	Yes	Yes	Yes	Yes	Sometimes	Yes	Sometimes	Yes	Sometimes	Sometimes	Yes	Sometimes

Dark—Positive Change in Attitude; White—No Change in Attitude; Light—Negative Change

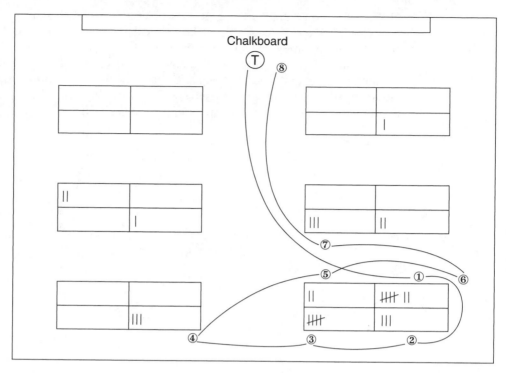

FIGURE C–7   Locus of Control/Teacher Movement

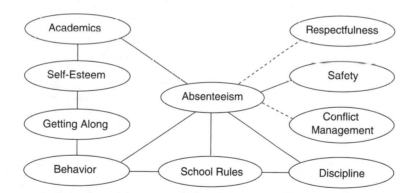

FIGURE C–8   Eastview's Concept Map of the Factors Affecting Absenteeism

Summary

The examples in this appendix have been extracted from preservice teachers' action research projects and are simple illustrations of how displaying data visually can enhance teacher researchers' data collection, data analysis, and sharing efforts. However, for the ultimate statement on the kinds of data displays that can be used to enhance data analysis, I would urge the reader to consult Miles and Huberman

(1994) who provide concrete examples of visual displays such as a context chart, checklist matrix, time-ordered display, critical incident chart, causal network, and partially ordered meta-matrix—to name a few!

Clearly, there are perhaps as many ways to display data visually as there are teacher researchers. The challenge for each of us is to "think display" so as to enhance our ability to work effectively and efficiently with the mountains of data that emerge from our qualitatively oriented research efforts.

References

Adelman, C. (1993). Kurt Lewin and the origins of action research. *Educational Action Researcher, 1*(1), 7–25.

Agar, M. H. (1980). *The professional stranger: An informal introduction to ethnography*. Orlando, FL: Academic.

American Psychological Association. (2003). *Publication manual of the American Psychological Association* (5th ed.). Washington, DC: Author.

Anderson, G. L., Herr, K., & Nihlen, A. S. (1994). *Studying your own school: An educator's guide to qualitative practitioner research*. Thousand Oaks, CA: Corwin.

Becker, H. S. (1986). *Writing for the social scientists: How to start and finish your thesis, book, or article*. Chicago: The University of Chicago Press.

Calhoun, E. F. (1994). *How to use action research in the self-renewing school*. Alexandria, VA: ASCD.

Christians, C. G. (2000). Ethics and politics in qualitative research. In N. K. Denzin & Y. S. Lincoln (Eds.), *Handbook of qualitative research* (2nd ed., pp. 133–155). Thousand Oaks, CA: Sage.

Cochran-Smith, M., & Lytle, S. L. (1993). *Inside outside: Teacher research and knowledge*. New York: Teachers College Press.

Conley, S. (1991). Review of research on teacher participation in school decision making. *Review of Research in Education, 17*, 225–266.

Creswell, J. W. (2002). *Educational research: Planning, conducting, and evaluating quantitative and qualitative research*. Upper Saddle River, NJ: Merrill/Prentice Hall.

Creswell, J. W. (2005). *Educational research: Planning, conducting, and evaluating quantitative and qualitative research* (2nd ed.). Upper Saddle River, NJ: Merrill/Prentice Hall.

Cronbach, L. J., & Meehl, P. E. (1955). Construct validity in psychological tests. *Psychological Bulletin, 52*(4), 281–302.

Cunningham, J. B. (1983). Gathering data in a changing organization. *Human Relations, 36*(5), 403–420.

Deal, T. (1987). The culture of schools. In L. T. Sheive & M. B. Schoenheit (Eds.), *Leadership: Examining the elusive* (pp. 3–15). Alexandria, VA: ASCD.

Eisner, E. W. (1991). *The enlightened eye: Qualitative inquiry and the enhancement of educational practice*. New York: Macmillan.

Elliott, J. (1991). *Action research for educational change*. Bristol, PA: Open University Press.

Flinders, D. J. (1992). In search of ethical guidance: Constructing a basis for dialogue. *Qualitative Studies in Education, 5*(2), 101–115.

Fueyo, V., & Koorland, M. A. (1997). Teacher as researcher: A synonym for professionalism. *Journal of Teacher Education, 48*(5), 336–344.

Fullan, M. (1993). *Change forces: Probing the depths of educational reform*. New York: Falmer.

Fullan, M. (1997). Emotion and hope: Constructive concepts for complex times. In A. Hargreaves (Ed.), *Rethinking educational change with heart and mind* (pp. 216–233). Alexandria, VA: ASCD.

Gay, L. R., Mills, G. E., & Airasian, P. (2006). *Educational research: Competencies for analysis and application* (8th ed.). Upper Saddle River, NJ: Merrill/Prentice Hall.

Greene, W. L. (2002). Ethnic identity and the sociocultural playing field: Choices made by ethnically mixed adolescents in Hawaii. In D. McInerney & S. Van Etten (Eds.), *Research on Sociocultural Influences on Motivation and Learning* (Vol. 2., pp. 23–56). Greenwich, CT: Information Age Publishing.

Greenwood, D. J., & Levin, M. (2000). Reconstructing the relationships between universities and society through action research. In N. K. Denzin & Y. S. Lincoln (Eds.), *Handbook of qualitative research* (2nd ed., pp. 85–106). Thousand Oaks, CA: Sage.

Guba, E. G. (1981). Criteria for assessing the trustworthiness of naturalistic inquiries. *Educational Communication and Technology, 29*(2), 75–91.

Gunz, J. (1996). Jacob L. Moreno and the origins of action research. *Educational Action Research, 4*(1), 145–148.

Hammersley, M. (1993). On the teacher as researcher. *Educational Action Research, 1*(3), 425–441.

Hendricks, C. (2006). Improving schools through action research: A comprehensive guide for educators. Boston, MA: Allyn and Bacon.

Holmes Group. (1986). *Tomorrow's schools of education*. East Lansing, MI: Author.

Hord, S., Rutherford, W. L., Huling-Austin, L., & Hall, G. E. (1987). *Taking charge of change*. Alexandria, VA: ASCD.

Imig, D. (2001). Back-to-school questions. *AACTE Briefs, 22*(9). Washington, DC: AACTE.

Jackson, P. (1968). *Life in classrooms*. New York: Holt, Rinehart & Winston.

Jones, J. H. (1998). *The Tuskegee syphilis experiment*. New York: Free Press.

Joyce, B. R., Hersh, R. H., & McKibben, M. (1983). *The structure of school improvement*. New York: Longman.

Kemmis, S. (1982). Action research in retrospect and prospect. In S. Kemmis & R. McTaggart (Eds.), *The action research reader*. Geelong, Victoria, Australia: Deakin University Press.

Kemmis, S., & McTaggart, R. (Eds.). (1988). *The action research reader* (3rd ed.). Geelong, Victoria, Australia: Deakin University Press.

Kennedy, M. M. (1997). The connection between research and practice. *Educational Researcher, 26*(7), 4–12.

Kincheloe, J. (1991). *Teachers as researchers: Qualitative inquiry as a path to empowerment*. Philadelphia: Falmer.

Lewin, K. (1952). Group decision and social change. In G. E. Swanson, T. M. Newcomb, & E. L. Hartley (Eds.), *Readings in social psychology*. New York: Holt.

Lortie, D. C. (1975). *Schoolteacher*. Chicago: The University of Chicago Press.

Lytle, S. (1997). *Action research keynote address*. Kansas City, MO: The Learning Exchange.

Maxwell, J. A. (1992). Understanding and validity in qualitative research. *Harvard Educational Review, 62*(3), 279–300.

McMillan, J. H. (1996). *Educational research: Fundamentals for the consumer* (2nd ed.). New York: Harper Collins.

Miles, M. B., & Huberman A. M. (1994). *Qualitative data analysis: An expanded sourcebook* (2nd ed.). Thousand Oaks, CA: Sage.

Milgram, S. (1964). Group pressure and action against a person. *Journal of Abnormal and Social Psychology, 69*, 137–143.

Miller, L., & Lieberman, A. (1988). School improvement in the United States: Nuance and numbers. *International Journal of Qualitative Studies in Education, 1*(1), 3–19.

Mills, G. E. (1985). Transient children. Unpublished M.Ed. Thesis. Perth, Australia: Western Australian Institute of Technology.

Mills, G. E. (1988). *Managing and coping with multiple educational change: A case study and analysis*. Unpublished doctoral dissertation. Eugene, OR: University of Oregon.

Mills, G. E. (1993). Levels of abstraction in a case study of educational change. In D. J. Flinders & G. E. Mills (Eds.), *Theory and concepts in qualitative research: Perspectives from the field*. New York: Teachers College Press.

National Council of Teachers of Mathematics. (1991). *Professional standards for teaching mathematics*. Reston, VA: National Council of Teachers of Mathematics.

Noffke, S. (1994). Action research: Towards the next generation. *Educational Action Research, 2*(1), 9–18.

Osterman, K. F., & Kottkamp, R. B. (1993). *Reflective practice for educators: Improving schooling through professional development*. Newbury Park, CA: Corwin.

Patton, M. Q. (1990). *Qualitative evaluation and research methods* (2nd ed.). Newbury Park, CA: Sage.

Pelto, P. J., & Pelto, G. H. (1978). *Anthropological research: The structure of inquiry*. Cambridge, MA: Cambridge University Press.

Sagor, R. (1992). *How to conduct collaborative action research*. Alexandria, VA: ASCD.

Sagor, R. (2000). *Guiding school improvement with action research*. Alexandria, VA: ASCD.

Sarason, S. B. (1990). *The predictable failure of educational reform: Can we change course before it's too late?* San Francisco: Jossey-Bass.

Smith, L. M. (1990). Ethics in qualitative field research: An individual perspective. In E. W. Eisner & A. P. Peshkin (Eds.), *Qualitative inquiry in education: The continuing debate* (pp. 258–276). New York: Teachers College Press.

Soltis, J. (1990). The ethics of qualitative research. In E. W. Eisner & A. P. Peshkin (Eds.), *Qualitative inquiry in education: The continuing debate* (pp. 247–257). New York: Teachers College Press.

Spradley, J. (1980). *Participant observation*. New York: Holt, Rinehart & Winston.

Stringer, E. T. (1993). Socially responsive educational research: Linking theory and practice. In D. Flinders & G. E. Mills (Eds.), *Theory and concepts in qualitative research: Perspectives from the field* (pp. 141–162). New York: Teachers College Press.

Stringer, E. T. (1996). *Action research: A handbook for practitioners.* Thousand Oaks, CA: Sage.

Stringer, E. T. (2004). *Action research in education.* Upper Saddle River, NJ: Merrill/ Prentice Hall.

Tickle, L. (1993). Testing for quality in educational action research: A terrifying taxonomy? *Educational Action Research, 3*(2), 233–236.

U.S. National Research Center. (1996). Third international mathematics and science study. Report No. 7. Washington, DC: Author.

Van de Walle, J. A. (2003). *Elementary school mathematics: Teaching developmentally.* New York: Longman.

Vockell, E. L., & Asher, J. W. (1996). *Educational research.* Upper Saddle River, NJ: Merrill/Prentice Hall.

Wells, G. (Ed.). (1994). *Changing schools from within: Creating communities of inquiry.* Portsmouth, NH: Heinemann.

Witte, R. S. (1985). *Statistics.* New York: Holt, Rinehart & Winston.

Wolcott, H. F. (1982). Differing styles of on-site research, or "If it isn't ethnography, what is it?" *Review Journal of Philosophy and Social Science, 7,* 154–169.

Wolcott, H. F. (1988). Ethnographic research in education. In R. M. Jaeger (Ed.), *Complementary methods for research in education* (pp. 187–210). Washington, DC: American Educational Research Association.

Wolcott, H. F. (1989). *Kwakiutl village and school.* Prospect Heights, IL: Waveland Press.

Wolcott, H. F. (1990). On seeking—and rejecting— validity in qualitative research. In E. W. Eisner & A. Peshkin (Eds.), *Qualitative inquiry in education: The continuing debate* (pp. 121–152). New York: Teachers College Press.

Wolcott, H. F. (1992). Posturing in qualitative inquiry. In M. LeCompte, W. L. Millroy, & J. Preissle (Eds.), *Handbook of qualitative research in education* (pp. 3–52). San Diego: Academic.

Wolcott, H. F. (1994). *Transforming qualitative data: Description, analysis, and interpretation.* Thousand Oaks, CA: Sage.

Wolcott, H. F. (1997). Ethnographic research in education. In R. M. Jaeger (Ed.), *Complementary methods for research in education* (2nd ed., pp. 325–398). Washington, DC: American Educational Research Association.

Wolcott, H. F. (2001). *Writing up qualitative research* (2nd ed.). Thousand Oaks, CA: Sage.

Author Index

Abit, H., 82
Adelman, C., 5, 142
Agar, M. H., 62, 72, 169, 172
Airasian, P., 3, 55, 75, 76, 95, 107, 113, 223, 225
Anderson, G. L., 56, 69, 90–92, 98, 103
Annice, Clem, 101–103, 137
Armstrong, Neil, 203
Asher, J. W., 96–97

Becker, H. S., 173
Bell, M., 81, 82
Berge, Z., 168, 172

Calhoun, E. F., 15, 56, 69
Carroll, W., 81, 82
Christians, C. G., 107
Cochran-Smith, M., 70
Conley, S., 156
Creswell, J. W., 17, 26, 55, 66, 107, 133, 134, 205
Cronbach, L. J., 84
Cunningham, J. B., 91
Curtis-Gramley, Mary, 189–191

Daugherty, M., 169, 172
Deal, T., 207
Dewey, John, 6

Edelman, B., 82
Eisner, E. W., 107, 113
Elliott, J., 6, 25, 26, 28, 44, 48, 149–150, 153, 154

Fagel, Lauren, 117–120
Flinders, D., 107, 109, 112, 113
Fueyo, V., 10
Fullan, M., 155, 156, 157, 158, 159
Funke, B. L., 169, 172

Gay, L. R., 3, 55, 75, 76, 95, 107, 113, 223, 225
Gorleski, John, 117–120

Greene, W., 133–135
Greenwood, D. J., 85
Guba, E. G., 85–87, 98
Gunz, J., 5

Hall, G. E., 156
Hammersly, M., 7
Hansen, L., 180
Harasim, L., 169, 172
Hendricks, C., 17, 18, 56, 121
Herr, K., 56, 69, 90–92, 98, 121
Hersh, R. H., 15
Holmes Group, 212
Hord, S., 156
Huberman, A. M., 231, 239–240
Hughes, Ian, 204, 205
Huling-Austin, L., 156

Imig, D., 3–4
Isaacs, A., 81, 82

Jackson, P., 12
Jones, J. H., 104
Jones, S. C., 81
Joyce, B. R., 15

Kemmis, Stephen, 5, 6, 15, 16, 26, 29, 44, 47, 48
Kennedy, M. M., 7, 11, 12, 13, 162, 178, 198
Kincheloe, J., 85
Koorland, M. A., 10
Kottkamp, R. B., 10

Lamott, 175
Levin, D., 168–169, 172
Levin, M., 85
Lewin, Kurt, 5, 15, 121, 142
Lieberman, A., 155, 156
Lortie, D. C., 12
Lytle, S., 2, 70

Malinowski, 173
Marland, Alyson, 81–83

Maxwell, J. A., 87–90, 98
McKibben, M., 15
McMillan, J. H., 58
McTaggart, R., 26, 29, 44, 47, 48
Meehl, P. E., 84
Migram, S., 104
Miles, M. B., 231, 239–240
Miller, L., 155, 156
Mills, G. E., 3, 43, 55, 60, 75, 76, 84, 95, 104, 113, 125, 137, 167, 168, 172, 180, 223, 225, 226
Mitchell, Cathy, 23–24, 57, 62, 135, 157, 158

Nihlen, A. S., 56, 90–92, 96, 98, 121
Noffke, S., 5, 6

Osterman, K. F., 10

Patton, M. Q., 65
Pelto, G. H., 56, 58, 76, 84, 230
Pelto, P. J., 56, 58, 76, 84, 230

Reston, Jack, 91, 130, 131, 141–142, 143, 149, 152, 156, 157
Rockford, James, 51–55, 56, 57, 66, 71, 158
Rutherford, W. L., 156

Sagor, Richard, 16, 26, 29, 56, 96
Sarason, S. B., 151, 155
Schrum, L., 168, 172
Senese, Joe, 117–120
Smith, L. M., 107, 108
Smith, Roland, 216
Soltis, J., 107
South, Deborah, 1–2, 19, 57, 122–123, 136, 153, 156, 157
Spradley, J., 58
Stenhouse, L., 17

Stewart, Jonathan, 211, 215, 216,
    218, 220, 221, 222
Stringer, E. T., 7, 16, 18, 56, 89, 126,
    129, 130, 131, 135, 207–208
Swanson, Paul, 117–120

Tickle, L., 205, 206

Valentin, D., 82
Van de Walle, J. A., 82
Vockell, E. L., 96–97

Wells, Gordon, 16, 17, 56
Whitehead, Jack, 204
Witte, R. S., 225

Wolcott, H. F., 20, 56, 57, 60, 61,
    87, 92–94, 95, 98, 107, 135,
    136, 137, 162, 175, 186

Subject Index

Absenteeism, 91, 141–142, 142–143, 152, 156, 158, 237

Accomplishment, as reason to write, 164

Accuracy
ethics and, 110–111
of on-line resources, 192–193

Action Plan, 170–171, 175–176, 182, 186–187
checklist for, 47

Action planning, 14, 140–160.
See also Action Research Plan
case study on, 141–142
challenges in, 151–152
change and resistance to, 152
collaboration and, 153
common elements, 18–19
definition of, 140
developing, 20
difficult truths and, 153
educational change and, 155–159
forums to share data from, 154
hurdles to, 151
individual, 145, 149–150
levels of, 145, 149–150
ongoing, 151, 208–209
questions, 160
in reading research, 219
reflective practices for, 151
resources scarcity and, 152
schoolwide, 145, 150
steps-to-action chart for, 143, 146–148, 218
steps-to-action checklist, 149
summary of, 160
teacher's gain in, 159
team, 145, 150
time for, 154–155

Action research, 1–20. *See also*
Action research on-line;
Action research plan; Action
research reporting
area of focus for, 23–49
article, sample, 166–172

case study. *See* Case studies;
Curtis Elementary School
case study
celebrating, 207–208, 222
central tenets of, 168
checklist of, 15
course, 167
criteria for judging, 204–206, 211, 220
critical, 6–7, 8, 20
as daily teaching practice, 14–15
definition of, 5
and descriptive statistics, 223–230
and educational change, 12–13
educational reform intractability and, 13
effects of teaching on Web, 166–172
emancipatory, 6
ethics in, 103–104
evaluating, 204
as fad, 13–14
goals and rationale for, 8, 10, 20, 155
grants for, 152, 219
impact on practice, 10–13
informed consent in, 104–106
journals, 176–178. *See also*
Journals, refereed; On-line
action research journals
justifying, 10–13
models, 15–17
ongoing, 151, 208–209
on-line. *See* On-line resources
origins, 5–6
outcome of, 142
overview, 2–5
personal bias in, 97
persuasiveness/authoritativeness of, 11–12
practical, 7, 9, 20
in practice, 211
process of, 5, 15–20, 19, 222
steps in, 19, 20

as reflective process, 17, 18
relevance of, 12
role of ethics, 107
sharing, 188–209, 219
student motivation research case study, 1–2
summary, 18–19, 20
teacher access to findings of, 12
team approach, 120
theoretical foundations of, 6–7, 8, 9
traditional research *versus*, 3–4, 223
Web sites for, 154, 194–196
writing up, 162–187

Action research article, 166–172

Action research cycle
Calhoun's, 15, 17
Creswell's, 17
Hendricks', 17
Lewin's, 15
Wells' idealized model of, 16, 17

Action Research Electronic Reader (on-line journal), 154, 200

Action research group
membership of, 45–46

Action Research Interacting Spiral (Stringer's), 18

Action Research International (on-line journal), 154, 200, 201
home page, 201

Action Research Laboratory, Highland Park High School, 117–120

Action Research Plan
area of focus statement, 44
checklist for, 47
data collection taxonomy, 73
implementing, 168–169
intervention/innovation description, 45
negotiations for implementing, 46
outline for, 175–176

preliminary data collection ideas, 47
refining, 76–77
research group membership description, 45–46
research questions development, 45
resources statement for, 46–47
steps in, 44, 166
structures in, 176–178
timeline for, 46
variables definition, 44–45
Action research process, steps in, 19
Action Research Process (Hendricks'), 18
Action research reporting
audience for, 220
as celebrations, 207–208
checklist for evaluating, 206
format for, 220
quality characteristics in, 205
Action research validity, criteria for, 85–91
Action research validity strategies, 92–95
accurate outcomes reporting, 92–93
candid approach, 93–94
complete recording, 93–94
early data recording, 93
feedback, 94
listening-to-talking ratio, 92
observational accuracy, 92–93
primary data recording, 93
Active participant observer, 58
Adequate Yearly Progress (AYP), 74
American Psychological Association. See also APA style manual
general ethical principles, 104
Analysis extension, data interpretation and, 135
Annotated action research article, 166–172
Annual Review of Psychology, 33
Anonymity of research subjects, 105
Antecedents/consequences analysis, 131
APA style manual, 187
abbreviations, 180
choosing a "journal" style, 179

conventions, 179–180
format and style, 165–166
punctuation, 179
reference formats (examples), 165
reference style, 180
spelling, 180
Appropriate sharing of data interpretation, 137–138
AR Expeditions (on-line journal), 200, 202
Archival documents, 78–79
Area of focus, 25, 26, 213, 215. See also Focus identification
Arlist-L (action research listserv), 196, 219
Artifacts, 72–73, 85, 170
AskEric Q&A service, 215, 219
Association for Supervision and Curriculum Development (ASCD), 36, 219
Assumptions, taken-for-granted, 7, 143
action research findings and, 13
origins of school-based, 10–11
Attendance at school, 141–142
Attitude scales, 74–75
as source of research data, 74–75
Audiotapes, 71–72
"Audit trail" for data collection, 86
Authority, restructuring relationships of, 155–156

Billabong Elementary School case study, 101–103, 107, 137, 156
Blind review, 177–178
Bottom-up strategies, action planning and, 156
Buckley Amendment, 105, 106
Buros Institute of Mental Measurements, 76
Bush, George W., and education agenda, 3–4

Calhoun, E. F.
action research cycle diagram, 17
California Achievement Test, 84
Candid approach to research, 93–94
CARN (Collaborative Action Research Network) Web site, 194–195

CARPP (Centre for Action Research in Professional Practice) Web site, 195
Case studies
in action planning, 141–142
action research collaborations, 189–191
action research in practice, 211–213
about area of focus, 23–24
about creating meaning in reading, 215–219
of Curtis Elementary School, 211–213
in data analysis and interpretation, 117–120
about data collection techniques, 51–55
in deemphasizing grades, 117–120
in interactive teen theater, 23–24, 135
in reflection on action research, 51–55
in student motivation, 1–2
Catalytic validity, 91, 92
Celebrations, action research reporting and, 207–208
Central tendency, measures of, 224–225, 226
Change. See also Educational change
educational, conditions for, 155–159
nature of, 152
Change agents, identification of, 157
Chapter One, 212
Chat room, 167, 171
Checklists, action
action plan, 47
daily teaching practice, 15
data analysis techniques, 132
data interpretation techniques, 138
ethical guidelines, 114
focus identification, 26
judging action research, 206
reconnaissance in, 28
steps to action, 149
validity of action research, 95
Wolcott's strategies, 95
Children, enhancing lives of, 8, 10, 221

Clarification, as reason to write, 164
Classroom
    and predictability, 12
    and routines, 12
    Web-based, 166–172
Coding for data analysis, 124–126
    demographic, 134–135
Collaboration
    action planning and, 150
Collaborative Action Research
        Network (CARN) Web site,
        194–195
Communication
    listserv, 169–170
    in Web-based education,
        169–170
Computer software
    for data analysis, 132–135
    NUD*IST 6, 133–135
Concept map, 130, 237, 239
Concept mapping, 130
Confidentiality, 105
    importance of, 109
Confirmability
    credibility checking and, 86–87
    of data, 86–87
Consent, informed, 104–106
Consequences analysis, 131
Contemplation, quality action
        research and, 205
Context descriptions, transferability
        checking and, 86
Control group, 3
Correspondence education, 168
Courage, quality action research
        and, 205
Credibility of research, 85–86
Critical action research, 6–7, 8
    values, 7
Critical friends' advice,
        interpretation and, 136
CSTEEP: The Center for the Study
        of Testing, Evaluation, and
        Educational Policy site, 34
Curriculum, altered, 213, 215,
        221, 222
Curtis Elementary School, 211, 212,
        213, 215, 219, 220, 222
    Action Research Fair
        (celebration), 222
    area of focus for, 213–214
    case study, 215–219

critique of, 220–222
on-line resources for, 214
setting of, 211–213
sharing findings of, 219
Stewart's action plan, 215–219

Data, visual displays of, 223–230
Data analysis, 14, 19, 20, 116–138,
        169–170. See also Data
        interpretation
    case study about, 117–120
    and descriptive statistics, 223–230
    ongoing, 121–122
    premature action and, 121–122
    role of, 122–123
    summary, 138
Data analysis techniques, 123–125
    antecedents/consequences
        analysis, 131
    checklist for, 132
    coding, 124–126
    computer software and, 133–135
    concept mapping, 130
    findings display, 131, 223–230
    key questions, 126, 129
    missing items statement,
        131–132
    organizational review, 129–130
    theme identification, 123
Data collection, 14, 19, 20, 169,
        180. See also Data collection
        considerations; Data
        collection techniques; Data
        matrix; Data sources
    preliminary ideas for, 47, 216
Data collection considerations, 80–98
    Anderson, Herr, and Nihlen's
        validity criteria, 90–92
    case study about, 81–83
    confirmability, 86–87
    credibility, 85–86
    dependability, 86
    ethics and, 103–114
    generalizability, 89
    Guba's validity criteria, 85–87
    Maxwell's validity criteria, 87–90
    personal bias in, 97
    reliability, 84
    transferability, 86
    validity, 84–96
    Wolcott's validity strategies,
        92–95

Data collection techniques, 50–78,
        143–145, 216
    from archival documents,
        68–69
    attitude scales, 74–75
    case study about, 51–55
    components of, 72
    direct observation, 57–61
    enquiring, 61–68, 73
    examining, 68–73, 73
    experiencing, 57–61, 73
    group interview technique, 62
    interviews, 62–65
    from journals, 69–70
    map construction, 70
    observation, 57–59
    qualitative, 55–57
    quantitative, 55, 73–76
        attitude scales, 74–75
        other measurements, 76
        school-generated report
            cards, 74
        semantic differential, 75–76
        standardized tests, 74
        teacher-made tests, 73–74
    questionnaires, 67–68
    summary, 77
    taping/recording, 71–72, 108
Data interpretation, 14, 19, 20,
        116–138, 169–170
    appropriate sharing of,
        137–138
    case study about, 117–120
    descriptive statistics for,
        223–230
    role of, 122–123
    summary, 138
Data interpretation techniques,
        135–137
    analysis extension, 135
    checklist for, 139
    critical friends' advice and, 136
    literature findings
        contextualization, 136–137
    personal experience connection
        to findings, 136
    theory for, 137
Data matrix, example, 52
Data sources, 68, 169–170
Deception and ethics, 106
    guidelines, 109–110
Democratic validity, 90–91

Democratic value of critical action research, 7
Deontological ethics, 112–113
Dependability, credibility checking and, 86
Descriptive activities, reconnaissance for, 27–28
Descriptive statistics. *See* Statistics, descriptive
Descriptive validity, 87–88
Developing Educational Standards site, 35
Dialectic Action Research Spiral, 19–20, 167
Dialogic validity, 91, 92
Discussion board. *See* Chat room
Displays of data, 223–230
Dissertation Abstracts, 32, 33
Documents, archival, 68–69

Eastview School, 91, 153
  concept map, 130, 239
Ecological ethics, 113
Education, correspondence, 168
Education Department, U.S., 35
Education Index, 31–32
Education Week site, 34
Educational Action Research (on-line journal), 154, 177, 196–198
  home page, 197
  publishing guidelines for, 176–177
Educational change, 3, 155–156
  and action planning, 140–160
  action research and, 12–13
  every person as a change agent, 157
  hope as a critical resource in, 158–159
  nature of, 157
  outcomes, and students' benefit, 158
  positive, 3
  power/authority relationships restructuring and, 155–156
  school culture and, 157
  teacher support during, 156–157
  top-down or bottom-up strategies for, 156
Educational Leadership, 36
Educational research, negative aspects of, 6–7

Educational Resources Information Center. *See* ERIC
Edward G. Begle Grant, 183
Electronic publication of texts, 188
E-mail, 170
E-mail interviews, 66–67
Empowerment, as a reason to write, 164
Enhancing value of critical action research, 7, 8, 10
ERIC (Educational Resources Information Center), 30–31, 37, 51, 214, 216
  AskEric, 215, 219
  best starting point for, 31
  on CD-ROM, 37
  Curtis Elementary sources from, 214
  descriptors, 31
  ED or EJ designations, 31
  Eric Search, 31
  getting information from, 31
  how to conduct a search, 31
ESL (English as a Second Language), 231–234
Ethics
  accuracy and, 110–111
  in action research, 103–114
  anonymity, 105
  checklist for, 114
  confidentiality and, 105, 109
  and deception, 106
  deontological, 112–113
  ecological, 113
  Finders' framework for, 112–114
  guidelines, 103–112
  informed consent and, 104–106, 107
  protection from harm, 105
  relational, 113
  social principles and, 109
  summary, 114
  utilitarian, 112
Ethnograph, 133
Evaluative validity, 89, 90
Excite (search engine), 34
Experiment, 3
Experimental group, 3
Experimentation in Professional Development Schools, 212–213

Explanatory activities, reconnaissance and, 28

Family Educational Rights and Privacy Act (FERPA), 105, 106
Feedback, 94, 150, 151
  writing for, 184–185
Fieldnotes, 59–60
  accurate recording of, 92–93
  early recording of, 93
  fresh perspective for, 61
  limitations, 59–60
  of paradoxes/contradictions, 61
  what to record, 60–61
Fieldwork strategies, 57
  enquiring, 61–68
  examining, 68–73
  experiencing, 57–61
Films, 71–72
Findings sharing/displays, 153, 188, 191–193
  Curtis Elementary School, 219
  data analysis and, 131
  visual display of, 223–230
Focus groups, 65–66
Focus identification, 19, 20, 22–49
  case study about, 23–24
  checklist for, 26
  clarifying general idea and, 25–26
  criteria for, 26
  interactive teen theater research and, 23–24
  literature review for, 29–45
  questions, 48
  reconnaissance for, 26–28
  statement, 44, 168, 180
  summary, 48
Forms
  student anecdotal record, 64
Forum to share action planning data, 154

Generalizability, 89, 96–97
  relevance versus, 98
Goals of traditional educational research, 3
Google (search engine), 34
Grading systems, research on, 117–120
Grants for action research, 152, 219
Growth, quality action research and, 205

Guidelines
  for ethics, 103–112
  for submission to journals,
    178–179
  for writing, 173–175

Highland Park High School, Action
    Research Laboratory case
    study, 26, 117–120, 129, 136,
    156, 195
Hope as critical resource, 158–159
HyperRESEARCH, 133
Hyperstudio (interactive multimedia
    software), 191
Hypothesis, 3

Idealized Model of Action Research
    Cycle, Wells', 16, 17
Independent learning activities
    (ILA), 190
Individual action planning, 145,
    149–150
Informal ethnographic interview,
    62–63
Information gathering, 26–28
    descriptive activities for,
      27–28
    explanatory activities for, 28
    self-reflection and, 26–27
Informed consent, 104–106, 107
    guidelines, 108–109
    parental consent form, 111
    sample cover letter, 110
    written consent, 106
Infoseek (search engine), 34
Institutional Review Board (IRB)
    membership and procedures,
      105–106
Instruction, Web-based (WBI), 169
    isolation and, 171
Interactive multimedia software,
    191–192
Interactive teen theater research,
    23–24
Interim analysis, 121
International Reading Association
    (IRA), 36, 183, 219
Internet, 136. See also On-line
    resources; Web sites
    action research chat rooms,
      167, 171
    ERIC, 30–31

getting connected via, 193
quality control on, 192–193
search engines, 34
searches, 34–35
sharing action research, 192
skills, 171
Internet Resources for Special
    Education, 35
Interpretation of data. See Data
    analysis; Data interpretation;
    Data interpretation
    techniques
Interpretive validity, 88
Intervention/innovation
    description, 45, 48
    reading, 215, 216–217
    writing, 231–234
Interview(s), 169–170
    attitude scales, 74–75
    coding, 126, 127–129
    components of, 64–65
    by e-mail, 66–67
    focus group, 65–66
    informal ethnographic, 62–63
    note taking, 65
    privacy and, 65
    questionnaires, 67–68
    recording, 64
    structured formal, 64–65
Isolation and Web-based
    education, 171

*Journal for Research in
    Mathematics Education,* 36
*Journal of Adolescent and Adult
    Literacy,* 36
*Journal of College Science
    Teaching,* 36
*Journal of Curriculum and
    Supervision,* 36
Journals. See also On-line action
    research journals
    data collection, 69–70, 93
    length, 183–184
    on-line, 154, 177, 196–202
    refereed, 37, 177, 188, 196, 204
    specific journals, 176–178
    submission guidelines, 178–179

Key Concepts
    action research
      critical perspectives, 8

practical perspectives, 9
    process, 19
components of effective
    observation, 62
components of interviewing, 66
components of records, 72
criteria for validity of qualitative
    research
      Anderson's, 92
      Guba's, 87
      Maxwell's, 90
      Wolcott's, 95
data collection taxonomy, 73
descriptive statistics, 226
on-line addresses, 202
quantitative data collection, 76
research comparisons, 4
Key questions for data analysis,
    126, 129

LAAP (Learning Anywhere,
    Anytime Project), 167
Learning styles, and Web-based
    education, 171
Lewin, Kurt
    Action Research Cycle, 16
Library, university, 36–37
Life enhancement, 10, 221
Life in Classrooms (Jackson), 12
Likert scales, 75, 223
Listening-to-talking ratio, research
    validity and, 92
Listservs, 167, 196, 209
Literature matrix, 42, 43
    sample, 43
Literature review, 29–45, 168–169,
    182, 215
    abstracting, 38–39
    analyzing, organizing, and
      reporting the literature,
      39–41
    concluding statement, 42, 44
    ERIC, 30–31
    evaluating sources, 37
    guidelines for technical
      writing, 40
    matrix, 42, 43
    professional organization
      membership and, 35–36
    promising practices and, 29–30
    in university libraries, 36–37
    writing, 42–44

Locus of control, teacher's, 237, 239
Lycos (search engine), 34, 204

Map construction, data collection
    and, 70
    example of, 70–71
Mapping concept, 130
Math, teaching with manipulatives,
    234–237
Mathematics Education Trust, 183
Mathematics Teacher, 36
Mathematics Teaching in the
    Middle School, 36
Matrix
    data, 52
        example of, 57, 78
    as organizing tool, 43
    triangulation, 57
Maxwell, J. A.
    key validity concepts of, 90
McKenzie School District, 226
Mean, statistical, 223, 224
Measure of variability, 226
Median, statistical, 223, 224–225
Member checks, credibility
    checking and, 86
Mental Measurements Yearbooks
    (MMYs), 76
Merriam-Webster Collegiate
    Dictionary, 180
Mills, G. E.
    sample annotated action
        research article, 166–172
    sample literature matrix, 43
Missing items statement, data
    analysis and, 131–132
Mixed-methods research designs, 4–5
Mode, statistical, 223, 224, 225
Model, action research, 167
Motivation
    case study, 1–2
    to read, 237, 238
Multiplication facts case study,
    81–83

National Center for Education
    Statistics site, 35
National Council for the Social
    Studies (NCSS), 36
National Council of Teachers of
    Mathematics (NCTM), 36, 88,
    101, 183

National Research Act (1974), 105
National Science Teachers
    Association (NSTA), 36
Negotiations for implementing
    action research plan, 46
Networking, 149–150
Networks (on-line journal), 154,
    198–199
    home page (screen-view), 199
    publication guidelines, 176, 177
NewJour site, 34
"No Child Left Behind" (NCLB), 3–4
    testing emphasis, 74
Note taking, 65
NUD*IST 6, 133–135
    description chart, 134

Objectivity, 6
Observation, direct, 57–61
    accurate recording of, 92
    early recording of, 93
    fieldnotes and, 59–60
    of paradoxes, 61
    by participant observer, 57–58
    by passive observer, 59
    persistent, 85
    purpose of, 57
On-line action research journals,
    196–202. *See also* Journals
    publishing criteria for, 176–177
Online Journal for School
    Mathematics, 36
On-line learning, problems in, 169.
    See also Web-based teaching
On-line resources, 171, 199–202,
    219. *See also* ERIC
    accuracy of, 192–193
    addresses for, 202, 214
    Arlist-L, 196
    challenges/concerns of, 202–204
    changing nature of, 203
    Internet connections for,
        194–196
    journals, 154, 196–202
    listservs, 196
    for literature review, 35
    for reading research, 219
    reflective practice and, 206–207
    technophobia and, 203
    time spent using, 204
    types of, 194–202
    Web sites, 154, 194–196

Openness, quality action research
    and, 205
Oregon Department of Education
    Writing Scoring Guide, 231
Oregon university system, 167
Organizational review, 129–130
Outcome validity of research, 91
Outcomes, students' benefit and,
    158
Outlines, 40–41
    Action Research Report,
        175–176
    other structures, 176–178
Overlap methods, dependability
    checking and, 86
Overview, quality action research
    reporting, 205

Parental consent form, 111
PARnet, 194, 219
Participant observer, 57–58
    active, 58
    fieldnotes of, 59–60
    purposes of, 58
Participatory Action research
    Network (PARnet),
    194, 219
Passive observer, 59
Peer debriefing, credibility and, 85
Personal bias in research, 97, 220
Personal experience connection to
    findings, data interpretation
    and, 136
Perspective, of participants, 88
Photographs, 71–72
Plagiarism, avoiding, 39
Portfolios, 72–73
Positivism, 3
Postmodernism, 6–7
Power, restructuring relationships
    of, 155–156
PowerPoint (interactive multimedia
    software), 167, 191
Practical action research, 7, 9
    components of, 9
Predictability, creating, 12
Prejudice in action research, 220
Premature action during data
    analysis, 121–122
Privileged, active participant
    observer, 58–59
Process validity of research, 91

Professional colleagues, action
research implementation
and, 15
Professional Development School
(PDS), 211–213, 222
principles of, 212
Professional organization
membership, literature
review and, 35–36
Professionalism, teacher, 10, 220
Promising practices, literature
review and, 29–30
Propositions, data collection
and, 97
Protection from harm, 105
Prudence, quality action research
and, 205
Psychological Abstracts, 32
PsycINFO database, 32
*Publication Manual of the
American Psychological
Association*, 166. *See also*
APA style manual
Publications. *See also* Journals;
On-line resources
electronic, 188

QSR (NUD*IST). *See* NUD*IST 6
Qualitative data collection
techniques, 56–57
list of, 55
triangulation and, 56–57
Qualitative research, 4, 57, 85–91
Quantitative research, 4
Queens University, action research
Web site, 195–196
Questionnaires, 24, 61, 67–68, 233
attitude scales, 74–75
checklist for, 69
considerations in, 67–68
Likert scales, 75, 223
semantic differentials,
75–76, 223
standardized tests, 76
Questions
closed, 64
open-ended, 64
research, 5, 168, 215
about Web-based education, 172

Randomly-selected groups, 3
Rapport building, 172

Readers' Guide to Periodical
Literature, 32–33
Reading
achievement, 211
activities, 215
instruction, 213
intervention, 215, 216–217
meaning in, 213–214,
215–219
references about, 214
Reading Research Quarterly, 36
The Reading Teacher, 36
Reciprocity in professional
development schools, 212
Reconnaissance, 26–28
critical activities checklist
for, 28
defined, 26
descriptive activities for,
27–28
explanatory activities for, 28
self-reflection and, 26–27
Records
archival documents, 68–69
artifacts, 72–73
components of, 72
journals, 69–70
making and using, 68–73
maps, 70
photographs and film, 71–72
video/audio tapes, 71–72
References, bibliographic
format examples (APA style), 165
how to prepare, 38–39
Referential adequacy, credibility
checking and, 86
Reflective practice, 15, 26–27, 220
action planning and, 151,
206–207
action research and, 121–122
credo for, 10
daily, 10
described, 177
quality action research and, 205
reconnaissance and, 26–27
teaching and, 53–55, 191
Reflexivity, confirmability checking
and, 86
Relational ethics, 113
Reliability, 94–95
validity versus, 95–96
Report cards, 74

Reporting. *See also* Findings
sharing/display
complete data, 93
forum for planning data, 154
of primary data, 93
Research. *See also* Action research;
Action research plan; Action
research reporting; Action
research validity
findings, access to, 12
influence on practice, 6–7,
10–13
integrative with teaching and
writing, 182–183
methods, 4–5
qualitative, 57, 85–91
questions for, 5, 45, 215
relevance of, 7
sample article, 166–172
scientific, 2–3
traditional, versus action
research, 3–4
Research article, sample
abstract of, 166
action plan, 171–172
area of focus statement, 168
context in, 167
data collection, 169
literature review, 168–169
research questions, 168
Research group membership
description, 45–46
Resistance to change, 152
Resources, fiscal
action research plan statement
of, 46–47
lack of, 152
Rituals and writing, 173–175
examples of, 174

Sample annotated action research
article, 166–172
Scales
attitude, 74–75
Likert, 75, 223
semantic differential, 75–76, 223
Schoolteacher (Lortie), 12
Schoolwide action planning, 145, 150
Science and Children, 36
Science Scope, 36
The Science Teacher, 36
Scientific method, 96

Scientific research, 2–3
Search engines, 35, 204
    updating links, 203
Self-assessment worksheet, student
    grading and, 118–119
Self-efficacy, teacher, 207
Self-esteem, teacher, 207
Self-reflection. *See* Reflective practice
Semantic differentials, 75–76
Sharing action research, 188–209
    case study in, 189–191
    criteria for, 204–206
    electronic means for, 192–193
    evaluating, 204–205
    informal criteria (sample),
        204–205
    interactive media software,
        191–192
    Networks and, 198–199, 199
Significance, statistical, 3
Site councils, action planning
    and, 150
Social Education, 36
Social principles, ethics and, 109
*Social Studies and the Young
    Learner,* 36
Software
    interactive multimedia, 191
    quantitative analysis, 133, 134
Southern Cross Institute of Action
    Research (SCIAR), 200
Southern Oregon University, 167
SPSS 12.0 Student Version, 223, 225
Standard deviation, statistical, 223,
    225–226, 227, 228–229
Standardized tests, 76
    as source of quantitative data, 74
Statistics, descriptive, 223–230
    central tendency, 224–225
    illustration of, 226–228
    interpretation of, 230
    list of common symbols, 227
    reasons to use, 223–224
    significance and, 230
    standard deviation, 223,
        225–226, 227, 228–229
    suggested procedure for, 228
Steps-to-action chart for action
    planning, 140, 143, 145,
        146–148, 150, 160, 175–176,
        218
    blank, 148

Jack Reston's, 146–147
Jonathan Stewart's, 218
table, 144
Steps-to-action checklist, 149
Strategies
    bottom-up, 156
    top-down, 156
Stringer, E. T.
    Action Research Interacting
        Spiral, 18
Structured formal interviews, 64–65
Student absenteeism. *See*
    Absenteeism
Students
    diversity in professional
        development schools, 212
    learning styles, 171
    motivation
        case study, 1–2, 122–123
        for reading, 237, 238
        unmotivated, 1–2
Student-teacher conferences, 119
Surveys, 169, 226
    of families, 142
    student self-evaluation, 53
    teacher, 54
Systematic inquiry in professional
    development schools, 212

Teacher as Researcher Grants, 219
Teacher as researchers, 3–4
Teacher-made tests, 73–74
Teachers' access to action research
    findings, 12
Teaching
    concerns, 169
    as craft culture versus reflective
        practice profession, 191
    daily action research in, 14–15
    integrating with research and
        writing, 182–183
    math with manipulatives, 234–237
    Web-based, 166–172
Teaching Children Mathematics, 36
Team action planning, 145, 150
Technology and mathematics
    achievement, 101–103, 137
Technophobia, 203
Teleconferences and Web-based
    education, 172
Testing, 4–5
Tests, standardized, 76

Theme identification, 123
Theoretical validity, 89
Theory
    critical, 6, 7, 8
    data interpretation and, 137
    definition of, 137
    postmodern, 6–7, 8
Thunder Cave, 216–217
Time
    for action planning, 154–155
    for on-line research, 46, 171, 204
    for writing, 173, 182–183
Timeline for action research plan,
    216
TIMSS study, 207
Top-down strategies, action
    planning and, 156
Transferability, credibility checking
    and, 86
Triangulation, 57, 86
    confirmability and, 86
    credibility and, 86
    matrix, 57, 78
Trustworthiness
    confirmability and, 86–87
    credibility and, 85–86
    dependability and, 86
    of qualitative research, 85
    transferability and, 86
    validity and, 85, 90

Uncover Periodical Index, 34
Understanding, 85
    descriptive validity and, 87–88
    evaluative validity and, 89
    generalizability and, 89
    interpretive validity and, 88
    theoretical validity and, 89
    validity and, 85, 89
University libraries for literature
    review, 36–37
URL addresses. *See* Web sites,
    action research
U.S. Department of Education, 35
U.S. National Research Center, 207
Utilitarian ethics, 112

Validation as reason to write, 164
Validity, 84–96
    Anderson et al. criteria for, 90–92
    catalytic, 92
    definition, 84

Validity (*contd.*)
    democratic, 90–91
    descriptive, 87–88
    dialogic, 92
    evaluative, 90
    Guba's criteria for, 85–87
    interpretive, 88
    Maxwell's criteria for, 87–90
    outcome, 91
    process, 91
    of qualitative research, 85–87
    reliability versus, 95–96
    theoretical, 89
    understanding versus, 89
    Wolcott's strategies for, 92–95
Validity in action research, 98
Variability
    measure of statistical, 223
    standard deviation, 223
Variables, 3
    defining, 44–45, 215
Visual displays of data, 223–230

Web sites, action research, 154,
        194–196. *See also* Internet;
        On-line resources
    changing nature of, 203
    quality control and, 192–193

Web-based Instruction (WBI), 169
Web-based teaching, 166–172
    action research class, 167
    communication in, 169–170
    criteria for success in, 171
    questions about, 172
    rapport and, 172
    teleconferencing and, 172
Wells, Gordon
    Action Research Cycle
        figure, 17
Wolcott, H. F.
    research-in-action
        checklist, 95
    validity strategies of, 92–95
World Wide Web
    searches, 34–35
Writing
    avoiding, 174, 175
    choosing a style, 179
    of ESL students, 231–234
    feedback, 184–185
    as a generative activity, 164
    guidelines, 173–175
        for technical writing, 40
    integrating with teaching and
        research, 182–183
    intervention, 231–234

    length of, 183–184
    polishing, 186
    rituals and, 173–175
    routine, 173
    for social sciences, 173
    style of, 178–179, 182
    time for, 182–183
    titles in, 185
Writing a literature review,
        tools and suggestions, 42–44
Writing up action research,
        162–187. *See also* APA
        style manual
    format and style, 165–166
    importance of, 164
    length, 183–184
    motivation for, 162–163,
        164
    publishing guidelines,
        178–179
    reference formats, 165
    sample article, 166–172
    self-assessment of, 180–182
        using rubric criteria,
        180–181
    summary, 186–187

Yahoo! (search engine), 203